Love
Joy
Trump

A Chorus of Prophetic Voices

by

BethAnon

Love Joy Trump
A Chorus of Prophetic Voices

by BethAnon

The chapters in this book are prophetic words and visions about Donald Trump shared by a variety of people the world over and gathered and curated by the BethAnon, a citizen journalist and Patriot.

While we do not claim to know the ultimate truth of God's will, we feel that collectively these prophecies suggest that Trump's election was part of God's plan. We pray for his continued health, well-being and leadership as corruption and dark forces are being revealed and those involved are brought to justice. We hope you will join us in saying prayers of protection for Donald Trump and his family.

We hope that sharing this book with others will help awaken the people you care about. Thank you for both your prayers and sharing.

Reviews are extremely helpful, and deeply appreciated. We are all in this together. WWG1WGA.

We have sought and obtained permission to publish all of the works in this book. However, if we have made an oversight, we are always happy to make corrections, updates, include missing sources, or to remove content used inadvertently without permission if requested. You may contact us at:

Published by Relentlessly Creative Books
http://relentlesslycreativebooks.com/
books@relentlesslycreative.com
Dallas, Texas, USA
303 317 2200

Love
Joy
Trump

Table of Contents

Foreword

Amanda Grace

We are at the most Crucial time in America's history. The Soul of our nation is at stake. We have witnessed major change in the United States and the world, that biblically coincide with events prophesied way before their time. The Lord in the midst has announced and raised up anointed leaders for such a time as this. Every trial they endured in their lives, was to prepare them in this crucial hour for their God ordained role. President Donald J Trump is one of these leaders.

The Lord does not call the qualified, He qualifies the called. What others harshly judge and may call ill equipped, those are the very qualities and characteristics the Lord will refine and use in an hour where evil and darkness are attempting an accelerated advance to take control before their time. Matthew 20:26 "but whoever desires to become great among you, let him be your servant." leadership that arises under the call of the Lord, desires to serve, at times putting the needs and safety of the people above their own.

King David is an example of a servant who was equally brazen in the face of evil while having the ability to be sensitive to the needs of the people. He was flawed yet called a "man after God's own heart." This public refining tests one's resolve, their faith, their will, their ability to clearly lead under pressure in ways they have never experienced before. They are refined in the furnace of affliction. This produces a deeply rooted faith to thrive, endure, and be victorious in the face of crises, danger, and evil exploits.

President Trump has endured the harshest of attacks, the most disturbing of crises, and the darkest of evils. He has been anointed to preserve life and set the captives free. Romans 8:31 "If God is for us, who can be against us?"

The Lord is making a way. We will continue to see Almighty God move and make a way even in the darkest of places as He continues to navigate the President on his ordained course to lead this nation.

Foreword
Mike Lindell

I am so excited to be a small part of God's plan for the Restoration of America. People all over the world are praying for President Trump as they recognize God's hand on him. We are at a time like no other and teamwork has never been more important. Like Mark Taylor says, "Time is up for the corrupt," and indeed it is. All of the Children of God are being called in this time to fulfill what we and our ancestors have prayed for: "Thy Will be Done, on Earth, as it is in Heaven."

President Trump is a modern-day Cyrus, and as Kim Clement says, "He has a heart like David." I have a calling from God to support President Trump. This election is not about politics. It is about good vs. evil. It is about freedom under God or slavery in a godless new world order. We must win and it is going to take all of us Children of God working together, giving it everything we've got, to prevail, by God's Almighty Grace, to reelect President Donald John Trump whose name literally means 'World leader under the Grace of God who excels and triumphs.' That's pretty clear, isn't it?

Everything works to the good for those who love God. President Trump and those who support him have made the decision to go "all in" to serve God and Humanity. Nothing will stop us with God on our side. *Love Joy Trump: A Chorus of Prophetic Voices* is ammunition for the Remnant to help wake our sleeping brothers and sisters who are still under the spell of the fake news narrative. It may also be the antidote for TDS (Trump Derangement Syndrome).

President Trump is working to bring a physical peace on planet Earth in preparation for the Spiritual Awakening and manifestation of Peace on Earth in our lifetimes. America First refers to restoring our Republic and maintaining our freedoms so our brothers and sisters from all over the world can do the same. We have been asleep to the massive deception that has been suffocating the individual pursuit of happiness and the search for God within ourselves, because of deliberate indoctrination and propaganda. Trump has put himself in a position of defending "we the people," by accepting his mission from God to serve humanity. His resilience against the slings and arrows of the enemy is remarkable and can come only through divine intervention and protection.

God bless those who surround the President and his family who take such good care. "Love Joy Trump" is a movement—the L J T Movement! We live in love and joy and support President Trump. I dare anyone to come against us in this enterprise. *Love Joy Trump: A Chorus of Prophetic Voices* reflects the unilateral worldwide excitement, understanding, wisdom, support and optimistic enthusiasm for President Donald J. Trump and what he is doing.

Faith without works is dead and President Trump is the perfect example of that with an energy and purpose that can only be considered divine. Prophetic voices speak today as they have always done. It is up to us to listen and take it deeper in our own discernment, and then to act with a fullness of purpose and in our full armor of God. This is a spiritual war and we can use all the positive force we can rally.

This book, *Love Joy Trump, A Chorus of Prophetic Voices* takes a stand for our chosen leader, and sings of hope and love to God, to Christ, to the Holy Spirit, a call to action, a rallying cry, a voice in the wilderness, asking us to arise and stand it our authentic divinity in this one lifetime now, to run with the Glory of our Creator and bow down on both knees to beg for forgiveness for forgetting God and to beseech Him for guidance to allow His Will to be Done. With love and joy; this is how Victory is achieved!

Introduction
BethAnon

P utting this book together has been an incredible journey, extremely inspiring and comforting in the chaos and current division and animosity of those who are trapped in the main stream media programming, willingly or otherwise. Anointed means chosen by or as if by divine intervention, producing a divine influence or presence. A person is anointed with a special purpose....to be a king, to be a prophet, to be a builder, being set apart for the service of God. God is the Big Boss and that's a good thing. It is only God who can anoint a person for a reason and a time unto His purpose. At the same time, spiritual anointing is available to all who love and serve their Creator, expressed in the same sanctifying influence and the Spirit of God, joy filled life.

God is true love.

Our publisher, Monica Rix Paxson, whose impeccable guidance was integral in putting this compilation together, made the point that spreading the Word of God's Decisions and how important that is, truly is the goal of this book. That, and to make a difference, to pay attention and conspire to inspirational unity. Faith without works is dead. People are finding God through QAnon and people are coming to God through resonating with the authentic prophecies of our time now. It's all about saving souls, sharing the good news for the hungry and thirsty hearts, filling in our inner dimensions, becoming holy, whole and saving billions of souls.

Monica also asked me about context...the circumstances that form the setting of facts, information and ideas in which something can be fully understood.

Context comes from the Latin for how something is made so you may say you cannot understand what happens without looking at the context ie. setting. For me this book and the compilation of good news about Donald Trump is the antidote to the poisonous lies that have been spread about the man by his enemies. These lies and disinformation have propagandized so many people who never had a chance to know the truth about Donald Trump as a candidate, a person or as a President of the United States of America. We basically want to set the record straight and this small attempt in that direction is a worthy effort of communication to all of our brothers and sisters who have never had a legitimate chance to witness and understand the deeper things regarding Donald Trump and his place in Our Great Awakening movement.

Another facet of this book is a gathering of information regarding different perspectives on the wonderful happenings in our time now. I hope to meet the President and his family at some point to be of further service in a myriad of ways as a strategic partner in connecting fellow lovers of God as we manifest heaven on earth in our lifetimes. Everyone is welcome. Join the party! Bring your wisdom and let's fill in this marvelous tapestry of opportunity and possibility that can become inevitable if we want it and make the effort towards fulfilling the will of our most awesome Creator. Nothing can stop us now.

The Trump Prophecies by Mark Taylor is the ace in the hole, so to speak, and is the original prophecy that woke me up to the hand of God being on Donald Trump. A prophet is an individual who is an empty vessel that can be filled with the Spirit of God in service to humanity and reveals a message called prophecy. It is also an awesome blessing that Mark Taylor is a living humble servant of the Most High God, who continues to speak out and share the Divine Message of God's Plan to clean up America and the entire Earth. MEGA...Make Earth Great Again!

This is reminiscent to me of John the Baptist and the Voice in the Wilderness preparing the path for Christ. It is a call for Repentance (to re-think, reconsider and have the courage to change, to align ourselves with God's Will) before Restoration, ie. Second Coming, though our Creator never really left. It is us who let go of His hand.

When the Archangel Gabriel spoke to Zechariah about Elizabeth's pregnancy with John (Luke 1:5-2:20), He mentioned, 'He will be your pride and joy and many people will be glad that he was born. As far as the Lord is concerned, he will be a great man. He will never drink wine or any other liquor. He will be filled with the Holy Spirit even before he is born. He will bring many people in Israel back to the Lord their God. He will go ahead of the Lord with the spirit and power that Elijah had. He will change parents' attitudes toward their children. He will change disobedient people so that they will accept those who have God's approval. In this way he will prepare the people for the Lord."

I am not saying Donald Trump is the reincarnation of John the Baptist, but I am saying there is a beautiful synchronicity in their two lives, and where we are now.

3

The fact that Donald Trump has never used any alcohol or drugs, because his older brother who warned him suffered from the debilitating progressive illness of alcoholism, and that he has raised such amazing children free from the petulance of drug and alcohol abuse is noteworthy. There will be no head on a plate this time, nor any crucifixion.

Also, he is the first President in history to actually confiscate drugs, making arrests, to end the flow of drugs into our country, instead of making money off of them like all of our previous Cabal owned presidents. Alleluia to that. He is doing the same with gun smuggling and most importantly, human trafficking, the biggest business and biggest scourge on our planet ever in history. Those paying attention can see how we are moving to save the innocents...closing Back Page and so many arrests of traffickers and pedophiles. You can keep up to date on the Department of Justice official website at www.justice.gov for these and many other criminal prosecutions. Fortunately, Trump has added innumerable just judges as we Drain the Swamp so convictions can proceed. Keep up to date with sealed indictments at www.pacer.gov. Military tribunals are in preparation and we are living in a time where Justice will be served! (over 8000 CEO Resignations at www.resignation.info and over 1200 pages of Seized Assets at www.tinyurl.com/y9mjufzm The Trump White House has an open door policy for faith leaders and prayer is a daily occurrence. Praise God.

This is the end of the worldly system and the beginning of the Reign of Christ and Heaven on Earth. And I am not talking about pictures and concepts of Christ. I am talking about a personal relationship within. Those with the eyes to see and the ears to hear, the Remnant, have been called by Our Supreme Commander God, to stand and bear righteous witness as we defeat the Luciferian New World Order Agenda (which goes back to Babylonian times), once and for all! I use the name BethAnon to call attention to QAnon (available at https://qanon.pub/) and all the digital army warriors who have made the Great Awakening possible by selflessly responding to their calling to discern and spread truth and nothing but the truth so help us God. I also like to remember to place Principles above personalities and focus on similarities, not differences, to join together in an authentic brotherhood and sisterhood of mankind.

WWG1WGA

"Have I now become your enemy by telling you the truth?"

—Galatians 4:16

Hope not!

Where We Go One We Go All

Teamwork is Divine.

Welcome to the Great Awakening Amen Selah

Recurring Theme
BethAnon

After reading as many Prophecies as I can lay my hands on, there seems to be a recurring theme and that theme is pretty simple and has been repeated throughout history. It is a call for Repentance...for changing our ways to align our self will with the will of our Creator. The Ten Commandments seem to be as relevant as ever. In fact, there was a meme going around that we wouldn't need the 17,000 laws in the law books if we could follow the ten on stone. True that. Doing unto others as you would want them to do unto you. The prophetic voices are speaking the glory and the sanctity of life, the importance of putting God first in one's life, as in, "Seek ye first the kingdom of heaven within, and all things will be added unto you."

The Prophecies address the sea of materialism and ego that humanity has chosen over an intimate relationship with God. It takes us back to the fall of Lucifer who wanted to be like God without God. We worship the Creation instead of the Creator. It is obvious to anyone that this formula has not served us well. In fact, it has practically destroyed the garden and its inhabitants through ignorance. Ignorance is based on the root word 'ignore' as in 'ignoring' the call of the heart.

When we ignore the call of the heart, we are ignorant.

The prophecies reflect the beauty and wisdom of the Sermon on the Mount. The Spirit of God speaks with authority against all of the sins of omission or commission that keep us from unity with Him. After all, it is our lack of obedience and discipline that cause separation from Source. We all live and learn and have free will. God is nothing if not a gentleman and the decision is ours to be conscious with every breath and choose wisely.

As crown of creation, we human beings have many gifts to live up to. We have been navigating a grand illusion. Like Christ said, "Walk through this world without being part of it." That direction has been a saving grace in my life for years and going within is the foundation of my conscious contact with God. Union is integral, to be able to participate in the battle of good versus evil which is happening in our time now. We must stand up in our authentic divinity and put on the full armor of God, not only for ourselves, but for our sisters and brothers who are still asleep in the mighty wave of propaganda and brainwashing that was unleashed upon us. The illusion is called an illusion for a reason. It looks real. It takes surrender, discernment, wisdom and grace to see through the veil.

As we live now in the time of the Great Awakening, the veil is being lifted and the light is shining in the darkness, exposing all kinds of demonic strategies that have imprisoned humanity for millennia. The Prophecies call for the dismantling and final fall of the Luciferian Agenda. We have been living in a matrix that has been seeking its own Godless New World Order, without understanding the spells and hypnotizing techniques we were tricked into accepting as 'normal'. We lived in 'idol worship' without comprehending that fact. Without realizing it, our power was being stolen, all in an attempt to mock God.

The call for an end to abortion is a huge part of the message from the Spirit of God. The sanctity of marriage and the appreciation for living in real relationship with those we love, united by divine service and directed by our Almighty Creator. The Prophecies call for an end to all the globalist created wars based on greed and power, stealing resources and dividing humanity for their own nefarious purposes, leaving poverty, destruction and death in their wake. The Prophecies also call out the Satanic practices of sodomy and child sacrifice in their warped religious rituals to gain power and spit on God.

This is a serious offense to our Lord and no politically correct moron can change that fact. Honesty, integrity, selfless constructive action, humility, serenity, peace, kindness, courtesy, love, forgiveness, service, generosity, appreciation, lack of cheat and deceit, ego deflation, sharing, freedom, liberty, personal sovereignty, and the fear (awe and relentless obedience) of the Lord are all gifts, practices, tools and methods to know one's true self. This is exactly what the Globalist Agenda has been distracting us from achieving. They don't want us in our full divine power.

The Prophecies are a call for souls to come home...to ourselves and to our Creator. It is time to sing the praises and rejoice in the gift of life itself and the ultimate blessing of union with God within, which completes us like nothing outside of us ever will. What we are looking for is inside of us and always has been. Now is the time to make it real and live "Thy Kingdom come, Thy Will be done, on Earth as it is in Heaven." Peace is not only possible, it is inevitable. This is the truth the worldly system has been distracting us from...but no more. We are awake and alive and thriving. Amen. (So be it)!

Destiny of
Donald John Trump
BethAnon

Donald John Trump was born on June 14th, 1946.

Donald is derived from the word Domhnall meaning 'world leader' or 'ruler of the world' (Gaelic dunno, 'world'; val, 'rule') John is a Hebrew name that means 'God is gracious.' Trump is a German surname meaning 'trumpet' or 'drum' and it is also an English verb meaning 'to excel, surpass, or outdo', as well as an early English variant of the word 'triumph.' As Mary Colbert, who co- authored *The Trump Prophecies* book describes, "Donald John Trump's name means 'World Leader Under the Grace of God Whose Leadership Will Excel, Surpass and Outdo in Triumph.'" Rings true to me. God chooses who He will use. Here are a few quotes from our beloved President.

"We will be one people, under one God."

"I judge people based on their capability, honesty and merit."

"We will be faithful stewards of God's glorious creation from sea to shining sea." —President DJT 7-8-19

"We all share the same heroes, the same home, the same heart, and we all are made by the same Almighty God" —President DJT July 4th, 2019 'Salute to America'

"Our republic was formed on the basis that freedom is not a gift from government. Freedom is a gift from God."

"Faith is more powerful than government and nothing is more powerful than God."

"Across our land, we see the splendor of God's creation. Throughout our history we see the glory of God's providence. And in every city and town, we see the Lord's grace all around us, through a million acts of kindness, courage and generosity. We love God."

Donald Trump's mother's name was Mary and his father's middle name was Christ. Another synchronicity in this revelatory story in these amazing times we are living in. According to Prophet Kim Clement, "Revelation is God's language. Revelation gives a forecast of history and also its conclusion. Revelations are a colorful pageant of the mystery of God. Prophecy is the power of seeing the future. Revelation is the telling of it." Kim also suggested, "Is it demonic or is it dynamic?" As in allowing something for a reason.

Saints all over the world are praying for President Trump. To the Pope, "I'm a Christian and I'm proud of it." —Donald John Trump

Trump is the only President who wrote entire books about what he would do to fix the problems facing America before he had any inkling of running for office. He was prepared by God.

Lance Wallnau, author of the book, 'God's Chaos Candidate', had a Word from God regarding Trump. "I heard the Lord say, 'Donald Trump is a wrecking ball to the spirit of political correctness." Amen to that! Wallnau also said, "Trump is like a child when it comes to the kingdom." He's open." That's everything that all of us could ask for him to be as well as ourselves.

Pastor Denise Goulet told Trump, "Yes, you are bold and this comes from God for such a time as this." Thank God for our President's relentless perseverance, anchored in God to serve.

In 1987 Richard Nixon wrote the following letter after his wife Pat was watching DJT on the Phil Donahue Show. "Dear Donald, Mrs. Nixon told me you were great on the Donahue show. She's an expert on politics and she predicts that whenever you decide to run for office you will be a winner!" Warm regards, Richard Nixon, 12/12/1987

There is a warning call for Repentance, a time to return to God or embrace further paganism and immorality. The choice is always our own with the blessing of free will and the opportunity to stand up in our authentic divinity and live in joy and peace.

God wants us to be in sync with Him. That is why He gives us His prophets. Trump is turning out to be a prophet as well, when you watch everything he says is going to happen, eventually come to fruition against all odds.

"You are about to see history in the making. Crimes committed on a global scale will result in full accountability. Justice is here, justice is taking place, justice is what many have prayed for, including those that have gone before us, and we get to witness it.

Victory!" Mark Taylor

"The Lord told me two years ago that another showdown between the Spirit of Elijah and the prophets of Baal was coming. It's begun! Judgment and massive exposures in the church system are taking place. The church age is over. A glorious and spotless bride will appear."—Mark Taylor

An Italian Connection
Father Giacomo Capoverdi

T om Zimmer was a Catholic devotee of the Lord, Jesus Christ, who prophesied in the 1980's that "Donald Trump would lead America back to God." Thomas Zimmer was known as the Hermit of Loreto. He was an American who had moved to Loreto, a town on the east coast of Italy, in the early 1970's, after a visit to the Basilica della Santa Casa compelled him to return. The Basilica is known for enshrining the house in which the Blessed Virgin Mary is believed to have lived. Pious devotees such as Tom Zimmer believe that the same house was flown over by angelic beings from Jerusalem to Tersatto (Trsat in Croatia) then to Recanti before arriving in Loreto. He was a man of deep faith and relentless practice. He wrote the Pieta Prayerbook which is a timeless masterpiece of traditional Catholic prayers and devotions and attended mass many times each day.

The month after Trump was inaugurated, an American priest named Giacomo Capoverdi posted a video on Youtube that tells the amazing story of Tom Zimmer, this Hermit of Loreto, as the locals know him. Capoverdi said it was around the year 2000 when a friend of his who is an Italian American physician, whose name is Claudio Curran, strongly suggested that he must meet this holy man. Capoverdi took the train from Rome to Loreto the next time he was in Italy. He arrived at the Basilica and saw an old man sitting on the floor hunched over in prayer at the Holy House, the home of Mary of Nazareth. To save the house from being destroyed by Arabs during the Crusades, angels transported it to Loreto, now a place of pilgrimage and veneration.

Capoverdi asked him in English if he was Thomas Zimmer and the two men had a wonderful conversation. Years later, when Donald Trump was elected, Claudio Curran called Capoverdi again and told him that back in the 1980's, Thomas Zimmer had said he had received a "premonition and that a certain man would lead America back to God and that man would be none other than Donald J. Trump." The doctor was incredulous upon hearing this news. "You mean the millionaire playboy from New York?", he said to Zimmer. "Yes", said the Hermit of Loreto, stating that, "He was so sure Donald Trump would become a great spiritual leader of America, that he wrote his name on a brick and had it placed in the Reconstruction of St. Peter's Holy Door after Jubilee so Trump would receive blessings from the many masses that would be said in the Vatican."

What does the Church do in order to determine whether a prophecy is true or false?

First: Was the prophet a good or virtuous person? Zimmer was that in spades.

Next: The prophecy must not contradict scripture or church doctrine. There is nothing in scriptural or church teachings that would suggest that a political leader cannot lead people to God; on the contrary, scripture points toward it as a duty. Finally, the prophecy must come true. Well, here we are almost four years in and all of the evidence points in favor of Tom Zimmer's premonition. Alleluia! Praise God from whom all blessings flow!

God and Donald Trump
Prophetess Nita Johnson

March 14th, 2016

"I want to share something with you that I believe will be very meaningful. However, before I do I want to ask all of you some questions. What are you looking for in a President? A Born-again Christian or God's choice? Do you want someone that will impress the Nations or do you want someone who will accomplish God's purpose? When you pray that God will put His man in office, what does he look like to you? There are two extremes (and everything in between) who are now vying for the Presidency."

"On your right, we have an outspoken and opinionated Donald Trump. On your left, we have a quiet, gentle and wise Ben Carson. Most of the rest look like varying degrees of the Republican Establishment.

I didn't know that the Republican Establishment had a look, did you? I suddenly saw it for myself. Once you stuck them up against Donald Trump and Ben Carson, it shakes you a little. They all act like a bunch of wolves protecting their dens from intruders, like Donald and Ben.

You see, it is no longer about what is right for America, but what this year's issues are going to be. They tell us what we are supposed to want and need, and then how they will provide it for us. Then we hear the other two men; Donald Trump and Ben Carson, and they tell us something so different that we have to pay attention."

"Four years ago (2012) the Lord spoke to me and told me that in the next election, He would put a Cyrus in the White House. In fact, He said that the mantle would flow out to many, and they would do the work to galvanize the people to liberate America. I believe He will do this if we pray. Everywhere I went I shared the vision of the Lord. I have had several dreams and visions about Donald Trump and each time, he seemed to come out of nowhere to take on the Establishment! Then it began to happen. I also felt that Ben Carson was supposed to be in office which the Lord confirmed to me in a dream not long ago. As time moved on the Lord continued to speak to me and something began to take shape that led me to this letter. If you want a religious man, you can have that in Ben Carson. He will be good in his place, in the season God has for him. However, God has not equipped him to do what our nation needs at this time in history. I look for that to come later. If you want a Cyrus that will turn America back to the land of promise and deal with the high-level wickedness, you must look for the one who is anointed for this purpose: Donald Trump."

"The man at the top does not need a Cyrus mantle to turn America around if he is a Spirit-filled Christian. He does, however if he is Trump. It's the mantle of Cyrus that will do the work. (The Mantle of Cyrus releases wealth and provision with no strings attached, restoring the Nation of the gifts that were stolen from her, via an anointing and alignment with the Spirit of God.) The man will simply be a tool in God's lofty and wise hands. I think a great pairing would be Trump as the President and Carson as the

18

Vice President. Trump may have the need of grace in particular areas." (Who doesn't?)

Nevertheless, he is not evil like all those in the shadow government. He will cause many of their tall and lofty mountains to fall."

"I promise you, as God is through Trump, doing that very thing. Trump is like a bull out of the pen, he sees red and heads for the target. He is as fearless as a lion being robbed of his cubs. With the Mantle of Cyrus and the qualities God gave him, Trump will achieve as much as we, through our prayers, make a way for him to accomplish. It will take the whole team fighting for this nation, for us to win the war. For our modern day Cyrus to achieve God's design, he will need more than just desire. He will need solid prayer covering and divine enablement. The Church cannot keep thinking that the world will take care of us just because we are the Lord's. The world wants their government, not God's. The Church will end up in a den of suffering if we do not fight now through prayer and our actions by voting for God's will."

"One person mentioned to me that they thought God could just put the Cyrus Mantle on Ben Carson. He could, but the Lord does tend to make the personality of the bearer fit the mantle. This being the case, why do we trifle with God's selection? He is so much more than our little and fearful boxes can visualize. I received many visions last night which led me to writing this letter and sending it out. Aim high in faith my friends, and let God be God. He won't disappoint us if we pray and trust Him. I stood for Ben Carson because I had several visions wherein I saw him taking on the Presidency. But, the Lord told me it is Trump's place now. We will not keep America if the Lord cannot have His way. I know it takes faith to receive this so, believe it and act on it. We will not be sorry!

In His Amazing Love, Nita Johnson"

Trump Revelation
Sadhu Sundar Selvaraj

S adhu Sundar Selvaraj is a former Hindu prophet turned Christian who received a Word from God regarding Donald Trump in August of 2016. "I was caught up in the Spirit and found myself standing before the Council. This was the very Council where I always used to go and I saw Father Abraham, and I was standing beside him. I was very surprised to see Donald Trump come and stand in that room. And this is what I was told. They said, 'Trump will become President. He will be used to clean and purify the nation. As hard as he is, he has been prepared for this. As Cyrus was used to discipline Israel and then restore Israel, likewise Trump will be used in the United States of America. He will be God's mouth and hand for this nation."

Sadhu Sundar Selvaraj revealed a vision he says he had of God where God told him He elected Donald Trump in order for America to "put away evil" in the land. The following is the revelation to Selvaraj in July of 2018. "I saw the Lord as a gigantic figure standing on the east coast of the United States. He was so huge. A map of the United States looked like an ant before Him. He had a shepherd's rod in His hand and He stretched it across the nation. He said that God told Him that He will "judge the nation for political crimes." "God elaborated," Selvaraj claims, "saying that the judgment will come "because of decisions that were taken in secret in the past to pass laws of unrighteousness and sin in the land. For example, like laws of abortion and same-sex marriage laws."

The former Hindu prophet says that God shared of "diabolical secret alliances and plans" that were made under the administration of former President Barak Obama, which would have continued if democrat Hillary Clinton was elected as President. (Google the 16-year plan to destroy America for details of the Obama Clinton evil agenda.) We really dodged a bullet here by God's grace and intervention.

Selvaraj added that he was invited to witness a 'Heavenly Council' where such matters were discussed and where it was revealed to him why Trump was chosen as the man to lead America in these times. "Why was Mr. Trump elected President? Because God had heard the prayers of millions of Americans who had prayed for this nation over the decades. He had heard their prayers and given them a chance, an opportunity, to put away evil and establish righteousness in the land." (Righteousness- acting in accord with divine moral law.)

So, Mr. Trump, being voted into office for a period of four years is God's opportunity. That He is giving them a chance because the Christians have prayed, so they can put away evil, put away unrighteousness and establish righteousness in the land." Selvaraj claims that the Church will "enter a New Era, a New Season and a New Dispensation when Signs and Wonders Would Increase, Angels would become Commonplace, and more people will become Christians and the Spiritual Realm will become very, very Visible to all Christians."

Evangelical Jim Bakker, was interviewing Selvaraj and asked him why some Christians still refuse to support Trump. Selvaraj replied that, "Such people are not really Christians at all, but are actually tools of the Devil. They appear like a sheep among the sheepfold, among Christianity, but they are not of God." Selvaraj said, "It's the Devil who has planted them, so they have the spirit of what the Apostle John calls the spirit of the Anti-Christ in them. So it is they who stir up the people and stir up the hornet's nest against a righteous king, a righteous man, so that either he is moved out of office or so he becomes so discouraged that he cannot stand up for righteousness and he will end up compromising. It is vitally important to pray for kings and President Trump is the king of this time. If the United States doesn't turn back to God, then that will be the end of the nation."

Televangelist, Jim Bakker, led his audience in prayer that God will protect Trump, end abortion and save America. Selvaraj added that, "Christians should also pray for Trump when he travels overseas carrying out God's mission of spreading righteousness. Why? Because he's God's chosen righteousness man. God will use him to effect righteousness on other world leaders and turn other nations around to righteousness." North Korea, China, Russia, Iran, Brazil, India? (President Modi of India just asked Trump to be a mediator for peace with India and Kashmir where a war of over 70 years continues.)

Beloved Prophet
Kim Clement

Who was Kim Clement? Many have called him a prophet, but to simply call him a prophet is not even enough. Part of the journey to understanding Kim Clement is a lesson in understanding the uniqueness of of his destiny. He was not a doom and gloom prophet with an apocalyptic forecast every three years; instead, he was a voice of hope to those who needed it the most. He was able to paint a picture of destiny that inspires instead of frightens those who catch a glimpse. He found a way to define again what it is to be a true prophet. He, along with his wife, Jane, was the founder of House of Destiny Church.

Here's how Kim Clement came to prophecy: In 1973, in a gutter outside a South African nightclub, Kim almost died from a heroin overdose and deep stab wound to the chest. He remembered an Anglican priest telling him that one day he would be desperate for Jesus. As the lifeblood drained out of him, Kim called out, "Jesus, if you're real, I need you now!" He was taken to a hospital by a stranger where he recovered. He dedicated his life Ministering the love and prophetic Word of God, the Father, to the broken and the outcast. For 16 years, all over the world, God used him as a voice of hope to the nations. On November 23rd, 2016, Kim entered his eternal glory. We know he heard God say, "Well done, good and faithful servant." Kim is sorely missed here on Earth, but his Voice lives on in the hearts of those who receive God's healing and understanding.

2006

"The people of Zion say, 'No, you shall not come and rape us as you have in the past. Babylon, you will not exist in our schools or in our legal system. The Babylonian spirit shall be brought to nothing, and Jezebel herself shall be down on her knees, says the Lord. For I have tolerated enough and now God says, 'Allow me to give you a four-year period of an extension of Grace.' An economy of Grace has existed, but now there is going to be an overabundance of Grace that is going to be granted to your children and your children's children.

Watch and see, says the Lord. I'll take them out of darkness, put light into them and send them back to darkness. And they will go as the lunatic that was delivered by Jesus and Jesus told him to go back. He was the first one that was set aside as a missionary in that place."

"God said, 'I'm raising up a whole troop of missionaries out of your children. I'm raising up Missionaries. They are going to go into the culture and they are going to take Babylon and say, 'You submit to us!' 'We don't submit to you!' The Daniels of this hour, the King Nebuchadnezzars and the King Darriuses, and they shall say, 'No, we will prove to your that our God is the only God." Watch ME, says the Lord, as I take the atheist and the agnostic and prove myself, because of the angel that has come to reveal the mystery, as in Revelation 10." (God is in control of all of Creation and time itself. His will be done.)

"It has been spoken by the Lord. But there is an angel that says we have blown the trumpet, the final trumpet. Now the mystery that was spoken by the prophets of old shall be opened up for this generation, to hear the secrets of God and take the Kingdom by force.

Says the Lord, Alleluia!" "And it shall come to pass that the news media shall change drastically. Hear what the Lord says, Church. TBN shall change drastically.

There will be a change of faith and a new name added to TBN (Trinity Broadcasting Network). They will not hold onto the old, they will not hold onto the old only. But they will have the old and the new and so combine them together. No more dullness for the youth of this day because I am going to rise up one that will take the youth by force. It shall not be called TBN. It shall be called something else and then another will rise up in the Spirit of God."

"The young men of this hour shall become like the Joshua and Moses of this hour. For you see God says, Moses prayer, what's scarier and more powerful than Joshua's fighting and Moses prayer?! Joshua never grew weary of fighting but Moses grew weary of praying. For God says, My people have grown weary of praying. Their arms have fallen down to the ground. But God says Moses grew weary of prayer but Joshua did not grow weary in battle."

"This generation shall go into battle against the faithless generation and the perverse generation. But God says the old order shall hold up their arms and they will pray and when they get tired of praying, they will lift their arms up and allow them to keep the arms extended. Joshuas shall stop winning the battles. Do you want to win the battles? Says the Lord. Do you want that?" "Then God says, 'I will take away the lethargy of the old. I will take away the Eli priest (Eli's indolence and failure as a father) and there will be deaths...there will be deaths over the summer.' But God said, 'Do not fear because I am taking out the old order. And I am taking those in the temple who are corrupting them with adulterous actions. What they are doing in the temple has brought an odor to me, says the Lord. I will remove them."

"But Samuel shall arise and Daniel shall arise and these will infiltrate the entire system. But the old order is precious to ME. I will take TBN. I will take some of the old and the glorious ones. And I will cause them to hold up their arms. If the arms are lowered the Joshuas will stop winning the battles. God says, It's not time to stop praying. It's not time to stop praying. It's not time. It's time for you to hold up your arms so the battle can be won." A miracle shall happen in the banking and stock exchange. Watch the oil...it will change. It will change because Greenspan (Alan Greenspan) will go. There is something different that shall come in it's place. And there will be an economic revival for this nation and you will not need the Middle East. You will not need their oil. You will not need them. But God says, it shall be in the soil of this nation that I will raise up my miraculous flood. Alleluia!"

"Do not say it is time for the old to be taken care of.

No, I am going to take care of those who have not listened. And some of them need to lay down their sword so a younger man can pick it up. Elijah shall arise. These are young prophets and apostles. These are young entertainers and sportsmen. This is the news media..the entertainment industry. The political industry.. kingdoms of sports, that I shall take by My hand and the Kingdom shall be in each one of these." "But the greatest kingdom to be involved, says the Lord, is the family of the United States of America. They shall be restored. Enough of this divorce. Enough of this putting each other away. God says, 'Enough!'" "Now I'll raise up the family and when I raise up the family, God says, there will be health and wealth in this nation. I will take exactly what I said and make it happen,' says the Lord."

"An economic revival is on its way as I take these kingdoms in My hand. I shall take the sword and Elijah shall walk to the same Jordan that was crossed over before. And God says, 'He will say, Where is the God of Elijah? Where is the God of Billy Graham? Where is the God of Oral Roberts? Where is the God of the greatest of yesterday? For God says, These men have already been accompanied by angels to bring them to My presence." "At this papal discussion, God said, there will also be confusion. But God said the Catholic Church shall be known as Mine. I'm about to take the Paracletos (paraclete-Holy Spirit) and give it to them,' says the Lord. "I speak of My Holy Spirit. I speak of the Holy Spirit. It shall be given to the Roman Catholic Church. God said, I will put it into the papal, into the pope, as a spirit of jealousy, for God said, He will be jealous. And He will say, God must be God. And they will say, you cannot change it. It's going to stay the way it is. But you watch, says the Lord, over a three-year period, how I will change things and they will say there is only one God. There is only one Saint. There is only one God and he is the Lord Jesus Christ."

For this shall be a miraculous invasion of millions of people who shall be taken care of. I will move in South America. I will move in Italy. I will move in France. When they repent for the disgusting things they have done. For God says, in the United Nations, I will pinpoint Russia, I will pinpoint France. I will pull their pants down and show their nakedness to the world. They have played with this nation. They have said we will bring shame to this nation. But God said, Now I will shake the United Nations. And God says, I will abolish it for it has done nothing but steal and bring corruption into this nation."

"The United Nations has housed Judas and now I have taken Judas out. And I am Revealing the lie. I shall abolish the United Nations. The only thing I shall keep is the refugees. I am going to

29

take care of nations financially. There shall be no more United Nations. I will raise up My Spiritual Force that will take care of it. And you know what that force is? It's My church, because My Church is supposed to bring Unity. My Church is supposed to bring finances. The economy is going to change because I will build My Church and the gates of Hell shall not prevail against it. Alleluia!" "Lift your hands up. I will expose Russia. And then the citizens of this nation that have acted the whore. I will bring them out and there will be one political upheaval after another. Because I placed a prophet in the White House. (Our beloved President Donald John Trump) Not a president, a prophet, who has stood the test of time, and he will be exposing all of this without even knowing it."

His anointing is exposing every corruption and America shall rid itself of leeches that take and give nothing back. Citizens who are not citizens but who are enemies of this nation. Let the prophet speak tonight in Nashville, Tennessee. You have allowed him to speak.

You have celebrated. Now, God says, I've sent Angels to watch over your children. I've sent Angels that will remove tumors. I've sent Angels that will stop the divorce. That will stop the breakups. And bring the children into a healthy economy, says the Lord."

January 14th, 2006

"And some of you said, when the Spirit said, 'Hillary Clinton', some of you shouted out, 'Yes!.' God said. 'I have already dealt with her heart, not to be President of this nation, but to be president in a Christian world. She will have a testimony second to none and will eventually come out with it and make a declaration that Jesus Christ saved her marriage, saved her child, and saved her life.

And when this happens, there will be a shaking of the Democratic Party So Powerful."

February 10th 2007

"God's Spirit says, "I'm waiting, I'm waiting for the response from My people throughout this land. Can somebody see victory? Can somebody see honor? For God says, Let Me remind you that I will place at your helm a President that shall pray to ME! Says the Lord. He will pray to ME! And God says, there will be a praying President, not a religious one. For I will fool the people, says the Lord. I will fool the people, yes, I will. God says, the One that is chosen shall go in and they shall say, 'He has hot blood.'"

"For the Spirit of God says, Yes, he may have hot blood, but he will bring the walls of protection on this country in a greater way and the economy of this country shall change rapidly, says the Lord of Hosts."

"Listen to the Word of the Lord, God says, "I will put at your helm for two terms, a President that will pray, but he will not be a praying president when he starts. I will put him in office and then I will baptize him with the Holy Spirit and My Power, says the Lord of Hosts."

April 4th 2007

The Spirit of God says, "I am God and you have called to ME, and many from this nation have said, 'Enough-Enough of religion and enough of dead speech." The Spirit of God says, "This is a movement of resurrection.' For the Spirit of God says, "Honor Me with your praise and acceptance of this that I say to you."

"This that shall take place shall be the most unusual thing, a trans-figuration, a going into the marketplace, if you wish, into the news media. Where Time Magazine will have no choice but to say what I want them to say.

Newsweek, what I want them to say. The View, what I want them to say." For God said, 'I have decided after your prayers and your faith, that this is the year where I shall use the media to destroy the power of control and manipulation.' Says the Lord.

"Trump shall become a Trumpet, says the Lord.

Trump shall become a Trumpet. I will raise up the Trump to become a Trumpet and Bill Gates to open up the gate of a Financial Realm for the Church, says the Lord.' "For God said, I will not forget 9/11. I will not forget what took place on that day, and I will not forget the Gatekeeper that watched over New York, who will once again stand and watch over the Nation, says the Spirit of God." "It shall come to pass that the man that I place in the highest office shall go in whispering My name. But God said, when he enters the office he will be shouting out by the power of the Spirit. For I shall fill him with My Spirit when he goes into office and there will be a praying man in the highest seat in your land."

April 20th, 2013

'The Spirit of God says, 'There is a man by the name of Mr. Clark (Sheriff David Clarke?) And there is also another man by the name of Donald. You are both watching ME, saying, Could it be that God is speaking to me? Yes, He is!" "Somebody, just a few minutes before you came on the show, you went out and you took the American flag, and you said, "I'm proud of my nation." "You raised it up and God said, 'You have been determined through your prayers to influence this nation. You're watching me. You're an influential person. The Spirit of God says, "Hear the Word of the Prophet to you as King. I will open that door that you prayed about. And when it comes time for the election, you will be elected.

February 22, 2014

The Spirit of God says, He says this man (speaking of Trump) will be associated with 'gold'. He will restore American prosperity. He will not be verbose like Obama, but will speak careful words. They will yell, 'Impeach, Impeach! But it will not be so!" "they will even say this President is not speaking up enough, but it won't matter because God has appointed him. The Lord says the plan

He has laid is So Brilliant! : it could only come from ME!' " HE says this President is a very stable genius." (Isn't that what Trump said about himself when they were questioning his mental status? Hysterical!) "He says there will be a second Snowden arising very soon." (Julian Assange) "God calls him 'His David for America.' " He says remember the name Stone." (As in Roger Stone?)

Prophet Kim Clement regarding a Woman

"There is a President who will come. And God says, "He will have absolutely no fear, absolutely no fear. He will be decisive; he will make decisions. And then in the middle of the Restoration of America, rapidly because of a source of Energy that shall come quickly, and because of medical breakthroughs, and because of agreements between nations. "(Specifically China) "God says, "Listen to ME. As the beginning of the Restoration, as it begins, there shall be a woman that shall rise up, a woman that shall be strong in faith; virtuous. Beautiful in

33

the eyes, her eyes shall be so beautiful. Her eyes shall be round and big." "I have crowned her says the Lord, as I crowned Esther. And the people shall receive her. She shall have the oil of gladness for the pain and for the mourning that has taken place, and she shall pour out the oil."

"She shall pour out the oil on this nation, and, God says, healing shall begin and then it shall flow rapidly. And God says, they will say, 'We hated her, but now we love her.' For she shall take the oil of healing and she shall pour it upon the scars of those left and those right and of the new party that has come forth and emerged, where they shall say, 'Christ will reign and we shall not implement socialism at all."

Kim Clement prophecy says, "that Trump will be baptized by the Holy Spirit, He will build the wall* and he will win the second term!!!"

Let not your heart be troubled.

*The importance of the wall is not only to curtail massive smuggling, trafficking and illegal immigration. It is to prevent an immanent invasion from all parts of the world who would use our southern border to breach our national security.

Hebrides Revival
BethAnon

D onald Trump has two great aunts that were responsible for praying in the historic Hebrides Revival down from Heaven between 1949-1952. The Hebrides Islands are off the west coast of Scotland. The story goes that the elderly sisters were too frail to attend the public services. Peggy Smith was 84 and blind and Christine Smith was 82 and almost doubled over with arthritis. As they were unable to attend public worship, their humble Scottish cottage on the Isle of Lewis in the small fishing village of Banas, became their sanctuary. They petitioned God night and day for a promise given to them from the Bible. "I will pour water upon him that is thirsty and floods upon the dry ground." One night, Peggy received a revelation that Revival was coming and their ancestral church would be flooded with young people again. Peggy sent for Reverend James Murray Mackay and told him about her revelation from God. She asked him to call his elders and deacons together for special times of waiting on God.

In the same area a group of men praying in a barn had a premonition of a coming blessing. One night the deacon was leading worship and prostrated to the floor begging to be rightly related to God. An awesome awareness of God filled the barn and supernatural power was let loose in the lives of the congregation.

One of those converted that night was a 15-year old boy named Donald Smith who was a righteous lad who had become a front-line prayer warrior. The Deacon recognized Donald's immersion in God and asked him to lead.

Donald made reference to the fourth chapter of Revelation which he had been reading that morning. "Oh God, I seem to be gazing through an open door. I see the Lamb in the midst of the Throne, with the Keys of death and of Hell at his girdle." He began to sob and lifting his eyes to heaven cried, "O God, there is a Power there, let it loose!"

With the force of a hurricane, the Spirit of God swept into the building and the floodgates of heaven opened. The church resembled a battlefield. On one side many were prostrated over the seats weeping and sighing and on the other side some were affected by throwing their arms in the air connecting to the Divine.

God had come to them. The widespread revival continued from 1949 through 1952 and came to be called the Hebrides Revival. This ties to Donald Trump as Mary Anne Smith Macleod, (Donald Trump's mother) who was the niece of the two intercessors of the Hebrides Revival, also cousin of Donald Smith, the 15- year old converted in the Revival, who emigrated to America and met a gentleman named Frederick Christ Trump.* Mary Anne met Frederick at a dance in New York City where they fell in love and married in January of 1936. Donald John Trump was born in June of 1946 after two other siblings. Little did the praying aunts know their great nephew would one day become President of the United States of America, bringing change and a move of God to the nations. As they say, the apple doesn't fall far from the tree, and it's beautiful to see his praying ancestors. We can appreciate their efforts as we stand with our President and pray for humanity.

*Donald Trump's grandmother, Elizabeth Christ, was born in 1880 and met Friedrich Trump in their hometown of Kallstadt, Germany. They immigrated to the United States and married in New York. They had three children, one of who was Fred, Donald's father. Fred founded his real estate company naming it after his mother, Elizabeth Trump & Son Co. Fred earned his fortune by building affordable housing for middle-class families at a better price and a better quality than his competitors along the East Coast in World War II. When Fred passed away at the age of 49, Elizabeth took control of the family business. She was a natural and was a big part of her grandson Donald's life.

Kindred Putin

BethAnon

"So you want to worship Satan? By all means, but leave Russia out of it. Rest assured that I will be your worst nightmare. You can quote me on that."

Vladimir Putin

There are some great YouTube videos of Putin speaking against the New World Order that I would encourage you to watch and here are some excerpts from the same.

Putin has not only delivered a scathing attack on the new World Order Globalists, he has warned Donald Trump that the secret Cabal is out to get him and has him in their crosshairs. "There is a secret cabal above elected rulers of your country and they have clear goals for the next couple of years. They do not want you to be President, and they are conspiring against you." Get behind us Satan! With all the Russia, Russia rubbish, President Putin never endorsed Trump, but any enemy of the New World Order is a friend of the Russian President's, and he had a few words of warning to share when they spoke on the phone in the run up to the election. Putin warned Trump to expect 'dirty tricks' like we've already seen, and much worse according to a Kremlin source, warning him that elite members of the GOP, his own party, are currently plotting against him.

Well, we have seen this for ourselves in all the fake investigations which fail at every turn as well as the numerous assassination attempts. The Swamp is deep.

Putin has not forgotten the torture and execution of the Romanov family, nor the Bolshevik Revolution, both backed by the heinous Illuminati. In Russia there is an old saying that roughly translates as, 'If you don't understand the past, you won't be able to understand the present, or shape the future." Putin lives by this saying. According to sources, he has been studying the history of the New World Order so he can understand their plans and destroy the invasive organization before its roots and branches spread too far and wide around the world and it becomes too late. This is why Democrats want war with Russia, to get them under Globalist control. (They even have commercials against the NWO as Public Service Announcements in Russia. Good luck with that in the West with Operation Mockingbird CIA NWO owned MSM.)

Fortunately, God is on our side and this NWO abomination is being completely dismantled and revealed by the Alliance, the White Hats, the Q Army, the Remnant, Patriots and all the free children of God around the world. Putin calls Trump a colorful man and appreciates his honesty and service to God and country.

According to The Trump Prophecies by Mark Taylor, Russia will be a strong ally in this coming destruction of the Luciferian NWO. Alleluia!

Putin has given public addresses where he mentions that, "many Euro-Atlantic countries have moved away from their roots, including Christian values. The family is under attack in so many ways. A faith in God and a belief in Satan are being accorded as the same thing. This is the path to degradation. In a State of the Nation address, Vladimir portrayed Russia 'as a staunch defender of 'traditional values' against what he depicted as the morally bankrupt West. Social and religious conservatism is the only way to prevent the world from slipping into 'chaotic darkness.'" Putin makes a crucial point in understanding 'that a nation cannot exist without objective morality, and objective morality cannot exist without God, the Creator, the Essence and Sustainer of the moral universe." (Couldn't have said it better myself, Vlad!)

When Putin makes reference to Satanism it is a political rebuke to the New World Order Elites, who, though they push militant secularism on the societies they are trying to under-mine, they are, in fact, closet Satanists. Darwinism, which has been a huge force in creating agnostics and atheists, is a giant hoax financed once again by, you guessed it, the Rothschild family. (Great YouTube on this: The Elite Don't Want You to Know God is Real—Here's the Proof!) Once you peek behind the curtain you cannot un-peek. New history books are being written now to tell the truth, according to Q, and according to my own knowledge of the many truthers and kindred souls who are busy sharing accurate, revised information, after years of the perversion of the truth by the fake news agenda pushers. In 2013 Putin said, "People in many European countries are ashamed, and are afraid of talking about their religious convic-tions. Religious holidays are being taken away or called some-thing else, shamefully hiding the essence of the holiday." Putin says that, "Russia will defend traditional values* that have made up the spiritual and moral foundation for thousands of years." Not unlike our President, Donald Trump. We love how President Trump Loves God and thanks Him every chance he gets. So this is why Globalists hate Putin* and Trump, because they are

41

saying, 'Enough is Enough'. Like Alexander Solzhenitsyn said, "Let us be bold, let each man choose: will he remain a witting servant of the lies, or has the time come for him to stand straight as an honest man, worthy of the respect of his children and his contemporaries?"

*There is a new documentary called 'The Putin Interviews' by Oliver Stone which is a must watch. Even with Stone trying to rile him up we see the real Putin, who is a common sense, righteous leader who wants a peaceful world. Oliver Stone asked Putin to be godfather for his daughter and Putin agreed.

*Russia forbids gay propaganda to children under 18 years of age. There is no problem with gay people choosing to be gay, but Russia does not want the indoctrination of children regarding gender before they can even think for themselves.

Donald Trump, Popping like Popcorn!

Elisheva Elijah (Eliyahu)

" I am called to minister the gospel of YAHUSHUA Ha MASHIACH with the anointing power of the HOLY GHOST. My goal is to see millions saved, sanctified, and filled with HOLY GHOST manifested power. I strive to obey YAHUSHUA and put HIM first in my life in every way."

+++

Below is the Prophecy as it came forth with Prophet Elisheva's "Holy tongues," as GOD'S SPIRIT gives utterance (Acts 2:3-4) of heavenly or earthly languages (1 Co 13:1). Elisheva speaks forth in tongues bringing Prophecy (1 Co 14:6).

It contains the HEBREW NAMES of GOD:

YAH / YAHUVEH is GOD'S HOLY, SACRED NAME as in "Alleluia" or "Hallelu YAH". Which literally means "Praise YAH": YAHUVEH / YAHWEH is GOD THE FATHER; YAHUSHUA / YAHSHUA is GOD'S ONLY BEGOTTEN SON (HA MASHIACH means "THE MESSIAH"; ELOHIM means "GOD.")

The Revelation of "SH'KHINYAH GLORY" as the PERSONAL NAME of RUACH HA KODESH, (in English The HOLY SPIRIT), is also on this site. (HA SH'KHINAH {SHEKINAH} is Hebrew for GOD'S ABIDING, DIVINE PRESENCE.)

43

Additionally, ABBA YAH means "FATHER YAH" and IMMAYAH means "MOTHER YAH."

Scripture quotes are KJV or NKJV unless otherwise indicated.

+++

YAHUVEH'S Words to Elisheva to be added before the Prophecies:

I warned you a long time ago Elisabeth [Elisheva], not to name this Ministry after a man or a woman. Even before there was a Ministry, I put it in your spirit.

For none of this has been done by your hands. None of this has come forth from your mouth.

It is from the Mouth of YAHUVEH that has given birth. It is from the Mouth of YAHUSHUA, your MASHIACH, that it has been given birth. It is from the Mouth of the RUACH HA KODESH, your IMMAYAH, that it has been given birth.

If it had only been by your hand, it would have failed long ago.

It is by the SHKHINYAH GLORY'S WIND that blows across this earth, the HOLY WIND OF REVIVAL. It is not by your breath, or it would have failed.

I AM the LORD YAHUVEH: that is MY NAME: And MY GLORY I will not give to another, Neither MY PRAISE to graven images. Isaiah 42:8

(Prophecy 105)

In July 2010, YAHUVEH GOD also said to add the following as a warning to those who mock:

But they mocked the Messengers of GOD, despised HIS Words, and scoffed at HIS Prophets, until the Wrath of YAHUVEH arose against HIS People, till there was no remedy. 2 Chronicles 36:16

Then, in July 2016:

Woe be unto anyone that dares to try to harm these two anointed ones. You will regret the day you ever were born. Touch

44

not MY anointed and neither do these two Prophets any harm (see Ps 105:15; 1 Ch 16:22). It would be better for you if I, ABBA YAHUVEH, would tear out your tongue!

(Prophecy 128)

And from Prophet Ezra:

I warn you, all those who are coming against this Ministry AND THESE PROPHECIES and Elisheva and I, all the Ministers of AmightyWind Ministry, I warn you now, Touch not YAH'S Anointed and do HIS Prophets no harm? (Ps 105:15; 1 Ch 16:22) lest the Wrath of the Rod of YAH come upon you. But for those who are blessed and are a blessing for this Ministry, and faithful, and who receive the Prophecies, much blessing will come on you all to protect what belongs to YAH in the NAME OF YAHUSHUA.

+++

This Prophecy was recorded via audio. Here is the transcription.

[Ezra prays in Holy tongues...]

Elisheva: ABBA YAHUVEH, in the NAME OF YAHUSHUA [we pray].

Ezra: HEAVENLY FATHER I ask YOU for us to be invisible-to cover us ABBA YAHUVEH-in the physical realm and in the spiritual realm, to be covered with the SHED BLOOD OF YAHUSHUA which is the weapon above all weapons (2 Co 10:3-5; Rv 12:11). We ask YOU ABBA YAHUVEH to do it for us in the NAME OF YOUR HOLY SON YAHUSHUA.

And satan I speak to you right now and all your principalities and the demons that are attached to you, I bind you from this conference call. I bind you from this Internet connection. Whatever I bind on earth is bound in Heaven (Mt 18:18) so you are bound on this earth, in this place in YAHUSHUA'S NAME.

I ask YOU ABBA YAHUVEH to send him to where he belongs, to all the place that YOU have prepared for all [of them], him and

45

his demons (2 Pt 2:4), until the day of Judgment in YAHUSHUA'S NAME (Mt 8:29).

Elisheva & Ezra: Amen.

[Ezra prays in Holy tongues; Elisheva joins]

Elisheva: [Whisper] What is it YOU want to say ABBA YAHUVEH? What is it YOU want to say YAHUSHUA?

[Holy tongues...]

Elisheva: What is it YOU want to say ABBA YAHUVEH? What is it YOU want to say YAHUSHUA? Hallelu YAH! [Holy tongues..]

ABBA YAHUVEH in the NAME OF YAHUSHUA, I thank YOU and I praise YOU right now. [Whisper] Please give me a Word about Donald Trump in the NAME OF YAHUSHUA. [Holy tongues ...]

We wait for YOU, MOMMA [RUACH HA KODESH]. We wait for YOU. What is it YOU want to say? What is it YOU want to say? [Tongues intensify...]

Prophecy 131 Begins:

June 29, 2016

I, YAHUVEH say I HAVE raised up Donald Trump for this time and this hour!

Elisheva: Oh my!

Prophecy Continues:

The satanic elite that fills the White House have so much blood on their hands (Ps 94:20-23) -the blood of a murderer, the blood of the unborn-but I've raised up Donald Trump, who values the sanctity of life. And it is his desire, and I have given him this desire: To wash that blood off the hands! To change the abortion laws! To give the rights back to the states!

Psalm 94: 20 Shall the throne of iniquity have fellowship with THEE, which frameth mischief by a law? 21 They gather themselves together against the soul of the righteous, and condemn the innocent blood. 22 But the LORD YAHUVEH is my DEFENCE; and my GOD is the ROCK OF MY REFUGE. 23 And HE shall bring upon them their own iniquity, and shall cut them off in their own wickedness; yea, the LORD YAHUVEH our GOD shall cut them off.

Elisheva, I changed your heart!

You only saw him where curse words filled his mouth. You saw him where he is a man that worships the material things of this world. But then as I showed you in a dream, the Prophecies he would come and he would read, and I AM drawing him even now as you speak!

TO BOW HIS KNEE TO ME!

-I, YAHUSHUA-

For although others look at him [negatively] and before you told the prayer intercessors to pray for him, you too-only saw the filth that comes out of his mouth-but I AM raising him up and I AM using a man who doesn't know righteousness yet. And yet I've put the desire in him for righteousness (Mt 5:6)!

Matthew 5:6 Blessed are they which do hunger and thirst after righteousness: for they shall be filled.

He wants to do what is right. He wants to stop the slaughter of the unborn! He wants the right of freedom of speech-back again! He does not want the transgender agenda! It is an abomination!

He has taken much persecution-as he tries to walk a fine line so he can win this election-so he keeps so much of his thoughts to himself. But when I tell him, and it's coming, to no longer care what people think and "Stop trying to walk that fine line. Keep speaking your mind!"-you are gonna' [going to] behold a changed man!

For this man has no blood on his hands of a murderer! In fact he wants to put those in the White House behind bars!

Elisheva: I see a vision of popcorn. He's going to be-he is like that. You put the kernels in a pan and YAHUSHUA is saying HE'S gonna' shake 'em [them]. HE'S shaking that pan. And where there was only a few kernels of truth allowed, it's going to fill that whole pan to overflowing-of popcorn, because that's what it's like-and he makes lots of 'noise'! ABBA YAH is saying...

Prophecy Continues:

He has been anointed to make the noise! You can't silence him-they've tried.

They've tried to intimidate him! They try to bring him shame! They've mocked him! They defiled his reputation! They try to make him look like he's lower in the polls. In reality, he's higher.

Elisheva: In fact it's ABBA YAHUVEH that has blessed him! For again, YAHUSHUA says...

Prophecy Continues:

Do not look at him with the eyes of the past. Realize during this time, I'm changing his heart-even with the new birth of his grandchild.

Elisheva: I see his desire is to rewrite-YAHUSHUA is telling me...

Prophecy Continues:

His desire is to rewrite so many laws and give the power back-to the states-that never should have been taken away. So Elisheva I give you this mandate this day. You & Ezra! Oh, no matter who it's gonna' offend, you're gonna' tell them.

There is no one else!

Just like I spoke out of the mouth of a donkey (Nm 22:22-35; 2 Pt 2:16) and MY will was done even though it appears he's on such a 'high horse' I, YAHUVEH, know how to humble him!

So, have the people who consider AmightyWind Ministry a blessing to start praying for him. Because just like you Ezra, was, drawn through the prayers (because of those around this world) when I gave the mandate to Elisheva to pray for Caleb to come-(she asked, "What is his name?" and I said, "You can just call him Caleb," but now she knows your name is Ezra) and she now understands-the same mandate, I give this Ministry this day: Pray for Donald Trump! To do all that he can! To wash the blood out of the White House!

Elisheva: There's so much blood! HE'S giving me a vision.

Prophecy Continues:

They serve the god of moloch (Lv 18:21; Dt 12:31). They sacrifice the unborn. And what's done in America has been a chain reaction that's around this world.

Leviticus 18:21 And thou shalt not let any of thy seed pass through the fire to Moloch, neither shalt thou profane the NAME OF THY GOD: I AM THE LORD YAHUVEH.

Deuteronomy 12:31 Thou shalt not do so unto the LORD YAHUVEH THY GOD: for every abomination to the LORD YAHUVEH, which he hateth, have they done unto their gods; for even their sons and their daughters they have burnt in the fire to their gods.

Elisheva: I just have these strange visions, Ezra. Again I see him with a [fire] hose. This is the desire YAH has put in his heart, to cleanse that White House! And I see him with a [fire] hose! And I don't-so much blood! He's got a [fire] hose and he's washing the floors of the White House and blood is just coming out of the doors! GOD is raising him up!

GOD, ABBA YAHUVEH says...

Prophecy Continues:

I've-I'm changing his heart! I've already begun!

And Elisheva if I would speak forth even more Words - and I shall when it's the right timing, but if I speak more of what I'm showing you - it would be used against him. For whatever "obamanation" has been for, he is against! They mock him about the birth certificate. They mock him about his stand on transgender.

But I YAHUVEH say, I've changed his heart during all this time-as he went before the people, as he genuinely cares about the people-I, YAHUSHUA say, I'm washing his heart, I'm cleansing his heart! He hasn't totally surrendered to ME. But remember the mandate I give this Ministry:

START PRAYING!

Remember Ezra, you were not even saved when I gave Elisheva that dream, when I gave her that love for you! Look what I've done for you! Look how I've promoted you!

Look how I changed your heart!

And I say this, as the prayers of the people-humble themselves and fall on their knees and repent: It is the prayers of the righteous that avails much (Jms 5:16). It is only by MY Hand alone that he is kept alive. For I have dispatched Holy angels to make sure that he survives! For there's already been attempts [on his life] that never came to fruition-never accomplished what the devil wanted, it to be done.

Remember this! I'm not done with Donald Trump.

As he was mocked for not knowing the Bible: He went to search in the Bible. He went to search for Scriptures. And some of them he hid in his heart (Psalm 119:11), and this is when the cleansing started.

Psalm 119:11 Thy word have I hid in mine heart, that I might not sin against thee.

As the interviewer said, "Give us some Scriptures! You say you're a Christian!" he had to go search. And I led him to where

I wanted him to read. And Elisheva, the dream that I gave you: He's going to read those Prophecies. He will want to know the meaning. He will ask.

I changed your heart Elisheva where once you just looked at him and you said, "He's an abomination! Look at him! So full of pride! Curse [words]-[he] mouths out of every other word."

But I remind you Elisheva, I, YAHUSHUA paid that PRICE at Calvary for Donald Trump!

It is I, YAHUSHUA that cleanses the heart. And your prayers-when you gave them to "YAHUSHUA'S demon stompers," I had to change your heart to a heart of love for Donald Trump before you would intercede and pray for him.

You see, it's not just about changing America. America has corrupted the world! It is not about making America great again! For America will never be great again. They are polluted with sin.

But it's about the prayers of the righteous who are crying out to ME and who are asking, "ABBA YAHUVEH do something! Help us politically. Give us a voice to change these laws!"

Where once only the minority believe-and now they force it to look like it's the majority and this goes from everything to abortion, to homosexuality, to transgender, [laws against] the morality, the freedom of speech-the lies, Donald Trump wants to turn to truth! He wants the truth spoken.

And, there's trembling knees! For he truly does have the facts! To put so many of the politicians behind bars-and this is truly a desire of his heart.

So I end this one more time.

As Elisheva, you warned about Obama. You warned and you warned - before the man was even elected - and a change came, but it was a change for the worse. And America was cursed in a way it had never been before.

Now I give you this mandate - with Ezra by your side, both of you, assemble the people who consider AmightyWind Ministry a blessing-to start praying for Donald Trump. That he stays in the forefront!

For he's in a horse race and not even the news is revealing the truth about him: how many people are supporting him! Why? Because the White House owns the media! But even this is going to change.

Elisheva: [Sees a vision] I really do see a horse race and he really does look like he's in first place. He really does. ABBA YAHUVEH I never, ever, ever thought that I would ever say such a prayer!

But we really do pray with all of our hearts for the salvation of Donald Trump; that he really will be in that White House (and although at one time he was so outnumbered-but YOU'RE telling me-even the negative press helped him to get in that first place).

So I stand in agreement-

Prophecy Continues:

He's coming to this Ministry. He will hear these Prophecies, especially those that stand up for the sanctity of life. He is so against abortion. He truly loves those little babies in the wombs.

Elisheva: Thank YOU BELOVED YAHUSHUA! We believe in faith that YOU will put him in that White House! YOU will give him that [fire] hose! And he is going to wash that blood out!

Prophecy Continues:

It's not only the blood of the unborn! It's all these wars that have been started! It's all of these-oh so much blood! So much blood (Ps 106:37; Pr 1:16)! Oh my, oh my, how evil, how evil the politicians are!

Psalm 106: 37 Yea, they sacrificed their sons and their daughters unto devils, 38 And shed innocent blood, even the blood of their sons and of their daughters, whom they sacrificed unto the idols of Canaan: and the land was polluted with blood.

Proverbs 1:16 For their feet run to evil, and make haste to shed blood.

This is why Elisheva I say to you, Donald Trump does not play the game of a politician. He speaks the words that the people would want to say-those that have any morality left. And those who love their country. He does not speak like a politician.

Elisheva: There's so much more that I would say right now but if I do, he'd lose! [Elisheva laughs.] That's all I'm gonna' say! There's some things a Prophet is not allowed to say. I won't do it!

But ABBA YAH showed me things about him. And Donald Trump truly, truly, truly is being drawn to YAHUSHUA. Um - the Judaism that his daughter married into he has a love for the Jewish people. And this is what ABBA YAH does give me permission to say.

Prophecy Continues:

He truly loves Israel. He truly - He truly, truly would be a friend to Israel.

Elisheva: ABBA YAH is saying-

Prophecy Continues:

- and it's his daughter who led him to have that love for Israel-

Elisheva: And I just keep hearing this one Scripture, "And a little child shall lead them" (Is 11:6).

Well ABBA YAH is there anything else you want to say? Today, whatever date this is, we stand in agreement. We will put some-thing-YOU tell us, tell Ezra what to write. And I will stand in agree-ment because he is a man of few words.

Elisheva: [Speaks what she hears from Heaven to say] And we will stand in agreement. And we will ask the people and we will put it in a video-that AmightyWind Ministry supports Donald

Trump with our prayers: FIRST for his salvation; and then that ABBA YAH YOU can use him-to wash the blood out of the White House.

End of Word.

Elisheva: That's what I hear.

Ezra: Thank YOU! We praise YOU, ABBA YAHUVEH! Thank YOU YAHUSHUA! Thank YOU IMMAYAH for the confirmation that he is the President that YOU have been raising. And I was talking to Elisheva and telling her and this came out. And that's the truth!

Elisheva: Yes!

Ezra: So we are supporting him 100% ABBA YAHUVEH because it's YOUR will for him to be as a president-to clean all the mess that has been done in that White House. So we thank YOU ABBA YAHUVEH for this Revelation and for the Word to the public. We bless YOUR HOLY NAME ABBA YAHUVEH in YAHUSHUA'S NAME! Amen.

Elisheva: And we just pray FATHER that people will under-stand-this is YOUR plan. This is, this is, this is YOUR plan. We're going out on this limb here FATHER. I knew. I knew, I knew, I knew about 'obamanation' in advance and told the people.

But now FATHER we are praying for the salvation of the soul of Donald Trump. People must take it very, very seriously and truly pray for this man! Because he's already-has the desires that YOU have put into his heart and he doesn't even realize how much he has already changed, in the NAME OF YAHUSHUA.

So this is a [Laughs] so one part of me says, "Oh FATHER I'm already on a shaky limb with the new leadership [announce-ment]," and YOU just, YOU just say, "Go out a little further on that limb Elisheva & Ezra!" But praise YAHUSHUA, YOU'RE the

ONE WHO keeps the limb from breaking! So we give YOU the Glory FATHER! We thank YOU and we praise YOU!

Precious-everyone, everyone who considers AmightyWind Ministry a blessing, no matter what language you are of, thank you for start[ing to pray]-praying that ABBA YAH'S will, will be done in Donald Trump and that the man is going to bow his knee and accept YAHUSHUA as MESSIAH!

Because when he does, he will be a President like none other. And it will be-it will affect . . . it will affect the countries around this world!

And we thank YOU ABBA YAHUVEH in the NAME OF YAHUSHUA. We praise YOU, we praise YOU, we praise YOU! We praise YOU ABBA YAHUVEH for raising up a man that no one would ever suspect! And you're doing it! And I keep seeing this horse race, FATHER, and he's definitely in the front in YAHUSHUA'S NAME! And that's what I had to say!

Ezra: Amen

Elisheva: What are you-? Oh yeah! Kathrynyah had visions!

More Visions

Kathrynyah: I was asking her [Elisheva] if I should share what I saw, just a couple things. I saw her [Elisheva] bowing before YAHUSHUA and HE had HIS Hand on her head.

Elisheva: Oh! Thank you! I needed that!

Kathrynyah: And then...

Elisheva: Well Ezra's right there, wherever I am.

Kathrynyah: So I'm listening and I see a loaf of white bread with the top and it has [black] pepper on it. At the top, is scraped off. I think it represents Donald Trump - like the top, maybe half an inch section scraped off and it's white underneath. Does that make sense?

Elisheva: Yeah! It's taking a layer of pepper-

Kathrynyah: -but there's pepper on top which is dark spots, you know?

Elisheva: Yeah. Well, yeah.

Kathrynyah: But underneath it's white. So we do, we lift him up to YOU FATHER.

Elisheva: I just pray FATHER, in the NAME OF YAHUSHUA-YOU know the secret dream that I am not going to reveal before the world. We can probably find out the date [of the dream], but when I told the YDS's to start praying.

I'm not. I'm not... Donald Trump has a secret that YOU entrusted to me. I pray FATHER that dream comes totally true in the NAME OF YAHUSHUA. And Donald Trump will become a friend of this Ministry. And he's going to learn through the Prophecies that which he has not known before in YAHUSHUA'S NAME. And I receive every part of that dream in YAHUSHUA'S NAME.

Ezra: Amen! Amen!

Elisheva: Awesome! Awesome, awesome, awesome! Who would know that would happen!

End of Recording.

I want to add this. It was cut from the audio. Pray and vote-and support him.

So it is spoken, so it is written in the NAME OF YAHUSHUA,

June 29, 2016

Apostle, Prophet Elisheva Eliyahu

A Mighty Wind Ministry: http://www.allmightywind.com/

https://www.youtube.com/results?search_query=yahsladyinred

https://www.youtube.com/user/YAHSservant777

https://www.amightywind.com/en/prophecyproof.html

Congratulations to YAH's AMightyWind for 26 years on the Internet!

The Trump Card
for Israel
Stephen Powell

My name is Stephen Powell. I was born and raised in the great state of Alaska, one of the most amazing places in the world. I was raised in the church but didn't really give my life to Jesus and start living for him until I was 14. From the very beginning of my conversion I was extremely devout in my faith. Although much of my immature expression of that faith was religious at the beginning, I had a pure heart, and God graciously visited me powerfully from the very beginning!

When I was fifteen I was filled with the Holy Spirit and received seasons of 'visitations' over the years while I went through years of character building and deepening understanding. I married an amazing woman, Amanda Kay Powell, and we have four beautiful children together.

We currently reside in Fort Mill, South Carolina and serve in a fulltime ministry in the Fresh Fire's School of Revival.

Be encouraged as you read this testimony that God can use anybody, that God always fulfills His Word, and that God never leaves you or forsakes you! JUST KEEP GOING! Trust that He truly will work all things together for your good as you love Him and keep accepting the call He has on your life!

The Trump Card for Israel

"The Lord would say to you Israel I've raised up a storm for you, and in this storm will stand a man for you from across the sea, and he shall receive blow after blow after blow for you Israel, but he is anointed to shed the arrows with justice, to resist the pressures from the wicked one to bend and to bow to nothing that comes against you, I will bless you, Oh Israel, for there is a man that I have given to you, to stand in My storm for you.

For in this storm I shall cause a shiver, a shake, a fear, and a dread to fall upon your enemies in this next season, Oh Israel, oh apple of my eye. I will shake your enemies, they shall be in disarray, they shall be in confusion, for I shall be a tempest against them. There is the storm of the enemy, and there is the tempest of the Lord, and I have raised up My Mighty One anointing, to stand in the storm, and stand for you Oh Israel. I'm standing with you, I'm standing for you, and I've raised up a man to stand in this storm for you, says the Lord."

"A fire goes before me, and also a fire goes before this man, and your enemies. Oh Israel shall be scattered before you. I shall drive you out of this land, for I shall put My fear and My dread upon your enemies, and they will will be clamoring after their own devices, they shall be utterly distraught by their own evil intentions and devices which they've formed against you, and those who find themselves in order aright, in this right order which I have set, which I have sent, which I'm revealing now in your time, shall find themselves flourishing in My harvest that I have set for the nations for this day."

"There is Jubilee for the nations, but there is Jubilee for My people Israel, and the land must be restored, and I the Lord am standing over this land, My land, Oh Israel, and I'm releasing the anointing which is necessary for your Jubilee, for your land, says the Lord. They shall drink from the cup of confusion, you Oh Israel shall drink from My cup of wisdom and strength, and you shall find strength in the vision, in the hope, in the leaping heart of joy which I shall sow to you in this season for harvest and strength, says the Lord."

"And now to you America, I've given you a brother in Israel, but you're giving your mouth to deceit, but I extend this invitation to you now, oh church, come out from among them, shed yourselves of that covering that is in the world, and see this word I speak to you. I've sent you a brother to Israel, a deliverer. Glorify Me in this season and watch as I rise in your land, and I fulfill My promise to My people Israel, and I will move with harvesting glory in the nations for such a time as this!

Your tongue is the framer oh church, don't weaken this foundation I've given you for the New Day, for it shall be a day of bright shining, of new light, of new inventions, even in Israel, as the anointing on you Israel for the witty inventions, the engines of war against the enemy's strongholds which shall devastate his corporation in the nations, says the Lord."

"Before your eyes consider your works, for I am watching, even from the White House, says the Lord. And I shall watch over My people Israel, and I will bless those who bless her, I will stand against those who stand against My Israel, says the Lord. I will set in order before your very eyes this divine establishment in the earth which I've chosen for My kingdom purposes, says the Lord. The heart of the prophetic shall rise and rise and rise, to make a strong port, for this strong anchor to go deep into My glory, says the Lord. For I am moving to establish an anchor for the soul of my people in this season, which shall be anchored to the heart and faith of Christ, which shall not be removed, henceforth, now and forever, as I bring a reviving of the Spirit again to My land of Israel. I will open the upper room again in Jerusalem, so pray, wait, tarry, watch, as I send these floods, for refreshing is yours, power is yours, presence is yours, for I will kiss you Jerusalem in this day, and you shall know that I am your Lord, and you are the apple of My eye, says the Lord!"

Trump is Unstoppable

"There is great momentum behind President Trump right now. Momentum can't be manufactured. It is part of a spiritual movement, which in this case, is part of a movie of God. This momentum enabled him to snatch the presidency from certain defeat, it enabled him to overcome the impossible, and he'll do the same while governing. Where people believe he won't be able to do this, he won't be able to do that, this momentum and this spiritual force behind him will cause him to break through barriers others failed to break through. I hear the Lord saying, this man is unstoppable because I'm unstoppable, my kingdom is unstoppable, and this man has a mandate from heaven, he has momentum that is not his own. His movement will not dissipate, it will grow, and it will reach beyond the borders of American governing. It will inspire, it will stir up a nest. As the eagle stirs up the nest, so the Lord will do through this man.

People are laughing at him, saying that his plans are too bold, his ideas are too big, that his plans will not work because after all, what President has been able to do these things before without gridlock? But the Lord is saying, this President shall not be in gridlock, for his strength is not his own. I have put a spirit of breakthrough on this man and on this land, and he will do these things that will be monumental for the generations to come. I will use him to stir up the nest and cause this young generation of young eagles to soar. Even a new class of young politician will see and say, I can do that, I can soar. I can be bold, I can be brave, and not bow to political correctness or the fear of man. I can fear God and be bold and stand up for what is right, and I can truly make a difference. For if God is for me, what Senator can be against, who can resist my agenda if my agenda is not my own? These senator, these congressmen, they are just men, they are just people.

Who can resist the hand of God when it is upon a nation, and God begins to stir up the nest?"

"Watch and see in this next season as I continue to do the impossible in the face of adversity, as I continue to show you signs and wonders, coming from this political sphere. There is a new faith available, a hope which I'm awakening right now, and it shall rise like the morning sun after a long dark night, and I shall rise with healing in My wings, even for the nations. This is My time of hope and healing, even from the womb of the morning, in the beauties of My holiness, to bring forth a New Day. But no, this shall not be gridlock, for nothing shall stop this man that I have anointed for this hour.

This is not just America's hour, but Israel's time as well. And this man whom I've chosen shall complete Presidential assignments for Israel going back even to the days of the Six Day War, for I the Lord have not forgotten the words I spoke to My presidents. I the Lord have not forgotten those mandates I gave to them for My Chosen people, Israel. Those mandates are still sitting here in Heaven, waiting for this man to rise up and take hold of them again, and move in My breakthrough, even for My people, even for My land which lies to the east, a place of destiny for these times, a place which I shall make My Peace."

"The Lord would say, continue to be unstoppable, for I will make you unbreakable, for even when they plot, and scheme, and shrewdly construct their ways against you, I will give you the upper hand. I will give you their next moves. The enemy will not outmaneuver you, Mr. Trump, for I am with you now in this time, in this hour, to move something forward which has been stuck for years. Yea, even this past generation could not complete their assignment because Israel could not possess their land, just as it was in Joshua's day. But as Joshua was preserved and matured for his hour of conquest, so have I preserved and matured you, Mr. Trump, for the time that would come to take the land. First you'll lead a charge to take back your own land, a land which I've given for this Republic which shall continue to stand, but I am the Lord, and I have purposed for My Chosen people, Israel to have their land, and they shall have their land, for I the Lord have spoken it, even before you were born. Israel, My Chosen people, shall have their land, and nothing shall stop this. You Mr. Trump I have made unstoppable, not just for your nation but for Israel too, for you shall minister to her, you shall protect her, and you shall set an agenda with her, partnering together for the next stage in My plans, and in this also you shall not be gridlocked like prior administrations have, for I am with you, and with the progress you make on the State's side, so you will carry this unstoppable anointing across the sea. I have commanded My people to hear you, to heed your voice, for the frequency I've given you is not your own. It's the frequency of awakening, it's the sound of freedom, it's a strength My people need, and they shall receive hope in this hour which shall be like oxygen to their life blood. The nation will receive fresh life again, because when you hope in Me you receive fresh life."

"And now I've come to deal with China, and with this nation, yes I will deal, for they have defied Me and My words for many generations, but they will not defy Me anymore, for I have purposed a Mighty Harvest in the East, and in this Harvest I will receive of their government, for what man can resist Me, what system can stand in the way of My Advancing Kingdom in this day? For the markets are mine, the steel is mine, the houses are mine, the land is mine. I will give My people in this land a House of Glory, a House of Freedom, a House of Safety, yes to worship in the days to come. And I will come in like a Covering Father to carve out a place for My people, a place of safety, a place of refuge, for this is the day of My Great Refuge, even refuge for the nations, says the Lord. But with you, China, I will contend, and you will not be able to resist Me, for I'm calling for a New Foundation in your land. It will be built on My Word, and My Agenda will come forth. And just as I've brought men forth that would be led by My Agenda in other lands, so I will bring this forth in your land, oh China. These men and women are being called forth now.

They're being harvested right now to carry My Heart in high places of authority. I'm unstoppable here as well, and I will find men and women to bear My Heart in this nation. I will do it. I Am the Lord."

Sound of the Trumpet Heard & Felt Around the World

"I hear the Lord say, I have chosen you, Mr. Trump, and you will be a leader to many, not just of your people, but of the world. You will not just be seen Mr. Trump, but you will be heard, for I have released a sound in you, and that sound shall be heard around the world. It will ring true and loud, and be like a shockwave in many countries where tyranny has reigned, and they will not be able to keep it out, says the Lord. For I will raise up this Sound in others, even as I have raised it up in you.

It's the Sound of the Trumpet of the Lord, a sound of Victory, a sound of Freedom, a sound of Faith."

"Hearts will rise to meet world problems based on the Sound I've released, says the Lord. Fear will be replaced with faith, doubt with optimism, for tomorrow will be greater than the former days, says the Lord. My people will hear the sound and they will believe it."

"I see this man's anointing being sent out like an electrical shock wave which will Awaken the Heart of Freedom in Nations that have not beat with it in generations, says the Lord. The Earth will see, and hear, and Seek Refuge in Me. This is the hour of My Refuge, says the Lord."

"America, America, I have called you in this hour, says the Lord. To stand tall, to stand free, to stand independent and sovereign, in the light of My Glory, says the Lord. You will lead the world into a New Day, My Day, My Vision, My Heart, says the Lord. As you honor Israel, I will honor you. As you feed the hungry, I will feed you.

And nothing will stop you, says the Lord. You are an unstoppable nation, a moving force for good and greatness, in the sight of the nations, says the Lord."

" I have chosen Donald Trump to forerun a new model of national leaders, says the Lord; yea, even a new form of world leader, says the Lord. This man will batter through demonic barriers, even on the world stage, which no man or woman in world history, has been able to have the breakthrough in before, says the Lord. But I have anointed him for this time, and his strength is not his own. I have assigned My Angels to assist him in the breakthrough, to remove every stumbling block, to extract every demonic levy, says the Lord. His sound will be heard and felt, and I will put My fear on entire nations who see, and fear, and do not understand my working in this man, says the Lord. For he will demonstrate something that I have chosen him for, a unique office, a unique position, a unique role, says the Lord. And many will follow after him, not just in America, but in the nations, says the Lord."

"Is My Arm shortened, has My Heart grown dim in the dark places of the world? Have I forgotten My people whom I love, whom I died for, whom I shed the innocent blood, even of My Only Begotten Son, to save them, says the Lord? No, I have not forgotten you, I have not forsaken you, in this hour of awakening you will know My Heart, and you will know My Strength, and you will know My Plan, says the Lord. Every child I see, every child I hear, and this man, whom I have chosen, says the Lord, will bear the weight of the world on his shoulders, and in doing so he will bear My Heart, says the Lord. I will move his heart while he's in office, and he will continue to sacrifice much, for my people, says the Lord. He will continue to give much of his fortune, and much of his life, for this cause which I have yoked his heart to, says the Lord. And this cause, which he has not yet fully understood himself, shall continue to take hold of him and consume his heart, says the Lord. I will make him a compassionate leader, a loving leader, but a strong leader, fearless in the face of the demonic, says the Lord. Let the Spirit of Breakthrough flow through this man's administration, as the breakthrough of Heaven's Armies continue to invade the earth, even Africa, even the Sudan, even the Far East, parts of the world broken, uncontended, I will contend for your Heart, says the Lord. I will release in the valleys of darkness, in the places of captivity, in the strongholds of religion and men, says the Lord. For it is time for the piercing light of My Word to go deeper and deeper, says the Lord. I will continue to go deeper into India, deeper into the Sudan, deeper into Saudi Arabia, deeper into Iran. I will break apart your foundations, and build new ones in the Apostolic, new ones in Love, new ones in

Me, says the Lord. And My Kingdom will advance, My kingdom will wage war, for the battle is Mine, says the Lord!"

Trump Will Have a Highway Experience

"I hear the Lord saying, 'Trump will have a highway experience.' He will find his way in this, in this presidency, for hidden in this season and in this hour is My Way, the highest way, says the Lord. And Donald Trump will find it. He will find a way to govern which has not preceded him for generations. He will find the Way of the Government of God in this season, for I the Lord have hidden it in his midst, and I will cause him to learn it, as I have taught him many other things along the path to the White House. He will not be outmaneuvered by the enemy; he will not be outsmarted. He will be given Revelation from the Heart of God, a Wisdom to rule, an access point to the ways of God, as Solomon was given in his time and in his day. From the thorns and thistles of our grounds will spring forth the Harvest in this day.

Donald Trump has been given a prosperity anointing, but the Lord says this anointing is the grace to "prosper in God's way", to prosper in the path which the Word of the Lord divides for. He will find access into a heavier portion of My Word in this hour, and in this Word will be given the prosperous way of a prosperous rider."

"The Lord our God has fashioned Mr. Trump into an instrument of breakthrough for America. In this breakthrough which has been opened in the Spirit, the Kingdom of God will come pouring back into America in an incredible way. Our way shall be made the way of the prosperous again instead of that of the debtor and the thief, for Donald Trump will continue to climb higher on the highway of the Lord, where he shall continue to learn the higher ways of God's Government. In this quick study he shall have the strength and the courage to implement into the earth what he learns at Heaven's counsel, and forever reform the office of the presidency. For from this time on every President will be held to this standard as such, for in this day a new standard will be formed out of the ways of God which Trump shall learn."

"With this breakthrough anointing which Trump is in, there comes access to the thoughts of God.

In these thoughts are hidden the ways of God. As he seeks ME, the Lord says, for Heaven's counsel, he shall find it, and again I say, he shall have the courage to bring the needed reform and implement what he's been taught of the Lord."

"Once breakthrough reaches a certain height there shall come the rains and the snows of God, which are the life of the Spirit for Harvest and the Glory of God to light upon this land. The land sings at the sight of this breakthrough, for from the thistles and the thorns of America shall spring forth new life in this day, and we as a nation shall once again have seed for the sower and bread for many eaters. Each man will eat from his own fig tree planted by his own hand. There will be a roll back on the bread and circus to manipulate the mob. Each man will eat of his own tree, says the Lord."

"In this breakthrough is the sword of the Lord. Found in His mouth, it shall go forth and make the way of this President prosperous, and in return the nation. Debt will become reserve, inferiority, prized accomplishment, for the days of roaring innovation shall come thundering back to these shores, loosed by the lifting of the economic fog our nation has been limping under for years. These words I put in this man's mouth are not useless, bringing back no profit, says the Lord. Indeed, they are full of life and purpose, and they will not return to his legacy lacking, for these are My words which I put in his mouth, to root out and to pull down, to destroy and throw down, to build and to plant a New America.

The Lord is ready to perform His Word on America, and this man will prosper in his way because the Lord will teach him the higher ways, the way of God's government on the earth. Pray for this man, and let your mind, your heart, and your tongue be single on this matter, concerning what the Lord has said about this President and what he shall accomplish. The Lord will fulfill His Word concerning this man. Believe the Word of the Lord!"

Trump Has God's Heart for North Korea

"In this hour of great tension, fear, and uncertainty, having nuclear warheads in the discussion, it's important to remember that our God reigns, and there has never been and never will be a nuclear bomb in play without God's direct involvement. North Korea may be out of most people's jurisdiction and oversight, but no one is out of God's jurisdiction and oversight. The nations may rage, evil may set itself against the Lord our God and the endeavors of good, but remember this, the Lord our God sits in the heavens and laughs. All of these schemes shall ultimately come to nothing; the enemy shall be filled with confusion, and our God shall have the last laugh."

My First Vision Ever of North Korea

"It was in the year 2012 when I happened to be in Seoul, South Korea, right near the border with North Korea, that I found myself having a vision of this nation. I was praying at the time in the greenroom of a church right before I was set to come out and minister to the South Korean people. I was praying for Revival, praying for God's Spirit to be poured out. As the prayers flowed from my heart I found myself praying also for North Korea. I knew that many of the South Koreans had relatives, family members, going back generations, who were living in that land under the iron fist of that demonic rule. I was asking for revival in North Korea, when suddenly I saw missiles being launched out of South Korea into the North taking out key strategic attack positions, disabling the North Korean's ability to attack Seoul. I was shocked when I saw this. Could it be in response to my prayers for God to move among the North Korean people that bombs would eventually fly? Yes, it could be and it will be if Kim Jong Un doesn't repent of his wicked ways and start serving his people the way God has called him to do."

Vision of Trump Receiving God's Counsel, His Heart, & His Strength in this Hour

"In this vision I was observing my President driving all over the place, in what looked to be a barren deserted place. The ground was brown and scorched, it looked like very little vegetation could survive in this harsh environment. He was driving himself around in a black car stopping at various spots talking to men and women, and then getting back in his car to go on to the next meeting location to talk and get counsel from these people. I perceived these individuals to be prophets in the night vision. I knew that Trump was receiving God's prophetic counsel in this place. As I observed Trump going here and there, I thought of the scripture which speaks of the Lord going "to & fro". (2 Chronicles 16:9) "For the eyes of the Lord run to and fro throughout the whole earth, to show himself strong on behalf of those whose heart is loyal to Him."

"It's interesting to note that in this scripture there was a conflict between the northern kingdom and the southern kingdom of Israel just as there is a north and south Korea. The northern kingdom of Judah was besieged in the story, just as North Korea is a closed state. Being cornered, Asa, King of Judah, reached out to a middle eastern nation for assistance in that of Assyria, and there was finance that flowed between those kingdoms. The Lord says that North Korea and Iran have had an alignment since the Iran-Iraq war sharing mutual interests in seeing western society fall. They've been partners and there had been technology and resources shared to elevate them to the position that they are both currently in as rising nuclear powers. In 2 Chron.16 when the time came for God to address the king of the North's actions, God sent a seer prophet named Hanani (whose names means 'gracious') to speak a word of rebuke for Asa's actions, to give him a plumb line word to repent with. In that Word the prophet uttered a scripture found in 2 Chron. 19:9 about how the Lord is searching for a ruler to show himself strong on behalf of. But as the prophet spoke, this only happens when you turn your heart to God and obey His Word.

I believe currently the Lord is speaking to Kim Jong Un in a similar way. God is being gracious in this hour to speak, as Hanani, the Seer spoke to the king of the northern kingdom in his day. This man wants to show strength, but it will only come to ruin if he doesn't submit to God in this hour. In the story of 2 Chronicles 16, Asa rejected the word of the Lord and the prophet was thrown into prison for his word. Then Asa's life ended in retched disease and misery. There are consequences that remain, despite the grace age which we live in, when you reject the word of the Lord, especially when the lives of millions of innocent people in a nation like North Korea are in the balance. God will answer the cries of those people going back generations. I believe the current events unfolding to be a manifestation of God's heart for the Korean people, and God has put President Trump in office for such a time as this to deal with this threat, and I believe also to liberate a nation. I also believe Kim Jong Un's actions to be a manifestation of the current demand for Justice coming from God's courts in Heaven. In his pride, his arrogance, and the hardening of his heart toward God's Word visiting him in this hour, he will lose his power and his regime will fall if he doesn't humble himself to God's Word visiting him now. The cup is full, the prayers have heaped up, God will answer the prayers of David Yonggi Cho going back to the 50's."

"The eyes of the Lord have run to and fro to find a man who could have God's heart and be mantled with God's strength to deal in God's righteous judgment, to the benefit of all, which He has been unable to find in a commander and chief for decades. The eyes of the Lord found Donald Trump many years ago and prepared him for this day. Make no mistake about it, saints, this is not happening randomly. This is a manifestation of God's dealings in the nations. What's happening now is an answer to prayers going back generations."

The Vision Continues

"Next in the vision, I saw President Trump get out of the car and walk out onto what looked like a playground. It was still the same scorched earth, still the same barren lifeless environment, yet there were tiny children running around playing. Most of these children were very small, barely old enough to walk. They were toddlers.

One of the toddlers with jet black fine hair walked up to Mr. Trump. I was behind the child, facing Mr. Trump, as this scene unfolded. I could not see the face of the child. This child waddled up to Mr. Trump, staggered like he had just learned to walk, and the President picked the child up and embraced the

71

child pulling him close to his chest. As this occurred I found myself walking around to the side of this scene, and as I looked into the face of that baby resting on the President's bosom, I could clearly see it was a Korean baby."

"God is Giving President Trump His Heart for Korea"

"It is a fearful thing to fall into the hands of the living God."

—Hebrews 10:31

"When we look into the heart of God we cannot see Him as one dimensional. As I heard one minister say one time, "You cannot flatten this multi-dimensional God." Our God is a loving God, a gracious God, granting mercy and giving abundant grace, but He is also Awesome, all- powerful, and all together just. The vision was clear which the Lord gave to me. Our God is giving President Trump His Heart for Korea, but understand that that heart is filled with love and wrath at the same time. Don't try and flatten Him. Don't try and water down His character and nature to fit your preferences of God. It's clear in scripture who He is and what is in His Heart." —Psalm 86:15

"But You, O Lord, are a God full of compassion, and gracious, long suffering and abundant in mercy and truth." —Nahum 1:2

"God is jealous, and the Lord avenges; The Lord avenges and is furious. The Lord will take vengeance on His adversaries, and He reserves wrath for his enemies;

The Lord is slow to anger and great in power, and will not at all acquit the wicked."

"Nahum's words here are a good reference because there is insight given into both the goodness of God's nature and the manifestation of His justice and righteousness. So God is good and He's not an out of control rage machine. He's actually slow to anger because of His gracious and loving heart. But having said that the prophetic utterance still comes out giving the complete picture of the Awesomeness of our God, and just what it looks like if you do not humble yourself to Him."

"The Lord says He's giving Trump a heart for North Korea. I believe the nature of God will be manifested through this man in this hour to deal with this situation according to God's love and justice for the North Korean people. I believe wisdom will be his, even supernatural intervention and assistance, because God's people are praying and have been praying for many years for God to move in that land. I believe those prayers have arisen and North Korea's time of deliverance is at hand. Kim Jung Un can either repent and agree with that word which is coming from heaven, or he can suffer the consequences of resisting the Lord at this hour when God is calling him to give an account of his actions and his ways. That aspect of God's judgment, when you're called to give an account and you receive the consequences of your actions. This I believe to be happening now in the North Korean regime."

"Understand, Our God is good, Our God is loving, our God is gracious, but he is also a righteous judge and king. The foundation of His throne is righteousness and justice. (Psalms 89:14) These are two powerful out-workings of His nature and character which cover the earth and cause one to rise and another to fall. It's time for North Korea to fall and for God to have His way in that land."

Trump Standing in the Spirit War

"Early in 2017, I witnessed both a darkness and a great light coming over our President as he took office in January. In my spirit I perceived this to speak of the glory conditions as described by Isaiah the Prophet in Isaiah 60 where with a great day of glory, light, hope and faith, there would also come great darkness. In this visionary encounter I also beheld two storms come out of both the light and the darkness which gathered around our President. I perceived this to mean that there would be storms, there would be raging, there would be great conflict in the spiritual realm over America which would spill over into the natural realm, and the storms would come from both light and darkness. I think we've seen that since this man first started running for President, and we've seen it escalating as he walked deeper into his first term. Trump is standing in a war and we must hold his arms up in fasting and prayer if we are to win this conflict which has ensued with the clashing of swords."

"Recently, as I was watching the news I saw into the Spirit to behold a spiritual bond, even bands that exist in this country connecting spirit to spirit, cause to cause, movement to movement. (Sounds like the Great Awakening QAnon WWG1WGA to me!) What I saw I believe to be this: There is a bond between Trump and the people, and there is a bond between the Political establishment, the Washington establishment and the Media establishment. This is not a right to left comparison. Why? Because that is a narrative which the enemy can no longer strongly support, for the attacks and the resistance which have come against Trump reveal fortitude by the enemy on both sides of the aisle. This is an alignment of the people with Trump against the elite, which I must say, I believe is a spirit war. There is a battle raging which is light against darkness, Christ against Anti-Christ, and this conflict is being revealed because of the power that is Donald J. Trump. Donald Trump is not God, but his power is not his own and it comes from God. He has brought the fight back into the soul of this nation, and that is what this battle is for, the very soul of a nation; the future being created in light or darkness, in God's blueprint or the enemy's. This is what the battle is over."

"Relationship is spiritual. It's a word we use to describe when a bond is made or broken, whether that bond is strong or weak. As I watched the news on this particular night I saw into the spirit to spirit bond between Trump and the people, and his and the people's divorce with the media and the political establishment.

Why does this bond exist between Trump and the American people? It's because there's a move of God's spirit among the people which Trump has tapped into, and that spirit is not compatible with the antichrist spirit which almost took over this country, and is still very much in power, through the Washington establishment, the courts, the intelligence community, and the media.

It was prophesied years ago during Obama's presidency that he would not let go of his power when his term was up, and there seems to be very compelling evidence surfacing to that effect, as talks of a 'shadow government' fill the conversation; as Obama had reportedly 'set up shop' only 2 miles from Pennsylvania Avenue after Trump was inaugurated. Things like this show that the spirit behind Obama, the left, anti-God liberalism, is not giving up power, and now that that spirit's lost its executive power. It's flexing its muscles through intelligence, the judiciary branch, the media, congress, and fake race wars funded by the elite designed to draw attention away from Trump's incredible triumphs so far."

"You see now, saints, that as this spirit has infiltrated all these branches so must we. We need people who are part of this move in the judge's seats, the intelligence chairs, and feeding us the news at night. It's not about a man, it's about a movement penetrating every part of this country's power structure. Trump has become a symbol of the restoration of Americanism, the revival of a nation founded for religious freedom, founded in the upheaval of religious powers out of the wave of awakening coming from the reformation renaissance era. Trump represents the current expanse of awakening, for his authority is not his own, his power which he holds with the people is not his own, his power comes from the anointing he carries, which God has given him to stand in the gap on our behalf for such a time as this."

"Christians still must stay very involved and connected to Trump's presidency in vigilance, watching, praying, blessing, and spiritual warfare with fasting as the Lord leads. There's a displacement of power happening, and Trump's campaign, his election, his inauguration (and reelection), and his first term is only the beginning. This displacement of high level demonic power which has been ruling on the tops of these mountains is a process, not a single act. Keep the pressure on the enemy, Saints, Until he's run out of this nation!"

Trump in Power for the People

"As Solomon asked for an understanding heart to better judge and serve the people, so has Trump asked for God's strength and blessing to serve America in these dark times. As David knew the Lord's intention in making him great, establishing him in governmental power, highly exalting him for the sake of the people, so does Donald Trump understand that all of his blessing, all of his power, his celebrity and business power gained through the years, was for the sake of God's people in this nation and many nations around the world. His acquiescence of this call has come from the Spirit's leading."

"As Trump continues to do rallies, bypass the media through powerful tools like Twitter to speak directly to the people, his bond with the people will strengthen and his power will grow, because this government, at the core, is still for the people and by the people. God never permitted the true American spirit to completely be taken because of the last line of defense which held strong, the praying and fasting Remnant church of America! But hear me on this matter saints. Some assuming conservative philosophers in this country have bashed the President for continuing with his campaign and holding these massive rallies. Hear me when I say that THE LORD HAS GIVEN TRUMP THIS STRATEGY, TO NOT STOP CAMPAIGNING DURING HIS FIRST TERM AS PRESIDENT. Why? Because this government is for the people and by the people, and the Lord has given Trump access to a wisdom which has eluded the enemy's agents."

"As long as Trump continues to lead these people, as long as he continues to take his case directly to the people, I believe that his movement will only grow; his strength and will to govern will only grow, because it is the heart of God-given Americanism which has sparked this revolution, and it is the heart that is driving the movement. Trump sees the people in this nation. He understands this, maybe not intellectually, but spiritually. Indeed, he has grasped this strategy and will continue to employ it being led by the Spirit."

"True representation for the people has been restored. The left's populace support is majorly blown out of proportion by the media, just like Hillary's projected crushing of Trump was greatly exaggerated. Even more, their projected strength is supported by the spirit behind them, which make no mistake about it, is anti-American and anti-God. It's the same antichrist spirit which John confronted in his epistles. (1 Jn.2:18-22, 4:3; 2 Jn.1:7) It's the same anti-Christ, anti-Israel, anti-Biblical spirit which overtook Germany during the Second World War. The inflamed Soros funded brigade shows more than a divided nation, but a contrasting spirit of war, which is good to see, because as the American church slept for decades it seemed all too one-sided, as we watched our liberties, religious freedoms, and moral clarity slowly erode before our eyes. What has dealt from the shadows for decades is being forced to deal in the light and it is truly showing its ugly demonic head."

"President Donald J. Trump is standing in a spirit that is currently, holding back a force of darkness you cannot possibly begin to grasp. The stakes have never been higher, Saints. So when you hear Christians bashing the ancient ways of the prophets such as fasting and prayer, do not listen to them. When you hear leaders in the body mocking those who would take up arms of the spirit, these mighty weapons of our warfare for the pulling down demonic strongholds, don't listen to them. Don't be beguiled through a false apostolic grace movement to lift a burden you were given by God. Take the burden to the courtroom of heaven and join with me in pleading the case of this nation before the Lord. You give Him your body of prayer and He will release his power through you as you willingly offer yourself before Him as the instrument which Daniel was on behalf of his people when they were in captivity. We're in this captivity, and God is working to break us free. I plead with you, saints, let us offer ourselves freely in the day of His power, and work with Him in union to see this nation through to freedom and deliverance which He has promised by the mouths of His prophets!"

Trump is a Modern Day Churchill

"I strive not to exalt this man above measure, as the Bible tells us, but I must speak what the Lord gives me to say about this man. This is what He spoke to me as I was putting my children to bed recently. "

"The Lord says that Donald Trump is a modern day Winston Churchill, holding back a force of darkness which once overran Germany and threatened to overrun Britain. If not for that man, empowered by the prayers of intercessors like Rees Howells (affected by the Welsh Revival and missionary to South African Revival, also founder of the Bible College in Wales) of the day, Great Britain most surely would have been overcome. And to think of the devastation, the extent of that war and the change of the course of history that would have been affected.

Make no mistake about it, that same spirit which overthrew Germany has grown in strength in America since abortion was legalized feeding the death culture, and it would have completely taken over this nation if not for this man, Donald Trump, which the Lord has raised up to stand in the gap. I'm not comparing Churchill's and Trump's experiences. They're completely different. But the war they are leading against that antichrist spirit coming out of Europe is the exact same." Ezekiel 22:30

"And I sought for a man among them, that should make up the hedge, and stand in the gap before me for the land, that I should not destroy it: but I found none."

"Donald Trump is as one who is standing in the gap, standing between an America consumed by the antichrist spirit and an America reborn through revival and awakening. The question is, what will we do? Will we hold up his arms at this time? Will we sacrifice to pray and stand in the gap with him so he doesn't fall?!

Stand with your President now, saints, for he has been raised up by the Lord, and he is standing in the gap. Oh that tumultuous gap, where he is torn to shreds daily, being pressured for impeachment, harassed with threats of prosecution, even death threats being made against him. (and acted upon!) Stand with him, fight this fight of faith, fast, pray and intercede for this man. The enemy is not resting, and neither can we until we see this move of God fully transform the nation!"

They Will Not Keep Trump Pinned Down

"I've seen this man in a vision as a huge horse who has survived many battles which have only made him stronger and more set for the victory. I see in this vision his tail pinned to the wall. Then suddenly he breaks free and begins running again. There's been some circumstances of late which have pinned this President down and have stalled him briefly, but he's about to have another break-through. He's about to break free from this current pinning, for the Lord will continue to give him victories in the eyes of the American people, and as he produces according to the anointing that's upon him, he will win more and more people over to his movement. More and more democrats and people who identify with liberal progres-sive ideas will be won over to this President, for he will truly be a President for the people, and this will show more and more as he continues. The way the media is attacking this man will ultimately not keep him pinned down. The way the enemy is painting him, satu-rating him in a barrage of word curses, attempting to chain him to a crafted identity which fits the plans to take him down, will not work."

"The enemy will make mistakes in the days to come for he will grow more and more desperate as Trump gains more and more victories. These mistakes which the enemy shall make shall only serve to further expose his spirit in this nation. With his loss of ground will come a greater reaction from the demonic and then truth will have its day. Truth will continue to expose evil in this nation and show the people what this evil is really for. This evil cares nothing for the American people but for power and control and lordship over these lands. But this is America, one nation under Almighty God, and this God goes by the name of Jesus! The Lord says there is a great purging, a great trial by fire occurring in the American bureaucracy right now. Prepare for the battle to become fiercer as the flames ignite hotter and hotter. These are the flames of reformation, the flames of awakening, and that which can be tested will be tested. From the testing will emerge a new govern-ment, a government born of the higher ways, the ways of God's government, restoring us back to the anointing on our Constitution, having a nation whose foundation is Biblical truth and their adherence to it! This man, Donald Trump, is like a fire to the Washington establishment, and he will continue to blaze in its midst putting it to the test, challenging these entrenched institutions which have existed for years under corruption and a shadow agenda. But their agenda will continue to be exposed, even by fire says the Lord. As we continue to fast, pray, and lift up this President and this nation, God will keep the feet of the enemy to the flame, and cause necessary change in this bureaucracy. Stay the course saints, keep the faith in God for our nation, and continue to believe the word of our Lord for this land and the words pertaining to this President no matter what your eyes may see or your ears may hear in the media, no matter how this man messes up. Look to Me the Lord says, and I will continue to deliver your nation from the hand of oppressors."

The Eagle Has Landed, Now The Prophet Will Soar "Something has changed in our nation in relation to the church's authority in the worldly system, and this change will continue as we step forward into the unfolding destiny of our nation. With the monumental victory of Donald Trump, our Cyrus chaos candidate, a spiritual shockwave has gone out across the nation and both the positive and the negative reactions are being felt and experienced now. But let not your hearts be troubled, saints! As God has begun a good work he will finish it. We just have to continue to walk with him in agreement, praying and staying engaged in this direction from the Lord for our great nation. Here are some words from the Lord based on visions I've seen and words spoken to my spirit."

The Eagle has Landed, Now the Prophet Will Soar

"The day after Trump's election I saw two peacocks come together as one mighty bird. This then massive bird took off into the air with an incredible sound of power, while a large eagle landed on the ground at the same time. I then heard the voice of the Lord boom from the heavens say, "THE EAGLE HAS LANDED AND NOW THE PROPHET WILL SOAR."

"I believe the eagle landing represents God securing the presidency in the Cyrus anointing which God's candidate, Donald Trump, has accomplished with the help of this movement. The double portion peacock is the double portion seer prophetic anointing being released in the nation right now. This anointing is for the nation, and is being offered to the nation, to be received like never before. PROPHETIC AUTHORITY IS RISING IN OUR LAND AND WILL INFLUENCE OUR GOVERNMENT IN INCREASING WAYS MOVING FORWARD."

"God is offering HEAVEN'S INTEL to governments in the nations, including our own. This prophetic authority will pierce the news media establishment as well as the entertainment mountain like we've never seen. This will continue to weaken the antichrist spirit's hold on these establishments and thus the entire nation, even the mind of the nation. The media is largely responsible for poisoning people against God and his ways, even conditioning them to resist the ever-increasing rise of Christ's tangible kingdom. Make no mistake about it, the current anarchist uprising of sleight, hatred and violence is DEMONIC, and it must be met with strength and be subdued and quailed. I was told more than a month ago that the enemy was planning civil war. He had many paths to accomplish this, and he's seeking to increase the depth of that current path until it becomes an inescapable guilt which denies the country any other direction. PRAY PRAY PRAY saints, and stay engaged at whatever level you can civilly. And remember, our greatest weapon against the spirit of antichrist is the LOVE of GOD!"

Governmental Authority is Being Added to America's Prophetic Ministry

"There is a major shift occurring right now not just in the nation, but in the church as well. It's already begun, but the Lord says it will increase as we walk through this next season of glory. This shift is of governmental glory.

The government of heaven and the governments of many nations are being aligned in an increased measure, and this will bring forth what I call financial glory for the church and an unprecedented release of harvest in all of the mountains of influence! This is happening in America saints, and I believe that of the increase of this governmental glory there shall be no end in our land!" (1 Samuel 9:9)

"Formerly in Israel, when a man went to inquire of God, he spoke thus: 'Come, let us go to the seer', for he who is now called a prophet was formerly called a seer."

"This is the first place the seer is mentioned in the Bible, and with its first mention is also included a revelation of its functional upgrade to prophet. Before, the role was in obscurity having never been named until this point, but it's real definition came with the rise of heaven's government in Israel. The seer became the prophet because of the apostolic authority that was added to the office, and these seers became advisers to the kings of Israel, shaping the direction and destiny of the entire nation, yea, even history itself. We've reached another key kingdom governmental shift in the U.S. (and therefore Israel and the earth) in which the prophetic authority of the church will play a greater role in shaping the destiny of the nations under the reign of Christ. Just as the seer function came out of obscurity into the forefront of directing national destiny, so is this happening for the prophetic ministry of America, which has been prepared for many decades for this moment. During Samuel's administration the seers came to the forefront and started to anoint the Kings who would emerge from that time on. THE LORD SAYS THE PROPHETIC MINISTRY WILL CONTINUE TO ANOINT AMERICA'S LEADERS MOVING FORWARD JUST AS THEY ANOINTED TRUMP IN THIS ELECTION, BUT THEIR VOICE AND AUTHORITY SHALL GROW."

"Right as the Lord spoke this to me today in a vision, I received by text message a link to an article by USA TODAY. The headline read 'MEET THE EVANGELICALS WHO PROPHESIED TRUMP'S WIN!' In it Rick Joyner, Jorge Parrott, and Lance Wallnau are mentioned. It's absolutely amazing because the writer of the article essentially says that when the pollsters got it wrong, the prophets got it right. I believe this was an absolute validation and confirmation to this word. The prophetic voice in America absolutely affected the outcome of this election in significant ways. I believe that is evident when considering the data that has come out since election night. Analysis shows that there were more evangelicals that turned out to vote for Trump than we have seen voting for any other candidate in two decades. I believe that God mobilized the church to take responsibility for the direction for our nation, and I believe this was largely because of the prophetic authority which rang out through the body from leaders like the ones mentioned above. Even ministries like the Elijahlist who specialize in releasing an ongoing stream of representation for the voice of God in the church, may have just experienced their timeliest and significant ministry season in their history. These 'prophetic press' organizations as I call them, came together in strength and fearlessly released the word of the Lord, despite the atmosphere of confusion and contro-versy surrounding God's man, Donald Trump."

Prophetic Justice

"The basic idea behind modern day prophetic is simply to hear the voice of God and understand His heart for His people. When we hear we see, and when we see as God sees we understand as He understands. This is the wonderful working of the spirit of wisdom and revelation in the knowledge of him (Ephesians 1:17)

GOD'S PROPHETIC PEOPLE ARE BEGINNING TO HEAR, TO SEE, AND TO UNDERSTAND GOD'S HEART OF JUSTICE

FOR THIS NATION IN THIS HOUR. THE ANOINTING OF THE FEAR OF THE LORD WILL RISE IN THIS HOUR AND ACCOMPLISH THIS SAYS THE LORD."

"There has been a wonderful release of the anointing of the fear of the Lord in our nation, and with this will come amazing righteousness and justice, and the church is going to lead in this anointing, even with the fiery prophetic witness which God gives! Look for great strides to be made in restoring the constitution, restoring religious liberty and protection of our faith under law in this next season, and look for there to be a strong anointing released to protect and save the innocent and the children in our country. The fear of the Lord is a fountain of life which provides a place of refuge for the children." (Proverbs 14:26-27)

"Whoever fears the Lord has a secure fortress, and for their children it will be a refuge.

The fear of the Lord is a fountain of life, turning a person from the snares of death."

"Look for God to cover this nation with his feathers, even for the covering and protection of the innocent and the children under law in this nation once again."

"Those who would harm these little ones, says the Lord, it would be better for you to tie a millstone around your neck and throw yourself into the waters, for you will not be able to hide from My justice as I release it on wings of the fear of the Lord in the days to come. I will be a terror to terror, a force against evil, a hindrance to wickedness, a plague against those who would bring harm to these innocent ones, says the Lord. You will not find a place to hide, a place to cover yourself, in My renaissance of justice, if you harm my little ones says the Lord. You will flee across the sea from whence you came, you will find no shelter, no harbor for your wickedness in my nation of liberty and justice for all, says the Lord. You will run for cover and I will chase you, because I will not rest day nor night, until all of my little ones are safe in this land, says the Lord. My prophets will speak and expose your ways, and My arm of justice will be extended in this land, to take hold of the syndicates, to take hold of the rings, to take hold of the cartels, the traffickers, even the power brokers, their evil shall not breathe, I will snuff out their funds, I will capture back their wealth, turn the flow of their riches for the poor, the widow, for those in need. And I will send you back from whence you came, watch and see, watch and see.

This is the Word of the Lord. So let it be established."

www.lionoflight.org

A Prophecy from Sydney, Australia

Matthew Robert Payne

Matthew Robert Payne was born into a Christian family and as a child, attended a traditional Baptist church with a strong focus on the Word of God. At the age of 8 he gave his life to Jesus and attended church every Sunday morning and evening until he was 17. Matthew had suffered abuse and trauma which resulted in some dark years of addiction away from the church and God, though Jesus proved a faithful friend throughout.

At 27, he joined a Pentecostal church and in a vision, Jesus instructed Matthew to be baptized in water and he came out of the water baptized in the Holy Spirit.

According to Matthew Robert Payne, "Trump 2020 Victory is assured by the results of the recent Australian election where Conservatives won by a wide margin. Just like the Brexit vote in 2016 in the United Kingdom was a signpost to Trump's victory, Australia's clean sweep for Conservatives demonstrate how things are swinging to the Conservative side. The Trump Administration will have a clear majority so that they can rule and reign without impediment. (Now Boris Johnson, Britain's 'Trump' has won the position of Prime Minister.)"

"In 2020, Trump will dominate and have a majority in the House and the Senate. This will give President Trump four more years to pass, legislate and enact everything that he chooses to do without obstruction.

Whether he knows it or not, Donald Trump has a prophetic edge and most of what he says seems to come to pass. Justice will reign and Trump will be able to step up and lead without further interference."

Transformation
Jorge Parrott

J orge Parrott is the President of Correll Missionary Ministries
which helps connect people who are hungry for genuine,
authentic relationships with the Lord for His purposes glob-
ally to fulfill the Great Commission of spreading God's love.

"President Trump, we thank you for your heart, for your fighting
spirit. I believe the Lord is calling you into this great transformation of your life, that this is what you were created for. I want you
to know that you have people of faith praying for you here and all
around the world. And that there are a great many opportunities
before you, even more than you can imagine."

"The Lord is sifting you and he is taking you through this time
of humility, but He is at work and He is with you. And I believe He
is going to anoint you in some very special ways in the next few
weeks to give you a fresh outlook. You will receive fresh revelations from Heaven, from the Throne Room of God, because the
future is at stake and it's more important than you or Hillary or
any of us. It's about the future of our great nation and that the
opportunity is there for you to become known in the future as
the father of the nation, one of the new fathers of the nation,
to really impact the generations of the future. To really rise up
young people full of entrepreneurial freedom and righteousness,
holiness and a love of truth."

"I saw the other day that after you are elected President you will have an opportunity to sign a treaty with Israel which will get a lot of resistance from all around the world, but it's going to go through and it's going to be a tremendous spiritual and financial blessing to America and to Israel. Thank you for your support of Israel."

Prophecy to Donald Trump

October 14, 2016

My wife and I were in Rhodes, Greece at a special gathering of the Knights of St. John of Jerusalem Investiture, with great friends. We had just heard of a Hurricane Matthew ripping through Haiti and Cuba as we prepared to return to the US. Having access to dear friends who are in the humanitarian aid ministry has been a huge blessing to many in times of disaster. Over the years, CMM has distributed $65,000,000 through our global network, to disaster stricken areas, sharing Jesus and restoration. During this disaster, we made social media and website requests for aid and friends back home began to also make appeals and within a few days the Lord brought in over $50,000 to be sent to Cuba and Haiti contacts.

We boarded the plane from Rhodes to Athens back to the US. I knew I needed to stay in touch and paid for the wifi service on the long flight.

Our friends and network members kept me posted in flight. During a time of rest the Holy Spirit spoke to me, "When you speak to Donald Trump call him Mr. President." I asked the Lord how would it be possible? Silly question which He did not answer. I answered 'yes, Lord.' This was on Wednesday October 12, 2016.

That week USA Today reported that Trump's poll numbers were 11% chance of being elected.

Two hours later I was back on my laptop helping coordinate disaster relief. I got an email invitation saying that Friday October 14th Donald Trump would be at a public rally in Charlotte. I was invited to a small private gathering ahead of the public rally with thirty local pastors. Replying yes to the invitation, I began to ask the Lord what He wanted me to say to Mr. President. Nothing came to me. We arrived back home and went back to work the next day. I continued to spend much prayer time seeking the words the Lord would have me to speak.

Our friend, Toby Kreiselmaier, an oft-misunderstood genius and author had previously sent a star chart for President Trump. Toby attended our CMM College of Theology and graduated with a Masters Degree. We then helped him get his Doctoral Degree from Primus University, where I had also been granted a Doctoral Degree in Global Leadership. I acknowledge Toby for sharing this which became a part of the word I would share if given the opportunity.

That afternoon I rode with fellow Pastors Justin Perry and John Boneck to the Charlotte Convention Center to meet with Donald Trump and local pastors. We arrived in the room and sat waiting for his entrance. Justin asked if either John or I had a word. I shared what I would say and they agreed that would be good. The 'Donald' came in. Frank Turek, noted Christian apologist, was the moderator and laid down the ground rules. Since they came in late I was praying for the opportunity to arise. They started with the questions and comments from the far side of the room and I knew only the Lord could make it happen.

Some in attendance were clearly not supporters of Mr. Trump. Slowly, they came around to our side of the room. Time was almost up and a pastor sitting on the other side of Justin asked a question, several in fact. As President Trump looked in our direction and Frank Turek was trying to wrap up the meeting I knew I had to get in there. While the pastor was asking questions and Trump was answering, I began to hold up my hand like a third grader, trying to get the teacher's attention. I left it up until I was called on by Trump.

Thankfully John Boneck recorded my word on his phone. USA Today later ran a story with the video clip about prophetic leaders who had prophesied about President Trump winning the election before election day. That week Trump's poll numbers were at a record low of 11% chance of winning the Presidency.

(This is the transcribed word) "President Trump, we thank you for your heart, for your fighting spirit. My name's Jorge Parrott. I'm the Missions Director at MorningStar Fellowship Church right in Fort Mill, a short distance from here. I go all around the world. Most of my adult life has been in the business world and the Lord called me out of that a few years ago, and I believe the Lord is calling you into this great transformation of your life, but this is what you were created for. But in my travels, the last couple of years in many nations, I've met with presidents of Dominican Republic, of government leaders in Singapore, other business and government leaders and ministry leaders in many nations, and the last two years, I hear consistently, "What has happened to your country?", referring to America. It's disgraceful; it's shameful what this liberal ideology has taken us through, and this vacuum of leadership is so dangerous with Putin calling all of his embassy employees and families home. It's very dangerous, but I do want you to know that you have many people of faith praying for you here and around the world. And that there are great, many opportunities before you, even more than you can imagine. But the Lord is sifting you, and He's taking you through this time of humility, but He's at work and He's with you. And I believe He's going to anoint you in some very special ways in the next few weeks, to give you a fresh outlook. Like you're going to receive like a fresh revelation from Heaven, from the throne room of God because the future's at stake, it's more important than you or Hillary Clinton or any of us; it's the future of our great nation. And that the opportunity is there for you to become known in the future as, 'The Father of the Nation'. One of the new fathers of the nation; to really impact the generations in the future, to really raise up young people, full of entrepreneurial freedom, of righteousness and holiness and a hunger for truth; a love of truth and I saw the other day that you will be, after you are elected president, you will have the opportunity to sign a treaty with Israel which will get a lot of resistance from all around the world but it's going to go through, and it's going to be a tremendous spiritual and financial blessing to America and to Israel. And thank you for your support of Israel."

I just did what the Lord said and so should we all when He speaks. Only the Lord could orchestrate this type of opportunity to declare and decree His heart. As the Word says, 'The Lord does nothing without first revealing it to His prophets.' Again, I am not saying I am a prophet but 'we can all prophesy.'

Birthing Clarity

Lana Vawser

L ana Vawser's heart is to encourage believers in deeper intimacy with Him, equipping them to hear His voice, so they may have deeper revelation of who He is and their inheritance in Him. Lana grew up in Australia and began her relationship with Christ in 1996 when she started to grow in her prophetic gifting. She is a gifted prophet and teacher and resides in Queensland with her prophetically gifted husband, Kevin, and three young boys, Elijah, Judah and Benjamin. They mostly journey and minister as a family, and hope to raise up other sons, daughters, mothers and fathers to journey with Christ in ministry and wonder.

I Had A Dream and I Saw The United States Of America Coming Out Of The Birth Canal

March 2019

"Last night I had a dream and and in the dream I saw the United States of America had been in a large womb, but now the nation was being pushed out of the birth canal and I watched as the nation was about to 'come out'." In the dream the sense of 'DELIVERY' was SO strong. As I have sat with the Lord on this dream I have been surrounded by the sense of 'BIRTHING' so strongly and the words surrounding me 'The nation of the United States is about to be DELIVERED!!!'"

"There is an INCREDIBLE birthing upon the United States right now, much of what the nation has been enduring are the labor pains of what the Lord has been growing and about to bring forth. As I sought the Lord's heart on this dream I heard Isaiah 66:9, 'Would I ever bring this nation to the point of birth and then not deliver it?' Asks the Lord. 'No! I would never keep this nation from being born,' says your God."

"This mighty birthing of the Lord's plans and purposes in the nation are going to bring forth a great move of His Spirit in the nation where all things that are not built in the Lord and founded in Him will not stand, things not built upon the Lord will be found wanting.

The labor pains and the warfare has been loud and relentless but the Lord is making a decree that what He has decreed to come forth will come forth in great power, signs and wonders. The Lord is causing delivery! The Lord is causing the birthing of the divine purposes and plans of His heart to COME FORTH. In the 'coming forth' and the 'birthing' there is great shaking and turbulence but the Lord WILL prevail."

Ready Or Not, Here I Come

"As I sough the Lord regarding this dream I heard Him say, 'READY OR NOT HERE I COME!!! and this decree of the Lord was not resounding just within the church, it was resounding in the entire nation. There has been major warfare against the birthing of God's purposes or plans but the demonstration of His power and revelation of Him as the God of breakthrough, the Mighty Deliverer, is going to be revealed like the United States has never seen before."

"There is a call upon the people of God to make themselves ready for the birthing. The Lord is calling His people to 'make room' for this birthing. The Lord is calling His people to remain deep in the secret place asking the Holy Spirit to prepare them and lead them in making room for the NEW that is about to come bursting through. New life is coming to the United States of America. The Lord is going to demonstrate that no one stands against the Lord Almighty."

The Mockiing 'Goliaths' Are Coming Down

"The Lord showed me that He is about to deal with a spirit of mockery in the United States with great power and vengeance. I heard Galatians 6:7 all around me: 'Do not be misled- you cannot mock the justice of God. You will always harvest what you plant.' In this mighty birthing that the hand of God is bringing forth, in this mighty demonstration of his power and the delivery He is bringing forth, the Lord will deal with this spirit of mockery through major demonstration of His VICTORY."

Definitive Deliverance

"Over the last week or so the Lord has been speaking to me about 'DEFINITIVE DELIVERANCE'. DEFINITIVE:

Conclusion or agreement done or reached decisively and with authority. SYNONYMS: conclusive, final, ultimate, absolute. There is about to be mighty demonstrations of the power of God in the nation in this New Era bringing forth MIGHTY deliverances of areas the enemy has occupied. There is going to be a powerful demonstration of the Lord's victory in His deliverance. He is rallying the troops, he is rallying His army together to stand together in a loud SHOUT of praise and victory in faith KNOWING that the walls are going to come down. I heard the Lord saying

97

that the generational walls are going to come tumbling down at the sound of the praise of God's people, declaring the faithfulness of the Lord, His Word and the POWER and STRENGTH of God to save and to deliver."

"The enemy has been working hard to stop this new and mighty birthing in the United States of America, but coming is a PREVAILING and UNVEILING of the Lord!"

"THOSE WHO HAVE ATTEMPTED TO BLINDFOLD WILL NOW BE BLINDSIDED BY THE POWER OF GOD AND ATTEMPTS OVERTURNED. The Lord spoke to me that where people and the enemy have attempted to 'blindfold', to 'hide' and to 'deceive' will now be blindsided by the power of God, the revealing of truth and their attempts overturned. I heard the Lord saying over and over, 'Haman will be hung on his own gallows.' (Esther 7:10)"

"The mighty demonstration of God's power, His truth and His justice will be SO profound and come UNEXPECTEDLY to those who have been attempting to 'blindfold' and 'cover up'-they will be blindsided by the mighty demonstration of His power and their attempts will be steamrolled by the hand of God and their attempts overturned as the mighty, glorious birthing of God's purposes and plans manifest like never before in the nation."

"The sound of Psalm 89:8-10 will be heard LOUDLY in the nation and cause it to shake: So awesome are you, Lord God of Angel Armies! Where could we find anyone as glorious as you? Your faithfulness shines all around you! You rule over oceans and the swelling seas. When their stormy waves rise, you speak, and they lie still. You crushed the strongholds of Egypt and all your enemies were scattered at the mighty display of your glorious power."

Those Who Have Mocked You and Spoken Against You Will Now Stand in Awe of My Blessing And Favor Upon You!!!

March 2019

"Recently I heard the Lord say: 'Those who have mocked you and spoken against you will now stand in awe of My blessing and favor upon you.' Those who have spoken against you, those who have mocked you for obeying the Lord, those who have mocked you for following the Lord's strategy, those who have spoken out against you and behind your back out of jealousy, the Lord showed me their mouths are about to be left open in awe at the hand of the Lord upon you releasing His blessing and His favor."

"The Lord spoke to me that there is a 'JOSEPH PROMOTION' upon many right now. Many have been in the place of facing the jealousy of their 'brothers' in many ways, but now the Lord shall bring forth a great promotion that will leave them in awe and wonder of the hand of God. The Lord spoke to me that is the 'JOSEPH PROMOTION' there is going to be a MAJOR surge of blessing and favor upon them to increase them to extend the Kingdom of God and for the Glory of the Lord to be seen. The mouths of the mockers will be SHUT. The mouths of the jealous will be left open wide by the hand and favor of the Lord upon you. The Lord is bringing forth a great vindication in your life."

"The Lord is releasing major promotion upon you for the sake of His Kingdom and His Glory. Those of you who have stayed away from the place of fame, or attempting to make a name for yourself but have remained true to what the Lord has called you to and stayed in the place of obedience and have been battling the mocking and word curses of others, the Lord is about to powerfully vindicate you, bless you and release great favor upon you."

"In these 'JOSEPH PROMOTIONS' not only is the Lord bringing about a 'shutting of the mouths of the mockers' but the Lord is bringing forth reconciliations in the promotion. He is bringing forth restoration in the promotion. The Lord will set up opportunities for you to bless those who have cursed you. The Lord will set up situations for you to show grace, love and forgiveness to those who have spoken against you and mocked you.

Continue to pray and bless those who speak against you like Jesus said in Luke 6:28."

"There has been great warfare many have faced because of these words spoken in the spirit, but the Lord is decreeing that 'no weapon formed against you shall prosper.' (Isaiah 54:17) For we wrestle not against flesh and blood, but against principalities, against powers, against the rulers of the darkness of this world, against spiritual wickedness in high places. (Ephesians 6:12)"

"The enemy has ridden on the words spoken against you, but there is a major breakthrough upon you where you shall see the Lord step in with His breakthrough, blessing and vindication. Many who have been battling these forms of witchcraft in the spirit over and over and over again and it has seemed relentless, there is a MAJOR breakthrough and promotion upon you right now where the Lord will release and demonstrate His favor over your life. Many of you have felt almost taken out by those who have mocked you and spoken against you, but NOW the voice of God shall be heard far and wide over your life by the favor He is releasing upon you as you have remained in purity, integrity and humility. Some of you are about to step into your greatest promotions of the Lord and you shall see Him move through your life like never before.

There is a great blessing ahead. There is great favor ahead. You are about to increase in blessing and favor of the Lord, not by your own efforts or hands but by the HAND of the Lord."

"Where you have followed the Lord, followed His voice and His Spirit, where you have walked the paths He has asked you to walk despite the unfamiliar territory, where the blessing and favor of the Lord has invoked jealousy in others, where your obedience has invoked mockery in others, do not apologize where the Lord is leading you. Don't apologize for the favor and blessing the Lord is releasing over your life. Continue in the pathway God has for you and bless those who curse you and pray for those who mistreat you. For the hand of the Lord is not only about to vindicate you but promote you into greater places to see HIS name lifted high and Kingdom extended. This is a major birthing moment for you and the Lord is decreeing these mockeries and words against you will NOT stop you as you stand in Him."

"The promotion and the blessing that the Lord is releasing is for the extension of the Kingdom and for the plans and purposes of the Lord to be extended across the earth. It is all for His name to be lifted high and His Glory to be seen across the earth and for all to come to know Him and His love and His goodness. It's time for you to step into greater advancement of your destiny in the promotion and blessing He is releasing so the name of Jesus may be lifted high across the earth."

www.lanavawser.com

I Heard The Lord Say 'I Am Capturing Many of My People's Hearts Again And Restoring Simple Devotion'

March 2019

"Recently I heard the Lord say "I am capturing many of My people's hearts again and restoring simple devotion. Friend, if your heart feels dry and weary and captured by the cares of this world and you feel like you have been weighed down by so many things lately that it's left you feeling discouraged and the passion you once had in your relationship with Jesus is just not the same as it was, I believe the Lord is speaking to you. He is going to capture your heart again by His love. The waves of His love are going to crash over you and your heart will be ignited and rekindled in passion and fiery love for Jesus and the restoration of simple devotion to Him. The Lord has seen how the trials and battles have weighed upon your heart, He sees how deep the weariness goes and He has heard your cries. He is restoring the divine romance of intimacy with Him to you taking you deeper than you have been before.'

"Where so many different things have battled for the affections of your heart, where so many trials have attempted to capture your heart and capture your attention and affection, the Lord is bringing you back into divine alignment. Areas where your heart has swayed from Him as true north, from Jesus being the lover of your soul, the fire of His love is falling upon you and it is His kindness and love that is bringing forth repentance.

For I hear the Lord saying: 'I am going to take you into the secret place with Me, to places you have never been.' There are new adventures awaiting you with Jesus and the wooing of His love is inviting you deeper than you have ever been. He is restoring the place of simple devotion and a deeper place of worship shall bubble up inside you like never before. The deep level of intimacy He is bringing you into that will catapult you into a deeper well of worship than you have known, will take you into encounters with Jesus like you have never experienced. He's removing the 'obligations', the places where you meet with Him out of 'religious duty', He is looking for friends. He is looking for those who will come before Him and delight in being in His presence, ministering to His heart and being with Him simply to know Him."

"Anything that has captured the attention or affection of the heart above the Lord, He is bringing down. He is releasing such deep, rich, encounters with His heart and His love that many will feel like they are meeting Him for the first time. This place of the 'recapturing' of the heart that the Lord is going is like a deeper divine reintroduction to his love, His nature and goodness. Everything that has not lined up with His character and revelation of His love and His Word will suddenly begin melting away. In this divine 'recapturing' the restoration of simple devotion and radical obedience will be restored. The deep cry that says, 'Jesus, you are my Lord! You are my King! Wherever You lead, I will go, whatever you say, I will obey." I heard His whisper: 'I am restoring the place of the JOY of My people's salvation.' 'Restore to me the joy of Your Salvation and sustain me with a willing spirit.' Psalm 51:12 The Lord is recapturing hearts. He is restoring simple devotion to Him and His ways. Joy is being restored in the revelation of who He is and in the deep places of intimacy. His whisper continued to surround me: 'It's the hearts blazing, living in the secret place and in deep communion with Me that will have the Courage to obey Me when I say, 'GO AGAINST THE GRAIN.'

It's A New Day Of Discovery!!! Can You Hear The Sound Of Clarity?

April 2019

"This week as I was talking to my son, Elijah, I said to him, 'Well, Elijah, it's a new day of discovery for you!!!' As I said it I felt the holy Spirit whisper to me, 'It's a new day of discovery in the body of Christ.' I began to ponder this with the Lord and again He reminded me of Jeremiah 33:3: 'Call to Me and I will answer you, and tell you (and even show you) great and mighty things, (things which have been confined and hidden), which you do not know and understand and cannot distinguish.' The Lord began to show me that BECAUSE we are in such a new day of discovery with the Lord and the revealing of mighty things that we have not known or understood before, such deep revelation of the Word, such specific blueprints, new pathways of pioneering and new strategies to unlock breakthrough, resources and the demolishing of strongholds, the enemy has come hard against the body of Christ with a fog. The enemy has been using confusion, distraction, and disorientation, attempting to knock people off balance and attack vision and forward momentum."

"This new day of discovery with the Lord is a place of deep revelation, a place of deep intimacy, a place of strategy that flows with the Holy Spirit and not the expectations of man. This new day of discovery requires radical obedience and living for an audience of One. For in this new day of discovery as the Word of the Lord comes to many to 'go against the grain' in how things have been or are expected, these are the pathways of the pioneer, the places never forged before. These are the places of discovery that in radical obedience to the Lord, the Glory of the Lord, the favor and the fruit that will be seen will be like nothing that has been seen before. This new day of discovery that we have entered into, as God's people place their hands on what He is building and the WAY He is building, there will be such a powerful demonstration of the new wineskins to bring in the harvest. In this new day of discovery, the Lord is bringing forth such a deep prophetic revelation and confirmation it requires us as God's people truly yielding to Him and His ways, NO self promotion, and having hearts that want to see what He is building and where He is building. For in this new day of discovery, things that have been built on foundations not of the Lord and things He is not building, things built on self-promotion in many ways will come down."

Dream—"Can You Hear The Sound Of Clarity?"

"I had a dream recently and I saw someone unable to open their eyes, they were trying and trying to open their eyes but they were almost sealed shut. As they kept pushing through to fight it to open their eyes, suddenly their eyes opened and I heard the sound of 'CLARITY' being released from heaven. The Lord is releasing divine clarity upon the body of Christ. Where a spirit of chaos and confusion has been assigned to hinder many of God's people, there is a major breakthrough upon the body of Christ right now where the SOUNDS and SHOWERS of CLARITY are being released."

'The unfolding of your words gives light; it imparts understanding to the simple.' Psalm 119:30

The haze is clearing and where there has been fogginess, confusion and chaos, the Lord is releasing supernatural clarity by His Spirit. The enemy has been attempting to use 'smoke and mirrors' against many to bring confusion, but I heard the Lord saying, 'I am releasing crystal clear Clarity in and through My Word.'"

Psalm 119 is a Key Right Now!!

'The Lord spoke to me a few weeks ago that Psalm 119 is a KEY right now for the body of Christ. There is SO MUCH that God is revealing and releasing through this Psalm and through the Word of God that is releasing significant Clarity. I heard the Lord saying: 'DO NOT LOOK OUTSIDE OF THE WORD FOR CLARITY. MY WORD MUST BE THE PRIORITY.' The Lord showed me that there's a temptation in the frustration many are feeling, the battle and the chaos that has been surrounding, to run to other places and people for Clarity, but the Lord is wooing His people deeper into the Word. For in the Word, especially in Psalm 119 and more the Lord is releasing specific revelation and His Spirit is bringing Clarity and THEN confirmation will come from the other sources. The Lord is realigning priorities in this hour."

"The Lord showed me that some of the things the Lord is going to have His people step into, build and create with Him in this new day of discovery will require a fire of deep conviction that He has spoken as there will be voices that will come to discourage saying, 'That's not the way it should be done. That's never been done before, do it this way, the way it has always been done' and in order to stand in obedience to the Lord and conviction there must be a deep grounding in the Word of God and what He has spoken to not bow to 'man' and 'man's way' when the Holy Spirit is clearly breathing on something new. It's important to be accountable, be in community and have covering, but when the word of the Lord is disobeyed because of 'expectations of man' there becomes a problem. The Lord will be confirming the revelation and His voice from the Word like never before, loud and clear with great CLARITY that will bring great conviction and peace within you that you are obeying the Lord. The hand of the Lord's favor will be upon you as you move in obedience to Him."

"Many of you are beginning to and will continue to now step into things that you have been feeling on your heart for a long time but you were not sure if it was the Lord because of fear, because of the voices of others, the attack of the enemy and intimidation, but NOW Clarity is coming like never before and that Clarity from the Lord's heart and the Spirit of God is GIVING YOU YOUR WINGS TO FLY! Can you hear the sound of CLARITY? IT'S RESOUNDING AROUND YOU!

Victorious Trump

Veronika West

Veronika West* of the Ignite Ireland Ministry describes her dream about Donald Trump in 2016, "I saw Donald Trump standing high upon a mountainside with both hands lifted high into the air and his eyes were fixed on an intense battle that was taking place in the valley below him. The battle was being one with victory assured and then suddenly I saw the enemy coming like a whirlwind upon the mountainside. I watched as he battled to stay standing and wrestled with the power and the might of demonic winds. His hands that were lifted high began to drop down low and his feet began to slip.

He was losing strength and seemingly overcome. As the dream continued the winds grew stronger and then suddenly there was a voice of the Spirit of God saying, Fear not, for I will brace up and reinvigorate and set the slackened and weakened drooping hands. I will strengthen the feeble and the tottering knees. I have pronounced victory and triumph over the enemy."

*Veronika is incredibly prolific, a true overflowing well of inspiration can be found at www.hiskingdomprophecy.com

A Word for America:

"He is Healing, Reviving, Restoring and Renewing the Broken Heart of America!"

"On a recent afternoon while walking on the beach as I do most days, I was suddenly overwhelmed by a deep sense of urgency to pray again for the American people. As I began to cry out to the Father for this great nation, suddenly the Holy Spirit showed me a very powerful and poignant picture. I saw the nation of America in the shape of a large heart. As I looked at the heart, I saw that it was made of stone. Then I saw the heart of stone begin to move, shift and change in appearance, and with every tear of joy that fell from the Father's face, the heart of stone began to be healed and fully restored. I watched closely as the heart became fully immersed and saturated with the Father's tears. Each tear of joy was life-giving. Each tear was a death blow to the destructive plans of the enemy. I then saw every deep crack and badly broken place within the heart suddenly and completely renewed, revived, restored and made whole."

Veronika says, "Rejoice, nothing can stand against the power and the authority that comes in the mighty whirlwind of Elijah which is now moving, advancing and being accelerated across this nation. God has raised up in this very hour who will stand to hold up the hands of Donald Trump through the power and authority of constant and consistent prayer and praise. The Redemptive plan of God over this nation shall prevail."

The Lord Said This is the Hour of Divine Reset

"A New Day has Dawned on My Beloved America! America, I hear the Spirit say, 'My Healing Oil shall now flow, flow, flow forth upon this Broken land, for this is the hour of Divine Reset, Divine Rehearsals and Divine Restoration," says God. "Beloved surely I tell you it was not by the power of your swords that you conquered the land, nor was it by the might of your strong arms that saved you, but it was by the Strength of My Right Hand and the Light of My Countenance and Favor that Brought you out of Captivity and Bondage and into the place of Great Victory and Manifest Promise," says God.

"Now Watch! As My Spirit Moves in this hour to turn, turn, turn the tide of Darkness, Division and Destruction that has engulfed the hearts and the minds of the people in this great land, watch! As My Spirit now moves to Heal, Restore and Reform broken lives and shattered dreams. Watch! As My Spirit moves to uncap the Ancient Wells of Healing and Revival in the land, Listen! For the Sound of a Great Awakening is Rising Up in the midst of you, Awake, Awake and Clothe yourselves with Strength, America Put on your Beautiful Clothes, Shake the Dust from your feet, For I Tell you, You are now free from the chains of iron that hung around your necks and that bruised your feet, Yes, get up oh you Mighty Warriors and Go forth to Rebuild the cities and the streets that lay in ruins, go forth and establish My Kingdom Purposes upon the Earth. America Rejoice and be Glad for My Courts have been filled with the cries of My Esthers and now My Golden Scepter of Favor is extended towards you in this hour." Says God.

"I declare for America's sake I will not keep silent, and for America's sake I will not remain quiet, till her Righteousness Shines out like the Dawn, her Salvation like a blazing torch. The nations will see your righteousness, and all kings your glory; America you will be called by a new name that the mouth of the Lord will bestow. You will be a Crown of Splendor in the Lord's Hand, a Royal Diadem in the hand of your God."

"America, no longer will they call you Deserted, or name your land Desolate America. But you will be called My Delight and your land My Bride; for the Lord will take delight in you, and you, America, will be married. As a young man marries a young woman, so will your builder marry you; as a bridegroom rejoices over his bride, so will your God rejoice over you America. Listen! America, you who call on the Lord give yourselves no rest, and give him no rest until He once again establishes the Body of Christ in America and makes her the Praise of the Earth," says God.

A Word for America

March 2019

"I had a dream last night where I was standing in the nation of the United States of America and I saw an elephant riding on the back of a donkey! Yes! I saw a donkey carrying an elephant, and the donkey's legs were breaking under the strain. As I looked at this strange thing, I heard the Spirit say, 'Watch! As I pay back seven times trouble to those who have brought trouble to My Anointed Trump!' I woke up! I decreed today that God is going to pay back seven times trouble to those who have brought trouble to American President Donald J. Trump. America, keep watching! Keep praying! For in the days ahead, you will see the 'breaking of the back' of the demonic agenda that is at work in the Democratic Party. Watch for a supernatural acceleration coming upon the Republican Party. They will become unstoppable and uncontainable. There will be an even greater shake-up both politically and spiritually taking place over the land.

Whoever remains stiff-necked after many rebukes will suddenly be destroyed, without remedy. When the righteous thrive, the people rejoice!"

America: An Elephant Stamped in 2024

March 2019

"I was led to pray for President Donald Trump. As I began to intercede for him, suddenly I heard the sound of a distant rumbling like thunder in the realm of the spirit.

Then I saw what looked like a dust storm moving slowly across the land (the United States of America). As I looked at the dust storm I heard these words, 'An elephant stampede that shakes and shifts the nation, for righteousness and justice will prevail in the land.' As I heard these words I saw the state of Florida come before me. I saw a great shaking taking place over that land then I saw flood waters rising across that state. As I looked again, I heard these words, 'Watch! For the state of Florida shall become a doorway to divine recompense and 7-fold restoration in the days ahead. Florida will be known as the state that turned the nation upside down and inside out! Then suddenly I saw the state of Florida appear as 'a door' and as I looked at this massive door, a keyhole appeared in the very center of the door. As I looked into the keyhole, my eyes were drawn to the top of the door where I saw the number '2024'. As I watched the door, I saw an ancient key being put into the keyhole of the door and watched as the key was turned. Then I saw the door open wide and watched a herd of stampeding elephants enter through the open door and through to the other side. The door was shut closed and I heard these words. 'The elephants shall rule the land and the donkeys shall reap what they have sown.'

113

A Word of Urgency for the United States of America and the United Kingdom by Veronika West: "Last night I had a powerful dream where I saw an image appear before me, where I saw the face of Donald Trump. I clearly heard him say, "Pray, your country needs you!" As I saw this and heard this, I began to pray in The Spirit and then the dream shifted and I saw the face of British politician, Jacob Rees-Mogg, and he said exactly the same thing. "Pray, your country needs you!" as I prayed over this strange dream, I felt an urgency to pray for both nations at this time. As I prayed for both nations, I saw what looked like three strands of cord in the realm of The Spirit. As I looked at the strands, it had the appearance of a DNA helix. As I looked at the DNA helix, I saw the nations of America and the United Kingdom, and at the center of both nations, I saw a strand of fire and I heard The Spirit say, 'A three cord strand cannot be broken!' Our destinies are joined!

Would you stand with me in this hour to pray fervently for both nations?"

An Urgent Dream Concerning President Donald J. Trump

"Watch! For the den has been prepared and the bloodthirsty lions lie in wait! At three in the morning I awoke from a powerful dream concerning President Trump where I was shown a great upheaval that is coming in the days ahead. In this dream I found myself standing in a dark dungeon type place and the smell of the air in that place is hard to describe—but it was the smell of blood and lions. (Having been brought up as a child in wildlife conservation, I know the smell of lions.) It is a smell so distinct, it is unmistakable. As I stood in that dark place, my nostrils filled with the smell (of blood and acid like tones) and I began to feel fear rise up within me. Suddenly, I saw a bright light appear round about me and an Archangel of he Lord stood before me in the dream and spoke to me saying, 'Fear not, for you have been brought to this place for what is about to take place.'

"As I looked through the open window, I saw President Trump knelt down upon his knees and looking up to heaven. As I looked at him, I saw a great battle taking place over the land, and as I watched him cry out to The Lord, suddenly I saw the Archangel Gabriel standing above him with a flaming sword lifted high above the president's head. I watched as the blade of the sword touched him as if he were being knighted, and then I saw President Trump stand to his feet. Suddenly I saw a mantle fall upon him, that flowed like liquid gold.

The mantle of gold covered him from head to toe and I watched as it became like a body of impenetrable armor, and the Angel of he Lord left him! I woke up, with my body covered in sweat and I was praying so loudly in the Spirit that my son had also awoken. As I reassured my son that all was well, I began to feel a great urgency to pray for the land of America and their President. As I began to cry out to the Lord, the atmosphere was heavy. It felt as if I was walking in thick sand. But as I prayed and warred in the Spirit, suddenly the Spirit of God spoke to me saying, 'Watch and pay attention! Pray! Pray! Pray for the nation of America and for the President Donald Trump, for it shall be like in the days of Daniel when My faithful servant was thrown into the lion's den! Watch! For they shall come together and they shall conspire with one another to destroy that which I have decreed and that which I have declared over the land. They shall look to catch him out and they look to grab hold of him to utterly destroy him. For surely I tell you, the den has been made ready and the hungry lions now lie in wait," says the Spirit of God.

"Watch and Pray! Call a fast! For they shall come together as one from the left and from the right. Yes! There will be those who shall come from the right, who shall say, 'How can this be?' But I tell you, many hearts will be turned cold by a strong spirit of lies and deception. Even a spirit of murder dwells in the midst of them, for they have hatched a plan and they have put together a plot to overturn and overthrow that which has been established. But listen! Stay vigilant in this hour!

Watch and pray, for surely I tell you again, just as the day they threw Daniel into the lion's den, so they shall come together in great unity and authority in this day to throw a praying President into the den of hungry lions. Tell My People, if they will look to Me and cry out to Me in this hour, I shall send My Angels of Protection into the midst of them. "

"Yes! Into the storm of rising lies and false accusations and into the midst of the roaring lions, and their bloodthirsty mouths shall be shut closed and that which was conceived in the womb of darkness shall not come to full term, but shall surely be fully aborted and brought to nothing," says the Spirit of God. "Now Watch! For I stand over My Word to perform it in this hour and in this day, for the nation of America shall see My Glory and they shall see My Hand move in mighty and yet more mysterious ways in the days ahead! For I have set My Seal upon My Servant and a mantle of kingship, and he shall become My Trumpet for Righteousness and Justice in the land and no man shall touch My Anointed and live." Says The Spirit of God.

Witchcraft and the Media Wolf

"The witchcraft released against the President has been unprecedented. Witchcraft is defined as spiritual INTIMIDATION, DOMINATION, and CONTROL. When it hits you it is a 'fiery dart' meant to cause panic and anxiety until you yield to the will of the spirit behind it. The President's personal fears and anxiety over the assault are revealed in the intimate moments revealed in the second part of the 400 pages hit piece compiled in the Mueller Dossier. The President has so few friends, even his own counsel has divulged juicy tidbits to destroy him. This is a huge alarm for those of us tasked to pray for him. Understand that the Mueller Dossier was written by Trump's political enemies with the intent of doing what it is accomplishing now—keeping the investigation going as a perpetual news cycle hit piece! It is a dangerous moment in American history. Media has merged with a political party to destroy anyone they do not want in office. It will backfire."

Collusion and the Spirit of Delusion July 2018 by Veronika West

"I heard the Spirit say this morning, 'Listen! For even now there are those who are plotting and scheming behind closed doors and under the shadows of darkness they conspire with one another against My Anointed one. Listen! They shout, 'Collusion! Collusion! Impeach! Impeach!', but fear not! For I shall set among them a strong spirit of delusion and they shall believe their own lies. For they have turned their backs on the Truth and the Light that I have given them."

"Now watch! For great will be their fall, their destruction is inevitable and their ruin irrecoverable. Watch and pray, for suddenly My Spirit will move like a mighty whirlwind to destroy their works of witchcraft and corruption," says God. "And to My Anointed in the White House, watch and pray! For he shall rise higher and higher and he will be known as a 'King' among the leaders of the nations, for I have set a seal upon him.

And those who would dare to touch My Anointed, will touch the Apple of My eye. For have I not said I have taken hold of his right hand to subdue nations before him? Yes! To strip kings of their armor! For It is I who goes before him to open doors. It is I who goes before him to level every mountain and to break down the gates of bronze and to cut through bars of iron. Yes! It is I, the King of Glory, who now gives him hidden treasures and riches stored in secret places so that he will know that I AM the Lord His Creator and God. For even while he was in his mother's womb, I chose him and anointed him for such a time as this." Says the Spirit of God.

Warning America! It Has Begun!

March 2019

"I woke this morning with the sound of groaning in the realms of the Spirit. As I pressed into the sound, I was caught in a vision where I saw the late and great prophets and apostles gathered together. I saw prophet Kim Clement, prophet Bob Jones, prophet Paul Cain, prophet John Paul Jackson. As I looked at these great prophets, there in the midst of them stood the great prophets Ezekiel and Jeremiah and the prophet Joel! I was unable to utter a word in this place as it was a great and sacred place, but as I watched, suddenly I saw Esther and the prophetess Deborah walk into the midst of these great prophets and in one accord, they lifted their voices, crying out for a notion of

Israel and crying out for the nation of America. In one accord they groaned together. Then suddenly I heard a sound of thunder and a great cloud descended among them I watched as they fell in worship, then I heard these words, 'It has begun!"

"Suddenly I found myself lying prostrate on the floor beside my bed! As I began to pray in the Spirit, the nation of America was brought before me and I heard these words, 'America, America, why have you forsaken your first love? Return, return to Me and I shall revive, restore and reform this nation.' As I heard those words a word I released in 2016 came to me, 'Heaven's Government Being Established on Earth.' Heaven's government is being established on the earth!"

The Army of God is Now Arising!

March 2019

"The Spirit of God says, 'Watch and pray, beloved! Stay alert and pay attention for the wolf is at the door. Yes! The enemy comes to rob, steal and destroy in this hour!' Friends, I see the powers of darkness increase in this hour, but I also see an increase, acceleration and manifestation of greater glory, super-natural power, greater authority, signs, wonders and miracles taking place across the nations of the earth. I see an unstoppable and an unquenchable fire of the Holy Ghost moving swiftly across the nations, the powers of evil and darkness cannot and will not hinder nor diminish it.

I see a mighty army of radical, fearless freedom fighters rising up I this hour. They are not deterred or distracted by the schemes of Satan. Their power, strength, skill and stealth comes from being deeply rooted and established in Christ Jesus. The weapons of their warfare are not carnal, but powerful to the pulling down of every stronghold and demonic structure in the land. These are the radical ones, anointed and appointed by God to pursue, push back, overthrow and overtake every power of death and destruction."

"They war not from the realms of doubt, fear or timidity, but they war in the realms of supernatural faith, courage, humility and victory, with the two-edged swords in their mouths. They are wise with their words, only speaking forth life, liberty and victory. They walk in the shoes of Peace and Prosperity. They command heavenly angels to come and to go. They love not their own lives even unto death. These are the glory carriers of heaven. New life, healing, hope and manifest promise flows forth from their bellies. The Spirit of Wisdom and The Fear of the Lord goes before them, making straight their paths and illuminating their way. Accelerated and mobilized by the Spirit of Might and Power, these brave hearts move with great accuracy and with spiritual vision and precision they take the land. I see Satan and his demons flee in a thousand different directions when these glory carriers step upon their territories. These demons of darkness know they cannot stand against the power of their unity and agreement in the Spirit. Listen! I hear the sound of great victory and jubilee!"

America: Revival Follows Retribution!

January 2019

"Today I have been greatly burdened for the nation of America. I just heard the Spirit say, 'Tell My People I have not changed My Mind concerning Roe vs. Wade.

Watch, for the giants will fall! Watch, as great revival comes on the heels of great retribution!' I suddenly saw the finger of God touch the Supreme Court of the United States this evening as I sat in his presence. I heard in the realm of the Spirit, the sound of the gavel of His Righteousness and Justice come down hard upon the block! Then I heard the Spirit say, 'Watch! For a death will soon make way for another and the one that shall arise to take their place will rule with great grace and like an iron fist in a velvet glove they shall go forth to demolish and destroy, overturn and overthrow demonic strongholds in the land!"

A Word Concerning America and Russia

November 2018

"Today I heard the Spirit say, 'Daughter Watch! For NOW My Word concerning the Eagle Nation and the Bear Nation will begin to manifest in the Earth, for a divine alliance and a divine convergence is now taking place over the nations. Watch, as I bring the two together in a new way, and many will say, but how can this be?

Bear and Eagle Come Together

Look! For the rise of the Eagle and the Bear will be seen across the nations as the two come together in strength and in vision to bring the beast of the east to its knees. Now do not lean on your understanding and do not question My ways nor My will, for My ways are not your ways nor My will your will. For I will have My way, and My will shall be established upon the earth. Watch! Pay attention! My governing hand is now moving suddenly, quickly and without warning in the earth! My

Truth, Righteousness, Unity, Mercy and Peace will now go forth to rebuild the broken bridges between the nation of Russia and the nation of America. For surely I tell you, the arm of the Bear and the eye of the Eagle will come together as one and the head of the uncircumcised giant shall be decapitated. Yes, the head of this snake shall be cut off and cast into the fire. Watch! For this shall take place quickly, suddenly and without warning. No longer will My justice and mercy tarry. Even now My Spirit of vindication is moving, shaking and shifting the nations, listen! For a battle cry of victory and freedom will soon be heard across the earth," says God.

A Word for America in This Hour

November 2018

"Why are you so double-minded, America?

Watch, for surely that which has been spoken that which has been decreed shall be established! Repent of your double-mindedness and look up to the hills, for greater are those that are with you than those who come against you! America! Fear not! There is a divine setup taking place over your nation. There is a divine unraveling of God's plans and purposes taking place! Look not with the eyes of doubt and unbelief, but see with the eyes of faith and expectation of that which is still to come, with great power and authority! Watch! For there is a divine turning in the realm of the Spirit. God is working a work of divine sifting and shifting in this hour. Things are not as they would first seem, for surely there is a divine uprooting and tearing down that is taking place over the land.

The demonic strongholds of the enemy will be totally dismantled and destroyed. The Red Carpet (blood of Jesus) has indeed been unraveled over the nation. The sound of victory will be heard going forth across the land as the enemy is sent running. America watch! For a spiritual earthquake draws nigh. 'The deep waters that have stood before you are now being parted. It's time to cross over and take possession of a new land!"

"Now in this dream, I saw President Donald Trump standing in the Court Room of Heaven, where he was standing before the judge of heaven. In the dream, I heard these words being spoken to President Trump, 'Fear not! Come boldly!' then I saw the president taking a step forward and I heard these words, 'This day, the Key of the House of David is set upon your shoulders. This day, the governmental authority of heaven is released to you for the purpose of advancing My Kingdom in this nation and in the nations of the earth. For this is the time, this is the season, of a great unlocking and locking in this nation. For this is the time, this is the season, of a great unlocking and locking in this nation. The doors he opens, no man can close, and the doors he closes, no man can open!'

"As I heard those words in the dream, suddenly I saw the numbers 2222 and it was quickened to me, Isaiah 22:22, 'The key of the house of David I will lay on his shoulder; so he shall open, and no one shall shut; and he shall shut, and no one shall open.' Then I saw a long purple robe fall, put upon his shoulders, and a silver sword being placed in his hands. Now, as I woke up from the dream, I quickly wrote down all I saw and heard and I started to pray, inquiring of the Lord for a deeper understanding of the dream. Then I heard the Spirit say, 'Watch! For there is a divine turning, turning, doors are opening. Watch! For there is a supernatural shifting.

Shifting doors are closing, for a great unlocking and locking is now taking place in the nation!"

"Then the Spirit of God quickened to me His Word which says, 'He who has the key of David, he who opens and no one shuts, and shuts and no one opens. I know your works. See, I have set before you an open door, and no one can shut it,' Revelation 3:7-8 A n d , 'this is what the Lord says to His anointed, to Cyrus, whose right hand I take hold of to subdue nations before him and to strip kings of their armor, to open doors before him so that gates will not be shut: I will go before you and will level mountains; I will break down gates of bronze and cut through bars of iron' (Isaiah 45:1-2) As I remained praying, again I saw many doors opening and shutting, both in the natural realm and the spiritual realm over the nation of America in this hour! I saw doors swinging wide open: doors over the Supreme Court of the United States, doors over religion, doors over education and family, doors over entertainment and media, and doors over the economy. But then I saw many doors being slammed shut: doors shutting corruption and wickedness, doors slamming shut on dictators and their works of darkness and destruction, and doors shutting on abortion and murder! Friends, keep watching and praying in this hour; for the Spirit of God is moving in great power in this hour. Many doors are being shut closed and many doors are being opened wide over the nation!"

America Watch! For Trump Will Become as a Heavy Anchor!

2018

"I just heard the Spirit say, 'Watch! For Trump will become as a heavy anchor that will bring great stability to the nation, for even now, I AM shaking the nation to its core! Tell My People to get ready! For everything that is not of My Kingdom will be shaken loose and will be cast down into the sea of forgetfulness,' says the Spirit of God. As I just heard these words, I saw a great ship being tossed violently by the winds and the waves at sea. The huge waves beat relentlessly against the sides of the great ship, and then I heard the sound of many who were crying out in fear and panic. But then suddenly, I saw the Hand of God take hold of President Trump and cast him like a heavy anchor into the violently heaving seas. Then again I heard these words, 'Watch! For Trump will become as a heavy anchor that will bring great stability to the nation, for even now, I AM shaking the nation to its core. Tell My People to get ready. For everything that is not of My Kingdom will be shaken loose and will be cast down into the sea of forgetfulness,' says the Spirit of God."

You Are His Divine Carriers!

2018

"I hear the Spirit say, 'Beloved, you are my carriers of My Glory! You are carriers of My Fire and My Favor! You are carriers of My Healing, Restoration and Redemption Power! You are carriers of My Strength and Might! You are carriers of My Knowledge and Truth! You are carriers of The Fear of the Lord! You care carriers of My Love and Grace! You are carriers of Divine Strategy and Clarity!

You are carriers of My Anointing and Authority! Now go beloved and impart what has been given to you,' says the Spirit of God. Always remember the more we give away the more we receive. This is your season to increase, expand and overflow!"

Trump is a Sharp Scalpel

June 2019

"I saw the Hand of God take hold of President Donald Trump and as I looked at the President he became a Sharp Scalpel in the Hands of a Skillful Surgeon. America, get ready for the Hour of Divine Transplantation is Now upon you! I had a dream last night that I feel led to share with you today. The timing of this dream I believe is Very Significant! Now in this incredible dream I found myself standing in a heavenly realm, it was a realm of Glory that was new and unfamiliar to me but somehow I felt like I had been in this place before. (It was strange but as I stood in this place, the Spirit of Revelation whispered to me, 'Daughter Fear Not! For you were here even Before the Foundations of the Earth were ever Built.') Now if that was not enough to blow my earthly mind, the best was yet to come! As I stood in this incredible place in the dream, suddenly I saw the Nation called America come up before me and I heard these words, 'Watch! For I Am Now Restoring the Old Foundations of Many Nations. I Am Taking the Nations Back to My Original Intent. Yes! I Am Taking Them Back to Their Ancient Roots. Watch! As My Spirit Now Moves Upon All of Creation to Restore, Rebuild and to Reform!'

"As I heard those words, I suddenly saw the Nation of America come up before me again and I watched as the Nation was placed upon A Large Wooden Table, a Table that had the Appearance of an Ancient Altar. As I stayed watching suddenly I became aware of a multitude of Angels that were surrounding the Ancient Altar. As I looked at them I saw that some were dressed in crimson garments and wore golden crowns upon their heads, while others wore garments of many colors like that of the Rainbow. Their faces shone like the midday sun, and their hair was like rivers of silver and gold. As my eyes looked upon them I knew by revelation that these were 'Guardian Angels Assigned to the Nations of the Earth'. Now as my eyes were drawn away from the angels and back to the Nation of America which stood before me, suddenly I saw the Hand of God move towards the wooden Altar where the Nation of America was laid bare before Him. Now I watched as the Hand of the Lord suddenly took hold of President Donald Trump and as I looked at the President I saw him Become as a Silver Sword in the Hand of the Lord and like a Sharp Scalpel in the Hands of a Highly Skilled Surgeon. I watched as a Work of Divine Reconstruction Began to Take Place Over the Nation."

"Then I heard these words, 'Watch! For these are the Days of Divine Restoration and Reformation in the Nations of the Earth. Watch! For I shall use My Anointed Like a Sharp Scalpel in the Hands of a Skillful Surgeon in the Days Ahead. For I Am Doing a Delicate and Intricate Work in This Land and in the Hearts of the People. Watch as My Sharp Scalpel Now Moves Strategically to Sever and Separate. Yes! For My Sword Comes Not to Bring Peace but to Bring Division. Watch! But Fear Not! For the Spirit and Power of Elijah Shall Come to This Land to Turn the Hearts of the Fathers Back to the Children, and the Disobedient to the Way of the Righteous. My Beloved

America, Watch and Pray for My Scalpel Now Moves Upon the Heart of This Nation to Bring Forth Healing, Restoration and Transformation, for Truly I Tell You that This is the Hour of Divine Transplantation in This Nation!' says God."

Bulldozer

John Paul Jackson

J ohn Paul Jackson (1950-2015) was an authority on Biblical Dream Interretation who revealed God and led people to Jesus. While the "Bulldozer" does not name Donald Trump, some suggest there is perhaps a similarity.

Prophetic Dream

2012

"God has chosen a Bulldozer to clear the mess and Implement God's Plan." John Paul Jackson interpreted a dream of a woman who had a dream about a 'bulldozer wrecking through the White House, bulldozing through the White House like it was a deck of cards.' "The great thing is this, the bulldozer,' says Jackson. "You're seeing man's plans, but you see God saying, 'I have a plan that will bulldoze right through the plans of men.' The Bulldozer says, 'I have a plan. Refreshing times will come. I want to refresh America but it has gotten so deeply convoluted that bulldozing is required." It's kind of like when you gut a house to renovate. It's a real mess, but then you have a clean slate for Restoration."

Trumpet Trump

"Trump shall become My trumpet to the American people, for he possesses qualities that are even hard to find in My people these days. Trump does not fear man nor will he allow deception and lies to go unnoticed. I am going to use him to expose darkness and perversion in America like never before, but you must understand that he is like a bull in a china closet. Many will want to throw him away because he will disturb their sense of peace and tranquility, but you must listen through the bantering to discover the truth that I will speak through him."

"I will use the wealth that I have given to him to expose and launch investigations searching for the truth. Just as I raised up Cyrus to fulfill My purposes and plans, so I have raised up Trump to fulfill My purposes and plans prior to the 2016 election. You must listen to the trumpet very closely for he will sound the alarm and many will be blessed because of his compassion and mercy. Though many see the outward pride and arrogance, I have given him the tender heart of a father that wants to lend a helping hand to the poor and the needy, to the foreigner and the stranger."

Repentance

Cindy Deville

C indy Deville is an author and prophetic speaker who pastors at Victory Today Family Church in Frisco, Texas.

Cindy Deville had a vision regarding Trump. It was in May of 2009 when Cindy had an open vision following a time of prayer for America. "I saw a map of America. I first saw youth gathering at schools around flag poles on the west coast, then I saw the same thing happening at universities and colleges. I began to see prayer sweeping across the nation from coast to coast. I saw people praying outside government buildings, in businesses, financial districts, on Wall Street, and in Hollywood. As I saw this Vision, I kept hearing what seemed like a loud cry from heaven, 'Pray, America! Pray!' Then I saw the Spirit of God descend upon the nation and I saw people begin running into the streets, crying out in repentance and for salvation, as they fell under the convicting power of the Holy Spirit. What I saw swept over every sector of society in America. It was a nation-shaking move of the Holy Spirit that began changing everything."

"If My people who are called by My name will humble themselves, and pray and seek My face, and turn from their wicked ways, then I will hear from heaven, and will forgive their sin and heal their land."

Chronicles 7:14

Protection & Strength
Todd Roe

T odd Roe "I gave my life to Christ 25 years ago and I've had a walk of faith ever since, like Hebrews 11 talks about. God made me a dreamer like Joseph from Genesis."

Todd Roe Faith YouTube Dreams

2019

"Trump was with a group of people that he was leading. He had a sidearm on his hip. It was an encouraging dream and he had people standing with him. He emanated protection and strength. The message was that the tide is turning. Trump won't back down. He is protected, supported and his leadership results in victory."

"President Trump and I were sitting at a table having a conversation about how God was using him. We prayed together for a long time. Then I ran into the President again in another dream, as a form of emphasis of the first dream. In this dream we conversed about the first dream. Trump knew it was important and he leaned in and listened intently. He was so focused and is seeking Godly Counsel. The message was that the President is seeking God on his own and in his own prayer closet."

"In a third dream, John McCain was on his death bed and I wheeled Trump into the room and they argued and after that had a tender exchange as human beings. And then on July 4th I had a Ronald Regan dream where Ronald Regan was dancing a happy jig on a big stage. He was glowing and radiant with Nancy. He was celebrating Trump's presidency. He was dancing with joy for the future of America with Trump leading the charge. Trump is being partnered by the Lord. He has a good heart."

Wedding Cake
Cynthia Kennedy

Love's Messenger Ministries with Cynthia Kennedy said "I saw the Lord laughing hard and it gave me such a deep peace that He was in control. I saw Trump in Congress and he was stirring them all up...especially the Rinos (Republicans in name only-not conservative).

He was pointing out every corruption and they were furious. An arrow shot into Trump's back but he had on a 'leatherback shield' that protected him so it didn't penetrate. The Lord said, 'Don't worry, I protect him.

He's a Leatherback."

"I saw a wedding cake that was a real mess, cheap and nasty, birds were picking at it. The Lord said, 'This is not what I had planned for the United States. Pray for the Congressmen. They will not set up another Tower of Babel. Look at what I have planned. (I saw a magnificent, incredibly beautiful wedding cake.) These are the dreams I have always had for this nation. It is My hope that they would all come to Me and I will Build a righteous city upon a hill when they get right with Jesus.' I saw that this is our chance to decide to be people of the Spirit of peace and love."

King Cobra & the Mongoose

Crystal Lyons

October 28, 2916

C rystal Lyons of Cowgirl Logic said on YouTube—"I think it's important to know Where these dreams come from. I was raised in a backwoods area of Southern Missouri. Spending so much time in the solitude of where I was raised, I started hearing the 'voice' of the Lord, mostly with dreams but occasionally open-eyed visions as well and of course, most of all just that 'quiet knowing' down inside. I got filled with the Holy Spirit in my 20's, started riding bulls and bareback horses in the Pro Woman's Rodeo Association when I turned 30. That is when all I'd been learning while being hidden away with God, working ranches and sale barns, thrust me into full time ministry on the Pro-Rodeo circuit, along with other horse related and western style events."

"I've now been in ministry for over 30 years, and travel full time with my Gypsy Vanner stallion and other assorted animals. I first started getting dreams about Trump before he became our President, while my heart was grieving over our nation and asking God about His plan for us."

"In a very vivid dream, I was watching a video recording on TV. There was this long, rectangular-shaped room with only two things in it, a large king cobra and a mongoose. The cobra was HUGE, supernaturally so. His body stretched down the length of the room, approximately 20 feet, with his head held high, several feet up the corner, overlooking the room. Obviously in control.

"The mongoose was at the other end of the room and with lightning-fast action, the mongoose sprung across the room and grabbed the cobra by the neck, shaking it fiercely. The cobra struck back and bit the mongoose on the right side of his neck and held fast. Not letting go, like a bulldog. Snakes don't do that. They strike and release, but this snake sank his fangs into the jugular of the mongoose and wouldn't let go.

"At this point in the dream I turned off the TV saying, "I don't want to watch this! I figured the mongoose would defeat the cobra. I don't want to watch the mongoose get killed!" Just then, a man's voice spoke. Chuckling, he said, "The mongoose DOES kill the cobra. The mongoose is immune to cobra venom and ends up killing the cobra."

"At that I woke up. I knew mongooses were immune to venomous snakes but wasn't sure about the King Cobra, so I asked Siri... (cause you know, Siri knows everything, right?!) Sure enough, mongooses are immune to King Cobra venom. I then asked the Lord the meaning of the dream. That it was a recording I was watching on the TV is very important. It means the end is already done... settled. Nothing left up to chance. The mongoose kills the cobra. I knew immediately the mongoose is Trump, who moved up in the Presidential race unexpectedly with lightning-fast speed. The cobra is, I believe, the spirit of witchcraft that rules within those corrupt politicians that have been long-time controlling our political system. Though Trump will face unrelenting attacks from the enemy, he WILL succeed and prove to be totally immune to the "political poison" of Washington D. C."

Magnificent Bull

Alveda King

Evangelist, Alveda C. King. uses her God-given talents and abilities to glorify God and uphold the sanctity of life, from the womb to the tomb. She currently serves on the pastoral team of Priests for Life, as Executive Director of its outreach called Civil Rights for the Unborn. She is also a voice for the Silent No More Awareness Campaign, sharing testimony of two abortions, God's forgiveness and healing.

The daughter of the late civil rights activist Rev. A.D. King and his wife Naomi Barber King, Alveda grew up in the civil rights movement led by her uncle, Rev. Dr.

Martin Luther King, Jr. Her family home in Birmingham, Alabama, was bombed, as was her father's church office in Louisville, Kentucky. Alveda was jailed during the open housing movement. She sees the prolife movement as a continuation of the civil rights struggle.

"During the first debate, I remember texting friends. 'Mr. Trump is like a bull in a china shop.' Then God revealed this to me. 'Yes, and bulls are beautiful and magnificent creatures, and china is fragile.'"

"In context of America's economy, the bull represents a strong economy. Even in the face of COVID-19 and the street riots of 2020, we must remember we entered this era with a strong economy and the job rate for African Americans is the highest in recent history. And yes, the China issue is very fragile."

True Grit: The Reasons We Elected Trump

David Stolinsky

D avid Stolinsky is a political conservative who does social commentary.

"There are two movies titled 'True Grit.' The first was released in 1969. It starred Kim Darby as a young woman whose father had been murdered, and John Wayne as the broken-down, drunken, profane U.S. marshal who helped her find the murderers. The second was released in 2010. It starred Halee Steinfeld and Jeff Bridges in the same roles."

"I have a sentimental pull toward the John Wayne version because, well, it starred John Wayne. In addition, the film had an upbeat and sometimes humorous tone.

Still, I have to admit that the 2010 film was deeper. It was more realistic, and therefore darker. And it had another advantage. Part of the soundtrack was a version of the old hymn 'Leaning on the Everlasting Arms,' sung by Iris Dement. Frankly, I prefer more vigorous versions, but hearing any hymn in a film was-to say the least- a pleasant surprise."

'Surviving and overcoming life's trials often requires true grit. But where does it come from? Tough, courageous people used to be said to have 'sand' or 'grit.' Perhaps this is related to the origin of pearls. The smooth, beautiful, iridescent pearl looks so delicate and fine, but at its center is a hard grain of sand. Without the sand irritating the oyster, there would be no pearl for us to admire. Mitt Romney? He didn't have the grit to face down Candy Crowley, when she abandoned her role as moderator and jumped into the presidential debate on the side of Obama. Then how could Romney be expected to face down potential enemies? Jeb Bush? While governor of Florida, he tried to prevent the slow killing of disabled Terri Schiavo by dehydration and starvation. But when courts insisted that she die, he stepped aside. He acted as a lawyer, not a leader. His focus was the law, not morality of murdering the disabled. Ted Cruz? He might have been the best law student Professor Alan Dershowitz ever had. But he failed to project a sense of strong leadership or clear purpose. Hillary Clinton? When four of her personnel were under attack in Benghazi, she did nothing-and blamed a video no one had seen. Then she had the gall to proclaim that we did not lose a single American in Libya. No, we lost four. Instead of 'leave no man behind,' she apparently believes in, 'cover your behind.' This is the very opposite of grit. Barak Obama?

He sent a message to Putin that he would be more 'flexible' after the 2012 election. Grit may take many forms, but flexibility with potential enemies is not one of them. John Kerry? He proposed a more 'sensitive' and 'thoughtful' war on terrorism. Those are words to inspire fear in our friends and confidence in our enemies. Oh wait, it's supposed to be the other way around."

"I could go on and on, but you get the idea. To paraphrase Teddy Roosevelt, concerning all these politicians, and so many more, one could say that they mean well...feebly. Perhaps they might suffice to lead a nation in a time of tranquility, when nothing much was happening. But now, in a dangerous and complex world plagued by international terrorism, someone else was needed-someone with grit."

"If everything and everyone fades into pale pastels, obscured by a moral fog, there are no bad people, but there are also no good people. If so-called leaders who wriggle out of responsibility aren't bad, then real leaders aren't good. If the Boston Marathon bombers aren't evil, then the first responders who aided the injured aren't good. If the terrorists who attacked our consulate in Benghazi and killed four American 'infidels' aren't evil, then people who welcome others with different religious beliefs aren't good. If the IRS agents who harassed political opponents of the Obama administration aren't bad, then dedicated, conscientious public servants aren't good. If the Department of Justice agents who spied on Associated Press reporters aren't bad, then agents who risk their lives to protect the public aren't good. If the Obama administration officials who stood by idly when Americans were dying in Benghazi aren't bad, then the military and civilian personnel who risk their lives to 'leave no man behind' aren't good."

'Every action and every person fades into a dull pastel, like a shirt washed too often in hot water and bleach. No vivid colors to rouse us. No strong beliefs to sustain us. No everlasting arms to lean on. No grit. No pearls. Just slimy, bottom-feeding crustaceans. Peter Druker wrote, 'Management is doing things right; leadership is doing things right.' To govern us, we were choosing people who would do neither. They were taking the country in the wrong direction, but-fortunately for us-they were doing so in an incompetent manner."

"Eventually we became sick of the dull pastels. We wanted bright colors-perhaps too bright, perhaps glaringly bright. We wanted someone who used the word 'terrorism' when it was appropriate. We wanted someone who could use the correct words when a Muslim extremist shot up a Jewish deli, and unlike Obama, not merely say that he 'randomly shot a bunch of folks.' Did Trump speak too loudly? Yes, but he didn't use weasel words. He used hyperbole to emphasize what he said, not euphemisms to conceal what had happened. Was he rough around the edges? Yes, but at least he wasn't slick and smooth. Did he look like a president, or at least like the president we had become used to? No, but at least he didn't look like a handsome, well-spoken actor who had been cast to play a president in a TV show. At least he doesn't exemplify appearance over substance. In short, we chose someone who looked like he had true grit. And as with the character in the films, we were willing to put up with his imperfections to get it. Now is the testing time, when we will see whether we chose wisely. My bet is that we did."

Trump Pulled the Sword from the Stone: Deal with It

January 2017

"Remember the story of how King Arthur came to be king? The young Arthur thought he was the son of Sir Ector and the younger brother of Sir Kay. Kay was to participate in a tournament, but Arthur forgot to bring Kay's sword. In his haste to obtain a sword, Arthur saw the sword in the stone and drew it out. The sword was Excalibur, which had been thrust into the stone by the late King Uther. Many had tried to pull the sword out of the stone to show themselves worthy of becoming king.

But they had all failed, while Arthur succeeded."

"It turned out that Arthur was the illegitimate son of King Uther. In those days, it was believed that 'blood' entitled some people to rule others. Now we believe that we should select our leaders. Still, 'the sword in the stone' remains as a metaphor for proving oneself worthy of leadership. And the point of the story is that the one who pulls the sword from may not be the one we expect, or the one who at first glance appears to be the best qualified to be our leader."

"There were 17 presidential hopefuls on the Republican debate stage. There were current and former governors and members of Congress. One was Jeb Bush, former governor of Florida, the son and brother of presidents, and the recipient of a huge campaign fund.

Others included Ted Cruz and Marco Rubio, who had the twin advantages of being senators and Latinos. But who knocked them all out of the race, as if he were a bowling ball and they were tenpins? Donald J. Trump."

"Trump then had to face Hillary Clinton, after she had defeated Bernie Sanders-with underhanded help from the Democratic National Committee. Hillary had spent eight years as First Lady, ten years as senator, and four years as secretary of state. Trump, on the other hand, had spent his career in real-estate development.

But who won the election? Donald J. Trump. Clearly, Trump was not the one most people expected to win. He did not appear to be the one best qualified by experience, or by personal qualities. Many found his demeanor to be rude, his speech to be loud, and his behavior to be ill-mannered. Like Arthur, some people considered him to be an uncouth bastard. Nevertheless, like Arthur, where others had failed, Trump pulled out the sword-and appeared to do so with ease."

"But the comparison goes further. In john Boorman's superb film 'Excalibur,' a knight complains that Arthur is unqualified to be king because he is not even a knight.

Unexpectedly, Arthur agrees, kneels down, and asks the complainer to dub him knight. We do not have knighthood in America. But we can agree that Trump is surrounding himself with cabinet members and other advisors who are eminently qualified. This is especially true in the areas of military affairs and national security, where Trump has little experience. In effect, like Arthur, Trump is saying, 'You have what I lack-give it to me.'"

"The recognition of what he lacks is the action of a wise man. In contrast, a narcissist like Barak Obama assumes that he is the smartest person in the room.

Surrounding himself with strong advisors is the action of a secure man. In contrast, a person like Obama wants to appear strong by comparison and surrounds himself with second-raters."

"For example, take Trump's candidate for secretary of state, Rex Tillerson, CEO of ExxonMobil, who for years has been negotiating billion-dollar deals with foreign nations including Russia. Compare him with Obama's secretary of state, John Kerry, whose 'reset' with Russia made things worse, and who proclaimed that our military effort in Syria would be an 'unbelievably small, limited kind of effort.' Now there is a threat to strike fear into the hearts of tyrants. The only risk to potential enemies is that they would injure themselves falling off their chairs while laughing uncontrollably. Trump chose a strong, experienced negotiator to help him deal with foreign nations. Obama chose a weak, silly fellow because Obama intended to be his own secretary of state. The results we see before us-disheartened friends, emboldened enemies."

"When Trump's ancestry is mentioned, people invariably refer to his paternal grandparents, who emigrated from Bavaria. For some reason, few mention Trump's mother, whose family name was Macleod, and who was born on the Scottish Isle of Lewis. Many natives of the Isle of Lewis speak Scots Gaelic as their first language. That is, on his mother's side, Trump resembles Arthur in his Celtic heritage. Come to think of it, Trump- like the idealized Arthur-has red hair as well as a long, straight nose, and in addition affects a stern expression."*

(*Look for Trump's lineage in another chapter of this book where Melissa from Freedom Force Battalion does detailed research with incredible results.)

"Whether or not a real King Arthur existed remains uncertain. The story may be based on a chief of the Britons who fought Saxon invaders. But in any case, the story itself is instructive. The one who pulls the sword out of the stone may not fit our preconceptions, but he did in fact pull out the sword. Sooner or later, we must all accept that fact."

Author's Note: "I have a personal recollection regarding the Isle of Lewis. I attended the university of California School of Medicine in San Francisco. We had several foreign -born professors. Our chief anatomy lecturer was a Scot from Glasgow, so I became familiar with a thick Scottish burr. Then I came into contact with another Scot, but his accent was different-more musical, much like an Irish brogue."

"Years later, I found out why. Dr. Donald Macrae was born in Stornoway on the Isle of Lewis, about 4 miles from the Tong, the village where Donald Trump's mother, Mary Anne Macleod Trump, was born. Like her, he probably spoke Scots Gaelic as his first language. In addition to being an outstanding teacher, Macrae had been awarded the Military Cross, the UK's third highest decoration for valor. He had gone forward into a minefield and treated wounded soldiers under heavy fire. The Isle of Lewis has a population of only about 18,500. But judging from Donald Trump's mother and my professor, it has more than its fair share of exceptional people."

dstol@prodigy.net
www.stolinsky.com

Trump Stands for
Religious Freedom
Blaise Joseph

B laise has a strong interest in social policy, writes on marriage
and family issues and is Assistant Dean at Warrene College
at the University of New South Wales.

"Christians are unable to speak freely. Religious freedom
is under attack. Society is materialistic and immoral. Western
civilization is facing huge threats, from within and without. And
Apparently the one powerful emerging leader is no saint. You're
thinking America 2016? No. Rome 312."

"The leader is Constantine, who is vying to become the Roman
Emperor. Constantine had many defects: he had multiple wives
and even put one of them to death, was extremely ambitious, and
was a ruthless general and politician. But the legend remains that
he had a 'Road to Damascus' moment, saw a vision, converted to
Christianity, triumphed over his opponents, and became a great
emperor of Rome."

"Constantine would go on to not only save the Roman Empire,
but also liberate Christianity. He signed the Edict of Milan in 313,
giving Christians the right to practice their faith and speak freely.
This was enough to allow Christians to engage in the public

sphere with freedom, thereby enabling them to spread the Christian message to the ends of the empire and Christianize a pagan culture. Constantine himself was no pillar of virtue, but he created the environment which gave Christians the freedom to influence society. The early Christians were perfectly capable of influencing society themselves; all they needed from the emperor was the freedom to do so."

"Fast forward to 2016, and we can see many obvious similarities. Western society has many problems.

Conservative Christians have the solutions to many of those problems, but cannot articulate them freely in the public square due to endemic political correctness and cultural Marxism. Conservatives do not lack will, good arguments, or articulate defenders; what they lack is the freedom to speak bluntly about social issues without being shouted down by the vindictive hordes of secular progressivism for 'offending' particular groups of people. Donald Trump is the only person who can give us that freedom."

"But first, consider the following:

Stating that children should ideally have a mother and a father because on average they will do best in that environment (as supported overwhelmingly by the relevant social science) renders you 'homophobic' (even though the statement has nothing to do with homosexuality) and a 'hater of single mothers'; Explaining that there is actually a biological and societal reason that marriage has been promoted and protected as between a man and a woman for millennia (hint: it's about children) makes you 'bigoted';

Arguing that the high divorce rate hurts children, and that no-fault divorce is responsible for many social problems, makes you 'living in the 1950's' and a dinosaur' (even though the social data on the effects of divorce is indisputable and President Obama himself has said as much);

Affirming the biological fact that men and women are inherently different makes you 'transphobic' (something that no one knew existed just a few years ago);

Pointing out that babies do not simply magically appear out of nothing after nine months, and may in fact have a right to life and dignity before birth, makes you an extremist (just because) and a sexist (even though this statement says nothing about women)."

"There are many more examples. The point is that making perfectly reasonable statements causes so much outrage that conservatives either give up or end up losing credibility and becoming impotent in influencing public opinion. Arguments are not considered on their merits but rather assessed based on the extent to which they offend particular groups of people. This makes the conservative Christian cause in the public sphere ultimately hopeless."

"And this is where Trump comes in. America doesn't need a president to make arguments for us. America just needs a president to give us the freedom to make our arguments without fear of being shouted down by the politically correct brigade. Whatever else you might say about Trump, he is definitely politically incorrect, and prides himself on that attribute. He refuses to back down after making controversial statements. He does not apologize for offending groups after making arguments.

He stands up to the media. He is defiant in spite of being vilified by political elites, journalists, and academics."

Let's consider the example of illegal immigration.

Trump is tapping into the understandable tendency for ordinary citizens to be skeptical of high levels of immigration, especially when there is little or not order to the immigration program. For many years, this was a no-go-zone, as those who raised the issue were shouted down by calls of 'racist' and allegations of offending immigrants, Mexicans, etc. Trump, however, in less than a year, has managed to kick-start a proper debate on the topic by refusing to be howled down and apologize for potentially offending minority groups. Regardless of your views on illegal immigration, it is clear that the tactics of the cultural Marxists, used in the immigration debate, simply do not work against Trump."

Or take the issue of terrorism. Unlike many other Christian leaders, Trump calls out the evil of Islamic terrorism and extremism for what it is; and seeks to sensibly scrutinize the policy of mass Islamic immigration in order to protect national security. In doing so, he has again overcome the slogans of 'Islamophobia' and 'racism' to actually discuss an important, sensitive issue."

"Christian conservatives need exactly the same thing to happen with other issues, like abortion and marriage. This is how Trump could be a great president for conservative Christians. Trump is the one presidential candidate who is capable of changing society to make it more tolerant of robust discussions on controversial issues. At last, with a leader who publicly holds the silencing tactics of the left with utter contempt, it would be possible to stand up to leftists on the hot-button issues."

"If Trump becomes president of the U.S. (thanking God every day that he did!) and the most powerful leader in the West, he can fundamentally change Western culture. The effects of his presidency would go far beyond the shores, and walls, of America. People would speak more freely about a range of issues. Political correctness, after being denounced by Trump over and over again, would become severely weakened. Cultural Marxism and the politics of victimhood would be crippled. Progressives who seek to shut down debate would realize that their tactics no longer work. And following this fundamental transformation of the political scene, conservatives could finally be free to make their case in the public sphere."

Everything else would follow from this. Our universities would become places of learning and free thinking again. (Trumps Executive Order to demand free speech on college campuses with the threat of losing funds is working!) Better judges, lawyers, and politicians would result. The population would be far better informed because public debates would take place with fewer impediments. This would lead to long-term successes on social political issues, like abortion and marriage, and also allow Christians to make Western society truly Christian once again. Now, many conservative Christian commentators and academics who oppose Trump are missing the bigger picture.

It's time to think outside the box and elect someone who might be able to deal a fatal blow to political correctness and cultural Marxism."

"Having a consistent conservative president of the United States would without a doubt be a welcome event. Publicly making the case for a number of Christian causes and nominating sound judges, for instance, would be good results in themselves. Coming from a commerce background, Trump is the 'high risk/ high return' option.

He could drive cultural Marxism out of the public sphere, allowing Christians to make their case freely for generations to come. After 4-8 years of Trump, political correctness will be a thing of the past. ('America will never be a socialist country!' President DJT)"

In any case, does anyone seriously believe that Trump has a bigger ego than any other politician? He just refuses to display the fake humility that politicians have come to perfect and the population has come to despise.

Here again is a similarity with Constantine: as emperor, he was an egotistical individual that named the capital of the empire, Constantinople, after himself. Trump wouldn't go that far. (Though we now have a Trump Heights in Israel thanks to the appreciation of the Israeli people.) Like Constantine, Trump is an imperfect human with flaws like all of us. But just as Constantine is now widely referred to as 'Constantine the Great' for his achievements as Roman Emperor and giving freedom to Christians, is it possible that one-day Trump may be remembered as the man who 'Made America Great Again' and revered by Christians as 'the Great'? "

"Trump could be exactly what conservative Christians need right now. We are currently constrained by a cultural Marxist environment of political correctness. If we want to take away this constraint once and for all, then Trump is the best candidate by far, in fact, he is the only candidate." (You were right, Blaise!)

"Pray that President Trump would put on the armor of God to withstand enemy attack. (Ephesians 6:10-20) Pray that President Trump would not be swayed by flattery or deceitful schemes. (Peter 2:3)

Pray for those around President Trump to rightly watch out for him and stand with him. (Proverbs 4:23)

Pray for the Trump household, that God's presence would overshadow relationships and family connections. (Proverbs 4:23)

Bless the Lord for the work He is doing in cleaning out corruption in high places. (2 Chronicles 19:7)

American Pharoah:
America Will Be Stronger
Johnny Enlow

Johnny and Elizabeth Enlow are social reformers at heart, as well as international speakers and authors of *The Seven Mountain Prophecy*, *The Seven Mountain Mantle*, and *Rainbow God*. As ones focused on the reformation of the 7 primary areas of culture, they are spiritual mentors to many in Media, Arts and Entertainment, Government, Family, Religion, Economy, and Education. Their passion is to awaken our generation to the reality of the God of all of life, Who not only cares for our souls, but also has practical solutions to offer through His sons and daughters for every problem that exists in society.

This prophecy, about the race horse American Pharoah, tells of our coming future, and while it does not mention Donald Trump, it clearly shares a future vision we may see under his leadership. "(Note: Due to a mistake in the horse's registration paperwork American 'Pharoah' is spelled incorrectly).

For many, of course, this can sound like something either not good or at a minimum confusing. Those with a Biblical foundation can easily think of Pharoah primarily in a negative light, as we remember the Pharaoh who would not allow the people of Israel to go free and thus came under severe judgment. However, it was also another

Pharaoh hundreds of years before then, who in essence, promoted Joseph to his position de facto ruler of Egypt. Without the Pharaoh, Joseph remains imprisoned and does not fulfill the promise of the dreams that he had after receiving the coat of many colors. "

"The word Pharaoh actually means 'big house' or 'palace' and I think that is significant. I believe that American Pharoah winning speaks prophetically of a place and role that America is about to more fully step into as it relates to world affairs and the world economy. The United States is in a position of world leadership not because of her level of righteousness, but because of the assignment of God upon her at this time."

"It is very parallel to the role Egypt had in Joseph's day when Egypt was the dominant nation in the world, despite not deserving it from a righteousness standpoint. This is important to see as so many Believers in America are always calling for her demise based on her lack of perfection in all aspects of morality, not realizing her lead role in world affairs is dictated by God rather than by having completely earned it."

37 Years: The Josephs Will Rise

"I see the 37 years (time since the last triple crown) as connecting to Genesis 37 when Joseph is first introduced to us and given the coat of many colors. In my book, *The 7 Mountain Mantle: Receiving the Joseph Anointing to Reform Nations*, I write much about this chapter telling of the coming Josephs who would arise in every mountain and be instrumental in the reforming our society. It's also significant that Joseph was 37 years old when the famine started that ultimately pushed Egypt to an even more lead nation status. Because of the Joseph solutions implemented by Pharaoh, it says that 'all nations came to Joseph,' Egypt, and Pharaoh for their own survival (see Genesis 41:57)"

"I believe that the United States position in world economics is about to be greatly strengthened and that there will also be a corresponding weakening of many other nations' economic positions, with the United States increasingly being in a place of dictating terms of economic rescue for many nations. Significant economic shakings are coming, but they will end up greatly strengthening the United States' position in the world and not weakening it."

"The Josephs will be bold as lions during this season and in the midst of much upheaval will greatly prosper. Fearful, self-protectionist, hoarders, (the pseudo-Josephs) will increasingly lose their status, their credibility, and even their resources. Make sure you're not one of them. There's a consequence to buying into fear and gloom. Boldness, generosity, and a carefree heart are Kingdom characteristics to embrace and walk in. Lose all self-preservation instincts that come from an orphan mentality. Walk in confidence as sons and daughters who know they are being looked after by the Father. Your best days are ahead of you, if you do."

http://www.restore7.org/

Trump Fulfilling Prophecies

250 Rabbis

Rabbis to Trump: 'You are fulfilling prophecies.'

"250 rabbis sent a thank-you letter praising Trump's decision to recognize Jerusalem, telling him 'You will be eternally remembered in the history of the Jews.' The letter, initiated by the Safed's Chief Rabbi Shmuel Eliyahu and delivered by Yossi Dagan, the head of the Samaria Regional Council, told the American president, 'You have a rare privilege to be the first president to recognize Jerusalem as the eternal capital of the State of Israel."

"We are privileged to be living in a generation that is repeatedly witnessing the words of the prophets coming true,' said the rabbis, 'Jews have made Aliyah and are continuing to come to the land of Israel from all corners of the world. Israel triumphs over its enemies time after time, the mountains of Israel offer generous bounty and the economy is booming."

"We are privileged to be seeing the rebuilding of Jerusalem," wrote the rabbis. "Children play in the streets' (Zechariah 8:4) and we are confident in the fulfillment of all the prophecies. The United States is privileged to be one of the first nations to support the establishment of the State of Israel. US presidents have had the privilege of being at Israel's side and being a partner in the fulfillment of the vision of the prophets regarding the return to Zion and the establishment of the State of Israel."

"They continued, 'We are confident that you will be remembered in the history of the Jewish people as one who stood at the forefront fearlessly. May it be His will that God's promise to Joshua (1:9) should be fulfilled in you: 'Have I not commanded you? Be strong and courageous. Do not be afraid; do not be discouraged, for the Lord your God will be with you wherever you go- Amen."

Dawn of a New Nation
Mike De Lorenzo

"This Painting is named 'Dawn of a New Nation'.

You can see Abraham Lincoln and George Washington praying over Donald Trump. The Lord told me in June, 2016, that America was about to celebrate its 240th year as a nation. 'I'm about to give you a double portion of 120, to reset America.' To be honest, I really didn't know how old America was when the Lord gave me the Word, but I quickly did the math in my head and said, 'Wow, we are 240 years old; God is right once again.' But I knew what 120 meant for the most part.

1. Noah took 120 years to build the ark, then the flood came and the world was reset.
2. Moses was 120 years old when the children of Israel entered the Promised Land for the first time in 400 years.
3. 120,000 people repented during the days of Jonah, when he called the city to repent.
4. 120 were in the Upper Room at Pentecost.
5. When God resets the world once again at the end of time, the Book of Revelation mentions the 144,000, and that is 120 times 1,200."

"In the background of the painting is Independence Hall, the place where the Constitution was signed. In May of 2017, while in worship, the Lord told me to put two angels in the sky blowing trumpets. Two weeks later I was talking to someone after church, and the Lord spoke to my heart, and said to put a mosaic of America in the cobblestones. Later, I noticed a cross and a face appeared in the outline of the United States, and the Lord said to put the Star of David under the Liberty Bell, for this year the scripture on the Liberty Bell is Leviticus 25:10, which talks about the Year of Jubilee, and proclaiming liberty and freedom throughout the Land."

"The Lord told me to finish the painting on my birthday 6/12/17. The number six is the number of man, 12 is the number of God's government, and 17 is the number of victory and triumph. The Lord said to me that He wants His government to have victory and triumph over the work of man coming against Donald Trump and this nation."

"He also gave me Psalm 89, about this nation and our new president, the day we dedicated this painting on June 12th. Here are some of the verses: 14 'Righteousness and justice are the foundation of Your throne; Mercy and truth go before Your face.' 15 'Blessed are the people who know the joyful sound! They walk, O Lord, in the light of Your countenance.' 16 'In Your name they rejoice all day long, And in Your righteousness they are exalted.' 17 'For You are the glory of their strength, And in Your favor our horn is exalted.' 18 'For our shield belongs to the Lord, And our king to the Holy One of Israel.' 19 'Then You spoke in a vision to Your holy one, And said: 'I have given help to one who is mighty; I have exalted one chosen from the people.' 20 I have found My servant David; With My holy oil I have anointed him, 21 With whom My hand shall be established; Also My arm shall strengthen him.' 22 'The enemy shall not outwit him, Nor the son of wickedness afflict him.' 23 'I will beat down his foes before his face, And plague those who hate him.' 24 'But My faithfulness and My mercy shall be with him, And in My name his horn shall be exalted.' 25 'Also I will set his hand over the sea, And his right hand over the rivers.' 26 'He shall cry to Me, 'You are my Father, My God, and the rock of my salvation.'"

'The time on the clock tower is 8:00 am, the start of a new beginning for this nation. Eight means 'new beginning.' I was impressed by the flowers forming a cross and the left side the number four. The four winds of the Holy Spirit are about to blow on the land, and the gospel is to go to the four corners of the earth. I was also given Proverbs 21:15, (New American Standard Bible) 15 'The exercise of justice is joy for the righteous. But is terror to the workers of iniquity.' God said that every paint brush stroke is exercising justice and joy to the righteous, but it's a terror to the wicked.'"

www.myfathershouseministries.com

Manifest Destiny
BethAnon

anifest Destiny is a phrase coined in 1845 by the journalist John O'Sullivan, expressing the philosophy that drove 19th century U. S. territorial expansion. Manifest Destiny held that the United States was destined by God to expand its dominion and spread democracy and capitalism across the entire North American continent.

It was based on a divine right of the American people to bring civilization and enlightenment to other races, usually associated with the massive expansion of the United States in just over fifty years from 1803 to 1853.

"American Progress: Spirit of the Frontier" is a painting by John Gast created in 1872 expressing the idea of Manifest Destiny. The painting is an allegory of Manifest Destiny. An allegory is a visible symbol representing an abstract idea. The Manifest Destiny painting conveys the idea of American Progress and Westward expansion using progressive transportation systems with people heading westwards who are guided and protected by the quasi-mythical goddess Columbia, as symbol of America. Columbia also represents Progress and Destiny, guiding the nation through a course of events that will inevitably happen in the future. Columbia holds the book of knowledge and enlightenment and also the wires of the telegraph enabling communication across the vast nation.

In spite of all the negativity espoused and inflicted by the enemy, the cause and direction were pure and resulted in incredible achievements and increased prosperity for humanity. Now that we are dismantling the Luciferian Agenda we will be able to amend and restore going forth in our full power to create the heaven on earth as we were directed over two thousand years ago. Praise God!

America's Purpose

Saul Alinsky propaganda, i.e. the Luciferian Agenda, has stolen our heritage from it's original design. Donald Trump has been chosen to lead the charge of restoration by bringing forward our true principles and putting them into action with the help of all of us children of God.

Jamestown was the first permanent English settlement in the New World. From its inception grew American civilization. What was America founded on? Why did we flee our oppressors in the British Isles? It was all about God, the freedom to worship God and live according to His Word.* We had to leave. We were being persecuted for our faith.

In the founding document of Jamestown called the 'Virginia Charter', it says this..."to the glory of His Divine Majesty in propagating of Christian religion to such people as yet live in darkness and miserable ignorance of the true knowledge and worship of God..." According to its earliest founding document, America was founded for the glory of God, the spreading of the faith of the Gospel, and to be a light to bring those in darkness to salvation.

Though much has been achieved, an underlying perversion of religion by the infiltration of the Luciferians has been a parasitic plague upon the true Christians and their efforts to spread the good news that Jesus loves you.

After centuries and decades, we have fallen further and further from our original true purpose of the founding vision of this country. And by the Grace of God we are deeply enmeshed in turning things around for the good by dismantling the deception wherever we find it.

This is our time, the time for the children of God to shine the light for all humanity to awaken and aspire to become our true selves and serve each other, seeing God in every human being. There is nothing more beautiful than a human being adorned in peace.

*There is a great movie about William Penn called 'The Courageous Mr. Penn' You can find it on YouTube.....a must see for every Christian patriot.

God's Message to Representative Mike Hill

Mike Hill

M ike Hill said, that he was at an anti-abortion rally a while back in Pensacola and "while the keynote speaker was delivering a speech, God spoke to me. As plain as day, God spoke to me. He said, 'That wasn't My bill, (talking about the heartbeat detection bill that I filed). He said that wasn't My bill.' I knew immediately what He was talking about. He said, 'You remove those exceptions and you file it again.' And I said, 'Yes, Lord, I will.' It's coming back. It's coming back. We are going to file that bill without any exceptions just like what we saw passed in Alabama."*

*Mike Hill is also campaigning to bring the Trump Star from the Hollywood Walk of Fame to Pensacola, the first settlement in America. Our President is a true gentleman who is a star with or without the acknowledgement of Hollywood.

Praying for the President

Rodney Howard-Browne

'Praying for the President, What Really Happened at the White House' By Rodney Howard-Browne (Founder of Revival Ministries International in Tampa, Florida)

"It was very surreal; we were in the executive buildings for planning and strategy meetings on the White House grounds. Vice President Pence walked in and told us the President wanted to see us, so 27 of us walked down to the Oval Office. The President was very relaxed. I've met him on several occasions and he is always the same calm person. Pastor Paula White announced that we were going to pray and the President welcomed it. Scripture says, 1 Timothy 2:1 'I urge you then, first of all, that petitions, prayers, intercession and thanksgiving be made for all people, for kings and all those in authority, that we may live peaceably in quiet lives and all Godliness and holiness.'"

"A lot of people were freaking out because 'they prayed in the Oval Office.' 'What about separation of church and state?' That's bogus! There is no such thing as separation of church and state. If there is such a thing it means that the government should not stick their nose into the church. So people misquote things all the time.

171

But the fact of the matter is, the founding fathers and all of our first initial presidents opened everything in prayer. The first mega church was in the Capitol Building. George Washington started that. The Marine band did the praise and worship. We have moved so far away from the founding of America that we don't even understand how our current nation was founded? Our initial founders looked to God....to Divine Providence. And our current President, President number 45, understands that. He realizes that he cannot go further in what he's doing without divine intervention in his life."

"So, this is imperative. When we were in the Oval Office we were surrounded by people of different faiths who all see things a little differently, but we can come together with one purpose, one cause, to pray for our President. We have set aside our differences. We decided to pray for one another and stand with one another. That is huge. I see the Body of Christ coming together because America needs another Great Spiritual Awakening. We had one in the 1700's. We had one in the 1800's. We need to have one now. Without divine intervention, it's over. God has given us, with President Trump, a last minute reprieve. But we have a window to see this thing turned around because the enemy is so upset with what is taking place."

"So what I saw in the Oval Office was a group of Christians coming together with no agenda other than to come together to pray for and bless our President. Our 35th President of the United States, John Fitzgerald Kennedy, said, 'Ask not what your country can do for you, ask what you can do for your country.' It's America's time to pray. We have to lift up our President in prayer because there are planned attacks on our President.

These have been planned by people that hate God, hate America, hate our President and we must stop this in Jesus name. I believe we have the power to do that."

"I believe that God is going to protect our President and that he will finish exactly what he was elected to do. The People of America elected the President. We have to pray for protection, wisdom and direction and that God would surround him with Godly leadership. The problem is that there are people all over the place, the Rinos (Republican in name only) and the Never Trumpers that don't like him no matter what he does. Then you have the media that keeps spinning lies, bias and agenda all the time. We have to come back to what the truth is. We need to pray that the hearts and ears of those surrounding the President would be attentive to Godly counsel and do what is right in God's sight. And that the wicked would be cut off and rooted out."

"We have to pray that the Word of God prevails and grows mightily in the hearts and lives of the people of the United States of America and Jesus is Lord over this great land. 2nd Chronicles 7 & 14 'If My people who are called by My name will humble themselves and spray, seek My face, turn from their wicked ways, then I will hear from Heaven and forgive their sin and heal their land.' Proverbs 14 & 34 'The righteous exalteth a nation but sin is a reproach to any people.' Galatians: 4 & 2 'Devote yourself to prayer and be watchful and thankful.' It is imperative that we pray. We do a 24-hour prayer room with someone in there all of the time just for the purpose of praying for our President, that God would protect him, that the plan of the wicked would be cut off, to stop the agenda of the enemy and that no harm will come to our President. Pray that if the enemy digs a ditch for the President that the enemy will fall in it themselves."

"This is about praying for our President. There is a fight on for the soul of the Republic and God has raised President Donald John Trump to be the trumpet that will sound in this hour. Thank God he is there. It is a huge, huge thing. There are many traps being set all the time.

So much has been averted already by the Lord since Trump has been in office. Join us and pray like never before. Pray, pray, pray. We lift up President Donald Trump to you Lord, his wife, his children. Everything that he is. Father, we pray supernatural protection upon him. I pray Lord that you speak to him in the night hours and show him exactly what to do. Give him supernatural wisdom. Father, please abide him in a wall of fire that no harm and evil will come near him. Thank you that we

will have peace in our country and peace on earth. Thank you for the peace of Israel. I pray every plan of the enemy will come to naught in the name of Jesus. Pull the wheels off of pharaoh's chariot. And we pray that you wake up the sleeping giant, the Church, and Lord, that they rise up and we see another great spiritual awakening in America. Father, we give you praise as your Holy Spirit moves across this land. Great shall be the Victory. We thank you for our supernatural weapons.

You magnify your Word and keep a Heavenly Host of

Angels and the Paraclete (the Holy Spirit) to comfort us. You understand all. Thank you, Lord in the name of Jesus.

www.revival.com

Prophetic Dream about President Trump

Wanda Alger

October 2018

Wanda Alger is five-fold prophetic minister, former field correspondent with Intercessors for America, speaker, and author.

My passion is to see the Church rise up to impact our culture and bring heaven's rule to the earth. "One of our intercessors sent this dream a while back and we believe it is a call to pray for President Trump as he continues to confront corruption and evil intent in the high places of our government. An intercessor is a person who intervenes on behalf of another by prayer. In the dream, this intercessor saw President Trump preparing to speak at an event and waiting inside the house of a woman who was down-trodden and poor. Parts of this house were being remodeled as it was in shambles. The room he sat in wasn't being fixed up and was horrible and dirty. In the dream, this intercessor began to clean out the trash in a corner of the room when she found a 'slipper'-a 'house shoe.' It was torn from top to bottom and smelled awful. When she looked inside, there was flesh still in it and it looked like someone pulled their foot out, leaving their flesh behind. There were maggots crawling all over it.

'In disgust, I threw it down hurriedly and it flipped toward the feet of the President. I ran over and got it and threw it outside and away from him. During this entire ordeal, President Trump was sitting alone in that room reading a paper and did not seem to be affected by any of this.'"

"We ask you to pray into this as the Holy Spirit reveals God's purposes. I would propose to you that the symbolism in the dream represents 'the swamp' and that Trump is trying to clean it out. The 'house' that he is waiting in refers to the underlying structures of the 'swamp.' The 'flesh' found inside the 'house shoe' could represent those sin and flesh issues that have made this place of government corrupt, thus drawing evil forces ('maggots'). Those who have served in this place have left such a stench that needs to be cleared out."

"Of even greater concern is the fact that these 'house slippers' tried to get on President Trump. I believe this is the focus of our prayers. We know a tactic of the enemy is to find a weakness or crack in someone's armor in order to attack and take hold. We must pray for President Trump to strengthen his own heart and soul in order to deflect any attempt of the enemy to take hold of him and cause him to 'slip' in his walk. We must also pray that he becomes aware of these spiritual attacks and not dismiss them prematurely (in the dream he was alone and totally unaware of what was happening.) The fact that Trump was even willing to sit in this crumbling house is telling."

"Realizing that this can be subjective in nature, we ask that you simply pray into this and ask the Lord to reveal His purposes in this regard. We know that President Trump needs prayer. We know that God is cleaning 'house' and that enemy forces are seeking to devour and destroy us. I encourage you to use these scriptures to lift up our president and those he works with in this season of clean-up."

"I AM" The Man Of War

July 29, 2019

You question this one I placed in the White House for this time?

You are offended by his speech and demeanor? I tell you, though his flesh often reacts and his ego feels threatened, it is MY zeal that I have placed in this one you have prayed for. It is MY righteous anger at the demonic forces swirling within this nation that I have burned into his bones. Though he may believe them to be his natural enemies, it is I who speak to the spiritual enemies that continue to assail this nation and My people. Even when his flesh rules his mouth, it is I who rule his destiny.

Do not question the Potter as to the clay He chooses to mold and shape.

I have placed this one as a David for he is a man of war.

Not a man to bring war or cause war, but a man who is not afraid to war against those who oppose Me in the high places of darkness and deception.

Many do not yet perceive the demonic battles raging for control of this nation and I need those who are not afraid to war for My cause.

This one I have placed in office is not fully aware of how I use him, but it is because of the prayers of the saints that I use even his weaknesses and missteps to champion the causes of My Kingdom and your salvation.

Do not allow any offense to blind your eyes to the realities of the unseen realm. Do not allow the distraction of his methods to turn your attention from what I am doing in higher places.

You think Me a tame God? You think My meekness and humility My only attributes? I tell you, in these days you shall see aspects of My character and My name that you have not yet seen.

You are going to see the Man of War that I AM, for I have not come to bring peace, but to bring the sword with which to rightly divide the sheep from the goats, the true from the counterfeit, and the religious from the pure in heart. Before there can be peace among men, the demonic forces warring with souls and deceiving minds must be overthrown and silenced.

My zeal is being unleashed and I am not afraid to offend minds in order to expose the flesh.

You must pray for this President.

Do not idolize the man, for in so doing, the ivory tower will surely fall.

He is new to this Kingdom and has much to learn. I will teach him as well as correct him. You must pray with eyes wide open and discernment keen. For this is not about a man. It is about My purposes being accomplished in whosoever will! He has made himself available and thus being steered by My hand.

You must keep your eyes fixed on the goal of My Kingdom being manifest and the realities of heaven coming to earth. Do not look to man or any whom I call in this hour. All are but vessels and parts of the whole. I will use many in the days to come that will not seem qualified by man's standards. I will use many that will shock the world, many that have been hidden from the opposition in order to unseat age-old principalities and powers.

Come up higher!

I say to come up to where I AM and the enemy is denied access!

It is only from this place before My throne that you can be changed by My presence and permeated with My Spirit. It is only through My Spirit that you will rightly pray and rightly rule. Your prayers are being answered. I am working on your behalf. Use My eyes with which to see and all will become clear.

(Isaiah 9:7, Romans 9:21, Exodus 15:3, Colossians 3:1,2)

https://www.facebook.com/TurningaNation/

The Earth Belongs to Us–We Are Q

Bulmaro Aguilar

ulmaro Aguilar (Komorusan Q714 on YouTube) said "The Deep State fuse is being defused and as indictments move forward, it will be over for many high profile individuals in the government, entertainment industry, Hollywood and Main Stream Media. Many will be shocked to see what has been going on deep in the shadows as pedophilia, child sacrifice rituals and human experimentation come to the surface. The government will be rebooted, so to speak. Fake news will be removed and replaced and every corporation tied to the fake news machine will be charged with treason and crimes against humanity"

"Our father in heaven chose Donald Trump for this time as an opportunity for his righteous sons and daughters to take back dominion of the earth. He was born for this task and most importantly has accepted his calling. Trump is not bound to any religious indoctrination and therefore is totally receptive to what has to be done. Trump's decision to run was not for political reasons or power. Trump decided to stand up and step in to stop the destruction of America which in turn will save the earth, something Trump knew he must do at least 28 years ago."

"He was born for this task and accepted his calling. What comes next will shock most because it hasn't been written and it doesn't conform to any written prophetic timeline of events that mankind has been conditioned to believe. Our Father in heaven denies any and all prophetic events as described in any books. We have free will and from this time forward, the righteous must regain total control and dominion of the earth."

"After the pedophile industry is exposed, the demonic satanic child sacrifice rituals will be brought to light, and every organization tied to it will be rooted out and assets will be frozen. It's not just the evil corrupt swamp in America, this encompasses all governments of the earth. So who are the righteous sons and daughters of the Most High? These are those who stand for what's right, those who have a moral compass, those who live in principle and teach their children to do so."

"In the beginning we were given dominion of the Creation, but we surrendered it to Lucifer. Now it is time to take it back because we are the guardians of our Father's Creation, and we must regain our posts with extreme prejudice. We must rid all genetic manipulation throughout all of Creation and we must keep this cancerous evil under full containment. Once we accomplish this the earth will heal, our bodies will heal and the quarantine will be over. Amazing discoveries await us."

"The good news of the Gospel will be understood as we learn to love one another. Jesus' commandment to love one another is the gospel that sets us free from religions and brings us together in righteousness."

(Following quote is from President Trump at a Faith & Freedom Coalition breakfast in Washington D.C.)

"As long as we have pride in our beliefs, courage in our convictions and faith in our God, then we will not fail. And as long as our country remains true to its values, loyal to its citizens and devoted to its Creator, then our best days are yet to come because we will make America great again. Thank you and God bless you."

"God is the conductor of the Trump Train. The Luciferian Reign is over. All Aboard!"

Trump Inspiring Youth at Turning Point USA 7/23/19 "As long as you keep your faith in God above, there is no limit to what you can do and achieve. You are the ones lifting our nation now and in the very near future, and I have no doubt that there is greatness in this room. You will look back and remember this day and see the greatness in each other. You are the ones bringing about the incredible rebirth of the human spirit. Your generation will make the light shine brighter than ever before. God bless you all and God bless America!"

https://www.youtube.com/user/714baguilar

Going All In for Trump
Mike Lindell

***

Mike Lindell had a word from the Lord in 2015 that Trump would win the Presidency. God told Mike, "to go all in to support President Trump." When Mike went to Trump Tower, he acknowledges that it was indeed a 'divine appointment.' "Meeting Trump at Trump Tower and seeing how much his employees love him speaks volumes!" exclaimed Mike. "In fact, everybody loves our President, some just don't know it yet!"

Mike played a cameo role in the Pro-life movie, 'Unplanned', as well as participating as executive producer. Mike has created a website where addicts can connect to other addicts for support and guidance, paths to sobriety, and offering jobs upon recovery. No more stigma to the disease of alcoholism/addiction...only solution at lindellrecoverynetwork.org. He is also involved in Dinesh D'Souza's movie Trump Card. www.trumpcardthemovie.com

Mike Lindell was branded by President Trump as someone that 'makes great deals.' In fact, Trump actually said that Mike was so good that Trump wanted Mike to become his ad buyer because, as Trump said, "I guarantee you that Mike makes good deals." And Trump knows that Mike makes a great product, declaring, "He is the greatest, he does make a great product, I actually use them," (the pillows) as the crowd applauded in approval.

Mike attended a North Dakota rally where Trump spoke and has been an incredibly strong Trump supporter from the very beginning. Mike will tell anyone who will listen, "Trump has accomplished beyond what I ever expected and this is only the beginning." In a quote in the Duluth News Tribune, Mike says, "Rest easy, Minnesota; Trump is winning for us."

Mike's favorite saying is "With God, All Things Are Possible" and Mike keeps proving this saying to be true day after day. Mike did a speech in Minnesota where he said, "When I met the president (before Trump became president), that was a divine appointment. And God said, "Go all in, Trump was picked for a time like this." Mike has 'gone all in' and encourages others to do the same. When people come up to Mike, asking, "Mike, what can we do?" Mike says, "Pray for our President to have wisdom, discernment, and protection." Plus, he tells everyone to go out and vote on election day and tell friends and family to do the same. Mike says, "So much has gotten done already. Last time we voted for Trump, we voted based on faith that Trump would succeed. Now we have proof that Trump will succeed. Let's keep going and get people into Congress who will support him."

Mike, as an entrepreneur (My Pillow), has seen business booming due to Trump. And Mike takes pride in his ever-growing business, with 1700 people working for him. And, he still runs his business as he started with this motto: "It's not just the product, your handshake is your word, and we treat every customer like our only customer." President Trump acknowledged Mike and his My Pillow business during a rally in Fargo, saying that he has Mike's pillows, and that, "They are very good, I've slept so much better ever since."

As a recovered addict alcoholic, Mike entered the White House meeting on the Opioid Crisis with personal experience. Mike has a platform called the Lindell Recovery Network, Which Mike says, "will wipe out this opioid crisis". Mike lost everything, found God, invented My Pillow and the rest is history. Sobriety is a redemption process. The disease itself is physical, mental and spiritual. The President's much loved older brother, Fred Jr. (Freddy), died of the disease of alcoholism at the young age of 43 and Donald never forgot his brother's stern warning, "Don't drink ever." Having a completely sober President is an incredible gift. Like Trump, Mike's life is an inspirational story and he continues to follow God by giving hope to all comers.

Mike feels strongly that Trump was 'anointed by God' like tens of millions of us do around the world with that number growing exponentially. As Mike says again, "Everyone loves the president, some just don't know it yet. God gave us a second chance on November 8, 2016, and it has been amazing."

(Mike may be running for office in Minnesota (hope so) but regardless, he is all in on helping our President win in 2020.)

www.lindellfoundation.org

Trump Does the Unthinkable

Liz Crokin

August 2017

Liz Crokin is an award-winning author, a seasoned journalist and an advocate for sex crime victims. Liz is a heroine who has led the charge to save the children from the pedo satanists and their minions.

"Donald Trump is a racist, bigot, sexist, xenophobe, anti-Semitic and Islamophobe—did I miss anything? HE is also deplorable. The left and the media launch these hideous kinds of attacks at Trump everyday; yet, nothing could be further from the truth about the real estate mogul. As an entertainment journalist, I've had the opportunity to cover Trump for over a decade, and in all my years covering him I've never heard anything negative about the man until he announced he was running for president. Keep in mind, I got paid a lot of money to dig up dirt on celebrities like Trump for a living so a scandalous story on the famous billionaire could have potentially sold a lot of magazines and would have been a Huge feather in my cap."

"Instead, I found that he doesn't drink alcohol or do drugs and that he's a hardworking business man. On top of that, he's one of the most generous celebrities in the world with a heart filled with more gold than his 100 million dollar New York penthouse. Since the media has failed so miserably at reporting the truth about Trump, I decided to put together some of the acts of kindness he's committed over three decades which have gone virtually unnoticed or fallen on deaf ears."

"In 1986, Trump prevented the foreclosure of Annabel Hill's family farm after her husband committed suicide. Trump personally phoned down to the auction to stop the sale of her home and offered the widow money. Trump decided to take action after he saw Hill's please for help in news reports."

"In 1988, a commercial airline refused to fly Andrew Ten, a sick Orthodox Jewish child with a rare illness, across the country to get medical care because he had to travel with an elaborate life-support system. His grief stricken parents contacted Trump for help and he didn't hesitate to send his own plane to take the child from Los Angeles to New York so he could get his treatment."

"In 1991, 200 Marines who served in Operation Desert Storm spent time at Camp Lejeune in North Carolina before they were scheduled to return home to their families. However, the Marines were told that a mistake had been made and an aircraft would not be able to take them home on their scheduled departure date. When Trump got wind of this, he sent his plane to make two trips from North Carolina to Miami to safely return the Gulf War Marines to their loved ones."

"In 1995, a motorist stopped to help Trump after the limo he was traveling in got a flat tire. Trump asked the Good Samaritan how he could repay him for his help. All the man asked for was a bouquet of flowers for his wife. A few weeks later Trump sent the flowers with a note that read: We've paid off your mortgage."

"In 1996, Trump filed a lawsuit against the city of Palm Beach, Florida, accusing the town of discriminating against his Mar-a-Lago resort club because it allowed Jews and Blacks. Abraham Foxman, who was the Anti- Defamation League Director at the time, said Trump put the light on Palm Beach, not on the beauty and the glitter, but on it's seamier side of discrimination. Foxman also noted that Trump's charge had a trickle-down effect because other clubs followed his lead and began admitting Jews and Blacks."

"In 2000, Maury Povich featured a little girl named Megan who struggled with Brittle Bone Disease on his show and Trump happened to be watching. Trump said the little girl's story and positive attitude touched his heart. So he contacted Maury and gifted the little girl and her family with a very generous check."

"In 2008, after Jennifer Hudson's family members were tragically murdered in Chicago, Trump put the Oscar-winning actress and her family up at his Windy City hotel for free. In addition to that, Trump's security took extra measures to ensure Hudson and her family members were safe during such a difficult time."

"In 2013 New York bus driver Darnell Barton spotted a woman close to the edge of a bridge staring at the traffic below as he drove by. He stopped the bus, got out and put his arm around the woman and saved her life by convincing her not to jump. When Trump heard about this story, he sent the hero bus driver a check simply because he believed his good deed deserved to be rewarded."

"In 2014, Trump gave away $25,000 to Sergeant Andrew Tamoressi after he spent seven months in a Mexican jail for accidentally crossing the US-Mexico border. President Barak Obama couldn't even be bothered to make one phone call to assist with the United States Marine's release; however, Trump opened his pocketbook to help this serviceman get back on his feet."

"In 2016, Melissa Consin Young attended a Trump rally and tearfully thanked Trump for changing her life. She said she proudly stood on stage with Trump as Miss Wisconsin USA in 2005. However, years later she found herself struggling with an incurable illness and during her darkest days she explained that she received a handwritten letter from Trump telling her 'that she's the bravest woman, I know.' She said the opportunities that she got from Trump and his organization ultimately provided her Mexican-American son with a full-ride to college."

"Lynne Patton, a black female executive for the Trump Organization, released a statement in 2016 defending her boss against accusations that he's a racist and a bigot. She tearfully revealed how she's struggled with substance abuse and addiction for years. Instead of kicking her to the curb, she said the Trump Organization and his entire family stood by her through immensely difficult times."

"Donald Trump's kindness knows no bounds and his generosity has and continues to touch the lives of people from every sex, race and religion. When Trump sees someone in need, he wants to help. Two decades ago, Oprah asked Trump in a TV interview if he would run for president. He said: 'If it got so bad, I would never want to rule it out totally, because I really am tired of seeing what's happening with this country. That day may come.'"

On the other hand, have you ever heard of Hillary or Obama ever doing such things with their own resources? Now that is really unthinkable! This is the Trump that won the election and will save America. He is our President."

https://www.youtube.com/channel/
UCL5QWloOWiD_H6nc_05PHBA

✧
Books & Saints
BethAnon

I n the 1890's, Ingersoll Lockwood, wrote books that have an interesting connection to the Trump Family. Lockwood was an American political writer, lawyer and novelist. He wrote Baron Trump's Marvelous Underground Journey & 1900 or The Last President.

Before Baron sets out on his adventure, the boy's father reminds him of the Trump family motto-"The Pathway to Glory is strewn with pitfalls and danger." In 1900 or The Last President, it begins with a newly elected President who is an outsider candidate said to represent 'the common man', amid claims he will liberate the people from the bankers, an anti-establishment candidate like our President Donald Trump.

The rallying cry of the people is this: "Our day has come at last. Down with the oppressors! Death to the rich man! Death to the gold bugs! Death to the capitalists! Give us back the money you have ground out of us! Give us back the marrow of our bones which you have used to grease the wheels of your chariots!" This chant is a foreshadowing of us, the Remnant, we the people, taking down the Luciferian NWO Agenda with Trump leading the charge. Trump is priming to finish off the Federal Reserve as well as the IRS and all the other evil corruptions that have been bleeding out the common man and woman. We will retrieve true capitalism that can work in our authentic Republic if we are not being enslaved by the Babylonian oligarchy."

"In America we don't worship government. We worship God." Donald John Trump

Donald Trump's Presidency was foreshadowed and 'prophesied' even by 'The Simpsons' television show, season 11, episode 17 called 'Bart to the Future'.

When Bart flashes forward into adulthood, viewers learn that Lisa not only becomes president, but inherits 'quite a budget crunch' from her predecessor, Donald Trump. "The country is broke?" she asks her aides in one scene. "How can that be?" (Opposite to how the truth is manifesting, as usual. We are more prosperous than ever and it is only going to get better as we are released from the parasitic hold of the Luciferian agenda. At least they got the President right.) At the time, the real Donald Trump Presidency was still 16 years away.

Snapshot by Cindy Munson of Tulsa, Oklahoma "Many years ago, a friend of mine entered Marble Collegiate Church in New York City. Sitting alone, in the balcony, he saw Donald Trump, head bowed in prayer. Those who judge this man are in peril. God always used sinners. We are all sinners. Hypocrites will always pass judgment. Make no mistake: God placed Trump in this position. Pray for our President."

Saints Melania and Our First Lady, Melania

BethAnon

S aint Melania, the Elder (325-410) was one of the wealthiest citizens of the empire, born in Spain and a Christian. She joined Christian asceticf monks near Alexandria after the death of her husband and two sons. She was described as "a very learned lady who loved the world and life itself." Melania, the Younger, was the paternal granddaughter, and a Roman Christian Saint who created a convent near the Mount of Olives giving all of her extensive wealth to the poor in the 5th century.

Our beautiful First Lady, Melania, whose name comes from the French form of the Latin name Melanie, meaning "black, dark" also meaning "rebellion", is the synchronistic image of these ancestral saints. What this kind hearted woman has to deal with is beyond comprehension, and yet she walks through all of it in grace and beauty, integrity and innocence, purity and magnificence. Her work as First Lady in her 'Be Best' program as well as the incredible strides she is making in the fight against opiate addiction are fantastic, but her most important job is to be the Woman behind the Man, the strength and gentle power that holds our beloved President in safe and devoted arms. There has never been a better example of that famous phrase, that "Behind every great man is a great woman.' Her love of God and her deeply spiritual connection allows her to shine and rise above all that the world tries to throw at her. I loved when she opened a speech with The Lord's Prayer and I hope she gets to do it again. This only empowers anything our wonderful President has to say."

Melania Trump was interviewed by ABC in 1999 Prophetically, Melania was discussing the possibility of being First Lady. When asked if she could picture herself as first Lady, Melania answered "Yes." Adding that she would "support" and "stand by" Donald Trump and emulate first ladies of America's past. "I would be very traditional, like Jackie Kennedy and Betty Ford."

Oh her attackers she said, "They don't know me." And she describes Donald Trump as "very kind" and "very charming." Even then she knew about the media, "The media can be very tricky sometimes. You need to be very careful." "I like to have my private life too. But I'm always open. I'm not shy of the media. But sometimes it can be very tricky, unpleasant and unfair."

When Donald Trump says things like, "Where's my super-model?" Melania responds, "It's his sense of humor. He's very kind and very funny." Melania also talked about, "What a great President Donald Trump would be, stating that she believed he would run for President one day." (Melania has a prophetic gift herself like her husband.) "He's very smart. He knows how to do business. He would be a great leader."

Melania said she thought of the United States as a "dream land" when she was growing up in Slovenia. "Your dreams could come true." she said. "You could do a lot of things, whenever you decide to do them."

Melania Trump Interviewed Again by ABC

2018

I n "Being Melania" the narrator mentions that people really don't know her like they know most first ladies. Melania Trump is the most private First Lady we have seen n the modern era. She is one of the most recognizable faces in the world, a stylish First Lady and a devoted mother. 'She is a person of few words.' She 'has that quality of mystery-almost regal.'

The interviewer asks Melania, "Finish this sentence for me. Melania Trump is......." Melania pauses and answers...."a mother, a wife, a daughter, a sister, a friend, first lady of the United States, caring, compassionate, strong, independent, very detail oriented and staying true to herself."

In the interview, Barbara Walters asks, "What was your first impression of Donald Trump?" Melania answered, "He had a sparkle." They married in 2005.

Melania said, "We have a great chemisty. To be with a man like my husband you need to know who you are, you need to have a very independent life as well, and be there to support him, to be very smart and quick to be there for him when he needs you." Walters asked, "Is yours a marriage of equals?" Melania said, "Yes." Then Trump leaned in to interrupt and said, "No, I think she is far greater than 50%."

When asked, "How has your life changed from before being in the White House until now? Melania answered. "I am the same person. I am staying true to myself. I want to live a meaningful life. That is the most important to me. I know what my priorities are and I am focused on that."

Melania's 'Be Best' is an awareness campaign dedicated to the most valuable and fragile among us, our children. 'Be Best' chooses to focus on the importance of teaching our next generation how to conduct themselves safely in a positive manner in an online setting.

"I wish people would focus on what I do and not what I wear." Melania (I did enjoy the 'I really don't care. Do U?' jacket which was a pointed message to the lying left wing fake MSM operation mockingbird media.)

"Nothing will stop me. I will do what is right." Melania Trump, our righteous and whole hearted FLOTUS and the spiritual ballast to our beloved President Donald J Trump.

"Melania walked down the aisle carrying only an ancient rosary, a family heirloom, to a vocalist singing Ave Maria in an exquisite soprano voice. In retrospect, so many clues to the future in validation of the past ie. 'future proves past. Q.'

Found Tribes of Israel
BethAnon

My kindred, Melissa, at Freedom Force Battalion, on YouTube, has begun a fantastic search about the Lost Tribes of Israel, or rather, now, the Found Tribes of Israel. I will do a little nutshell here but please follow up with her YouTube channel and on Freedom Force LIVE. What does this have to do with Donald Trump? Only that he could be the heir to the Scottish throne which has been hijacked by the fake British monarchy. That would blow some minds.

There is a large rock called the 'Coronation Stone' which England says is their number one possession even though they have owned 1/6th of the wealth of the world. This stone is the same stone that Jacob was blessed with at Bethel (meaning the House of the Lord). This is the stone that was the pillow for Jacob when he had his vision from God. He poured what oil he had on it and God interacted with the world through this stone from then on. When his clan passed through Bethel, they took the stone with them. This was the same stone that saved the Israelites in the desert. As the Israelites defeated the Amalikites, Moses sat on the stone as they held his arms up in prayer with the rod of Aaron to win the battle. They made an 'I AM' banner because the Lord saved them. (The Hebrew letters were 'aleph x' and 'tah t' combined to express Eternal God and turns out to be the original Symbol for the flag of Ireland.)

Next we see Solomon seated on the coronation stone. "Then Solomon sat upon the throne of Yahweh as king in place of his father, David. He prospered and all of Israel obeyed him." The coronation stone was passed down through the generations with the righteous kings. Joash and Josiah were coronated on this same pillar stone, seated upon it.

When the rightful heir would sit on the throne, the coronation stone actually spoke their name. Remember folks, so the natural lies within the supernatural. All things are possible with God.

When Zedekiah was king, his sons were murdered by Nebuchadnezzar and then he was taken captive. The prophet Jeremiah had hidden away Zedekiah's two daughters and they became the rightful heirs of the Pharez line of Judah. Tea Tephi and Scota were their names and this is the beginning of the question of the Lost Tribes of Israel. Where did they go? Who are they? The rest of the Israelites who were taken captive to Assyria were set free by King Cyrus. Their names had been changed so it was difficult to track them, hence, "the LOST tribes of Israel." But now they are identified by their heraldry, language, artwork and names by E. Raymond Capt. They migrated through the Causus Mountains and became called Causasians. The Caucus Mountains became known as the 'Pass of Israel. They settled throughout Europe and some tribes became Celts and ruled in Ireland, Scotland and England.

When you take a look at Ireland's coat of arms you see David's harp and Zarah's hand. Jeremiah took them to Ireland where the Zarah line of Judah was already ruling. The two sticks rejoined as Tea Tephi married the Zorah King Heremon and they were coronated on the stone at Tara, Ireland.

The Ulster flag contains the Star of David, and the Royal Crown symbolizing the two lines of Judah. (Danite, the third tribe of Israel is now known as Tuatha de Dahaan). Tea Tephi was proclaimed Queen by the Gadite Israelites and as she was coronated the Coronation Stone of Jacob sang her name. Tea Tephi established rule based on the righteous Torah law. These are some of the 'lost tribes' of the house of Issac in the British Isles. (Issac-sons, "saxons") Other tribes migrated throughout Europe, others to Russia, and India—scattered all over the world just as the Lord planned. So the whole earth would be filled with the knowledge of the Lord.

The Lost Tribes were never really lost. They only lost their identity as they moved west to become Anglo Saxon Viking Jews Celts Pics. The royal house of Stuart are descendants and as God has promised there would always be a descendant of David on the throne. The legitimate rulers always initiated righteous Torah law and all Scottish Kings were crowned on "the stone of destiny" or "Stone of Scone" or "Jacob's pillow" until King Edward stole it and built it into a Coronation Chair placed in Westminster Abbey. This was the beginning of an illegitimate monarchy and what William Wallace in Mel Gibson's 'Braveheart' was fighting for, as well as Robert the Bruce. (see The Outlaw King) They couldn't surrender and put up with tyranny just like we can't. This is why we came to America to follow the Lord. We are fighting the same tyrants today.

In 1950 the Coronation Stone was stolen from Westminster Abbey by Scottish patriots and they replaced it with a fake one which Queen Elizabeth the Second was falsely coronated on and she knew it. She told them to place a curtain around the fake stone to prevent scrutiny. Elizabeth is not God appointed ruler and she has not kept her oath to keep and do only God's law. She has definitely multiplied her personal wealth to the extent that she is now the richest woman on the earth and owns one sixth of it! Until President Trump! True monarchs and true leaders who rule as God's ambassadors from Saul forward are commanded that they 'shall not multiply silver and gold.'

The Stone of Destiny, was taken to Edinburgh Castle but was supposedly returned to Westminster Abbey, but it is a poor replica. Ezekiel 21:29 recorded a Word from God on Jacob's Stone, "I will overturn, overturn, overturn and it shall be no more until he comes whose right it is and I will give it to him." The first turning was the transition of rule from Jerusalem to England, second was the transition of rule from England to America, and it appears that now is the transition to the rightful heir, Christ Himself. Is that what we are seeing?

Here is an interesting discovery in President Trump's lineage. The two lines of Judah emerge through the John Stuart line, and and connected with the line of King Christian of Denmark. Trump has ancestry in both lineages.

The Stuart and Lennox royal lines tie directly to the two royal lines of Judah!) Trump is the rightful heir to the throne of Scotland, England and Ireland! This is all from the Lord, all the way back to King David and to Jacob. What a wonderful blessing! This is the Lord's doing! FYI, they almost used this stone in the temple but the builder's rejected it, yet it has blessed us all since Jacob received it. This Stone represents Christ as he crushes all the false kingdoms, when God's Kingdom manifests on earth. (Much of this information comes from 25,000 Assyrian tablets passed down from an ancient library and translated into English. "Missing Links" is covered in *Assyrian Tablets* by E. Raymond Copt. Again, check out Melissa and Freedom Force Battalion on

YouTube for all the details and so much incredible information she has uncovered.)

As the Lost Tribes transplanted into England, we see the Merovingians, who are in the line of Judah. These are the long-haired kings, like Samson. President Trump is in the Merovingian line of long-haired righteous kings of course! The media makes the Merovingians the villain in the The Matrix and everywhere online. The enemy inverts everything.

Remember, the enemy cannot create, only invert and pervert. We were never taught about the Merovingians in school.* They seed our minds with negativity about positive things. The way they make Christians look crazy in films and use the Lord's name in vain all of the time.

One of the best things about Trump and Q and all of our digital warriors, is the pursuit of truth through research, understanding and discernment, which is what real learning is all about.

We are to have no fellowship with the unfruitful works of dark-ness, but instead expose them and root them out. This is the exciting times we are in. Alleluia! This genealogy that Melissa unearthed shows that the real founders of Western Civilization are the Twelve Tribes of Israel and not Roman's. History books will be rewritten to reveal the truth according to God's words and Q. The twelve tribes continued on to America as well as many other places throughout the world. But the ruling tribes transplanted to American and are distributed to set the whole world free from the evil line of Cain.

This is the time of revelation and deliverance. We will no longer be suffering under the Luciferian Agenda, but will instead be ruling in righteousness in the millennial Kingdom of Christ. Praise God!

*FYI There is a list of names of Satanic bloodlines but one can only access who-is-who one human being at a time.

It's ultimately not about names, but about souls.

Word of the Lord
Amanda Grace

Amanda Grace of Arc of Grace Ministries endured a 16-year battle with an uncommon autoimmune neuropathy called small fiber neuropathy that ended her up in a wheelchair in 2014, unable to move from the waist down. With mountain moving faith and God's intervention she miraculously got up out that wheelchair and started an incredible Journey with the Lord to health and Redemption from what she lost. Prophetically Charged Mountain Moving faith is what Amanda Grace preaches as she teaches the Word of God to Others and brings encouragement to those enduring a difficult time. She also has an animal sanctuary, Noah's Ark, that she frequently incorporates into her you tube channel and Biblical teachings. Amanda desires to see those persevere with the help of the Lord and truly turn their trials into testimonies.

January 30, 2020

Word Of The Lord

The Spirit of The Lord is upon those who have been anointed, appointed, and ordained to speak My Word, preach My Word, and deliver prophetic utterance that will truly light a fire in this hour says the Lord of Hosts this day. For I the Lord thy God do nothing until I reveal My secrets To My servants the Prophets according to Amos says The Word. I am the Word says the Lord, in the beginning was the Word and The Word was with God and The Word was God says the Lord. For I the Lord God Jehovah, El Shaddai in this hour shall encompass with Strong anointing, wisdom, council, might, and power from the most High God, including reverential fear of the Lord, that shall encompass and be activated with a concentrated precision and power By those who truly have been ordained and have had a Mantle placed upon them by Me Almighty God to deliver in This Hour the Roar of the Lion, the Fire that encompasses My throne, as well as the lamb, the Love, the Grace the Mercy. For truly My Children it is needed, both working together, operating in sync, I am God, I am the Lion, I am the lamb and neither overpowers the Other says the Lord, however there are seasons where more of the Lion, of the Fire, of the power is necessary to destroy the Works of the Kingdom of darkness, to light a fire within the souls of My people, to penetrate and deal with the heart of an issue.

Then My Children there may be seasons where more of the lamb emerges, where truly My love, the precious sacrifice of My one and only son, gentleness, meekness, emerges in order to build those up who have been torn down and tattered, rebuild their lives, for My love and the blood of the lamb to cover their wounds , to begin to heal those deep soul wounds that have been used by the enemy to truly anchor them where they become stationary and an easy target for the enemy. Remember My Children a moving target is much more difficult to hit says the Lord God Elohim. However, You will always see both emerge, the lion and the Lamb, fire and Grace, as My Word goes forth to those who I have anointed with the Holy Oil from My throne in this Hour to become ESTABLISHED says the Lord, keyword. I the Lord have trained, and I have begun to build up and have been building up those who are anointed in this time to speak My Word, to be sent into various areas in this world including business, ministry, churches. I have taken them through what the armies of this earth would call boot camp, basic training, and then advanced training. Now in this hour I am ESTABLISHING those who truly have been about the Father's business, speaking My Word, setting their own feelings aside to deliver what I the Lord say to deliver to the people. It shall be made very clear says the Lord I am establishing, I am equipping, I am solidifying foundations so the enemy and the Kingdom of darkness cannot so easily move them says the Lord. For as Job endured a long grueling battle of trial after trial, test after test and he was found faithful, I the Lord rewarded that faithfulness with a wealth of blessing, only after he walked through that season of trial and testing with nothing, with no benefit, with no security except his faith that Almighty God is faithful and will watch over His word to perform it. He was more blessed in the latter than in the former.

My children do not let your identity in Me your worth in Me suffer because of scoffers and those who point the finger and unrighteous and unjustly judge. For they judge from their own preconceived ideas that are NOT founded upon Me or My Word. All they see is what I the Lord am blessing you with now HOWEVER, they DID NOT SEE the long grueling, trying, season of stripping, and removing, and trial you walked through without any of what I have now in My mercy and doting love for My children who I call faithful, am allowing to flow into your lives now. They only see the latter and completely disregard that you have walked through valleys that many would have run from. Would have of abandoned the call, would have found an exit for an easier road. That is why many are called but FEW are chosen My children, because the few walked through the valley of the shadow that the many did not want to endure says the Lord thy God Jehovah!

You are watching and witnessing in this hour a shaking, a shifting, a friction says the Lord as the armies of the Living God and the soldiers in the Kingdom of God on this earth drive back the forces of darkness attempting to advance upon the earth before their time says the Lord! I the Lord have ruled against them and I have ruled against those who serve them! This shall become very evident in the natural says the Lord that those who serve mammon, who serve principalities, territorial spirits, will lose the power and position that these wicked spirits lulled them, and manipulated them promising these children of darkness if they did their bidding against the anointed Children of the Most High God. However, says the Lord it was a trap! They walked, willfully out of selfish ambition and lust for more and more power into a trap.

They shall be caught in a trap that snaps down upon them now says the Lord and they will not so easily be able to pull themselves from the snare as now they will have to face the reaping upon their lives and households of the corrupt decisions they made in rebellion against the throne of the Living God says the Lord God Jehovah. I The Lord am releasing Wisdom from My throne in greater measure upon My Children, receive it in Jesus name.

NOTE: Watch the amazon, that area says the Lord.

A terrorist attack against the U.S. will be thwarted and exposed right before it occurs for I the Lord shall expose to those who serve me within the Govt the plans, locations, and details to orchestrate a take down. Allah Akbar shall NOT get the Glory says the Lord, I the Lord shall.

One may be attempted against the New York city subway system, the hub says the Lord

Oklahoma City, and San Bernardino, watch says the Lord.

The friction is building under the ground, beneath the earth in California in those areas of concentrated sin and rebellion, the ground shall bear witness to the outcry of the earth from the sin and rebellion in those areas and it will shake in more ways than 1 says the Lord, I will protect My Children in those areas as I protected Lot says the Lord. The Major fault lines, underground pressure building, a shift, the event shall run along a major Fault line and impact multiple states says the Lord. Pray now My children for your spiritual family in these areas for there shall be signs of miracles, miraculous protection that come forth from these areas.

I am pulling things from the deep says the Lord.

Special doors are being unlocked for such a time as this. You will hear "uncharted territory"

Canada says the Lord. There is a tug of war happening, and a new leader shall arise from it, by the book, Fresh ideas. A leak in Canada.

There is a Cruise Ship Company, a MAJOR event will occur, hearing OUTBREAK, it will be newsworthy says the Lord of Hosts.

NOTE: Hearing onyx and Beryl

There will be a medical Breakthrough for Burn Victims, New Skin. I the Lord have a heart for Burn Victims because their flesh has been impacted and harmed By fire says the Lord.

There will be an uncommon meeting between two leaders of nations that has not taken place in a very long time.

NOTE: Eagle eyes, eagle eyes. You will see a change:

Watch Russia with Ukraine says the Lord, testing the waters, psalm 35 take hold of shield and buckler and stand up for their help, also drawn out the spear and javelin and close up the way who pursue and persecute them, the Lord is their deliverance.

NOTE: The word SMITE with the enemy.

Huge discoveries shall come forth from the water! The oceans shall give them up at My Word says the Lord-The Dead Sea -watch the Dead Sea!

As I the Lord parted the red Sea there shall be a parting in the area of the middle east

Pray for those who are underground in their faith in Iran, parts of Russia, China and various surrounding areas. I the Lord am bringing areas of China to their knees. For their crimes against humanity and crimes against My Creation the outcry became too great against them and the door was opened wide for the enemy to attack all of china says the Lord, however I am operating through these events to begin to force those resisting the gospel to yield. To close the door of idolatry and return unto Me and I will return unto them says the Lord. There are MANY worshipers in Iran, in turkey even says the Lord, their prayers in secret are affecting the balance of powers in that country. The people shall continue to Erupt, they would rather no longer live on earth than live under such a dark territorial oppression from those advancing the radical ideas of that principality set by lucifer to keep that whole area steeped in a religion, in radical ideals where the principality is served not Almighty God, for they do not KNOW ME and My Sheep KNOW MY voice and a STRANGERS they will not follow. Pray for the believers, the pastors in Iran for this shift shall cause paranoia on the part of the govt however I the Lord thy God am hiding the remnant as I hid the prophets in caves when jezebel ad Ahab sought to destroy them all and in their wicked rebellion signed their own death warrants with the blood of those they illegally shed for the kingdom of darkness. I the Lord shall raise up Obadiah's within the govt and area to hide the remnant to protect the pastors says the Lord thy God. The IA tolah says the Lord time is about to run out, taken out because of recompense the blood they shed must now be accounted for says the Lord there must be a reckoning! They have been weighed and found wanting. And when I the Lord God give the order there is not a principality that can secure the continued rule of their hosts says the Lord of Hosts this day.

Seek me while I may be found. 2020 will be a monumental year of one event after another that will set this year apart. However, do not fear My children I am delivering you and protecting you. You shall emerge victorious, triumphant and deeply rooted as you are now established this year for what I truly have created you and called you to be. Man has no right to say whether you should have your position or not. I Almighty God giveth and I Almighty God can taketh away it is not for them to decide it is more me to decide says the Lord. This is a year of great change, transitioning into new chapters, in some cases the door being closed on the former to make room for the latter. The latter bears depth and weight and needs much room for the growth that will come forth from Me the Lord God Jehovah speaking into that growth in My Children's Lives. They have been called faithful, the anointing they carry bears weight and is sharp and precise. Watch as I the Lord carry this out and there will be those who MUST recognize only God could have done this and will bow in submission under the weight of The Holy Spirit. Go Forth My Children, Be strong in the Lord and in the power of His might, put on the whole armor of God so as you grow you will stand against the scheming of the devil and cause a retreat to make the way straight now for those announcing, "prepare ye the way of the Lord!' thus sayeth the Lord of Hosts in Jesus name.

February 10, 2020

Word Of The Lord

I am God! I am the Alpha I am the Omega; I am the beginning and I am the Ending. I rule and I reign forevermore, says the Lord! I am Almighty, I change not says the Lord Thy God. I watch over my Word to perform it, for I am not a man My children that I should lie says the Lord of Hosts this day!

For you shall see My plans, you shall see evidence of My promises spring forth now My children, it shall spring forth, behold I do a new thing says the Lord in the lives of My people, do you not see it?!! This is the time of the builder and the bulldozer says the Lord thy God this day.

The bulldozer will dig up and forcefully pull up the ground, will by force move the obstacle in the way, by force it shall move says the Lord. And the builder says the Lord the builder is a visionary, the builder can come in and look at barrenness, can look at demolition and envision what to build upon that area that has now been torn up and brought down, the builder knows the proper FOUNDATION MY children, the builder can envision the restorative process and the builder goes step by step building upon what was once destruction, what was once confusion, what was once brokenness, and built up at My word a new structure, a better structure, a solid structurally sound building that will not so easily be torn down again says the Lord. The builder is not afraid to approach a mess and raise it up to be a message that exudes the glory of God that brings forth and testifies to the power of Almighty God that nothing is impossible to those who believe My children.

There are those who looked to take the bulldozer and tear down the very foundations and principals of the United States, while claiming with a megaphone that was programmed with deceptive tones, they were attempting to save and stand for the very ideals the very foundation they were with all their might attempting to tear down.

I the Lord says this day that the bulldozers they were attempting to use in an attempt to tear up the foundations has right before them, as they were blinded by the spirit of mammon, that bulldozer has indeed dug a hole for them says the Lord of hosts this day. A pit right before them it has turned and dug for you cannot curse what I the Lord thy God have blessed. They are not for the Lord but against Him and every Holy Godly principal that I the Lord laid a foundation of stability for those who wanted to surrender to My plans, My way and turn their hearts over to My son Jesus Christ, and accept Him as Lord and Savior. I the Lord have given that chance I the Lord have given us the grace; I the Lord have given time.

However, now I the Lord say the scales of justice have ruled against them and it is time to ACT it is Time to Release the penalty in measure in accordance with their rebellion. For the principality of Confusion was released over the airwaves to infect like a virus like a contagion those listening with confusion and madness, so they ramble and bumble their words making no concise thought or sense leaving them in an altered world from reality. This is exactly where the devil wants them to stay and wants the younger generation to stay says the Lord thy God.

That serpent, that snake puts his trophies on display with their symbols, and their songs, and their satanic rants and dances that are meant to entice and to lure as the sirens so lured the sailors says the Lord thy God so this was meant to lure those into constriction of the mind, into blindness and lust where they cannot see the clear picture and the truth that has been clouded by fancy hosts and glittery distractions along with African sun worship and Congo dances that are pawned off and manipulated and packaged as entertainment says the Lord thy God Elohim.

There have been tampering says the Lord "accidents" are not what they appear says the Lord thy God and the tampering will be exposed says the Lord for there are those embedded deep sold out to a pagan counterfeit of people who attempt to over-shadow the Work I the Lord have set forth to do. However says the Lord thy God as King Cyrus was operated through Mightily By Me to issue a decree that protected My people and put the builders to work rebuilding My house of worship, rebuilding what is Holy, rebuilding what had been bulldozed by pagan nations before them so I the Lord Thy god am giving the builders and the visionaries the materials, the vision, the Words or prophecy as I sent the prophets Haggai and Zechariah to encourage and speak into Zerubbabel, Ezra, and those who were with him building so I the Lord thy God am doing the same and I have raised those up and am raising those up in the younger generation who will speak to a nation and bring those who once opposed Me and My will, will turn them for My glory to build for the Lord of Hosts to Speak forth and encourage those fighting to build the Holiness back up in the United States of America and around the world for My Glory says the Lord thy God this day. AS I OPERATED THROUGH King Cyrus so I the Lord God Jehovah shall operate through leadership to issue decrees, and edicts and orders to build up and begin to push out those who want to ensnare, entrap, entice says the Lord. There are those on the airwaves whom I the Lord am silencing, there will be those this year BEFORE the elections that will suddenly be taken out and lose their positions. They have laughed at Almighty God and His plans for the LAST time, their smugness has testified against them, they have chosen to serve their Father the devil and so they shall be handed over so perhaps their souls may be saved says the lord thy God this day.

I am building up Holy Strongholds in Europe, in Australia, in Indonesia and the Philippines says the Lord. In Spain in England there are Holy Strongholds strong towers that the righteous will run too will flock to and will be safe and will call on the name of the Lord God Jehovah and I will answer then and show them and demonstrate great and mighty things in their countries that will baffle those nations. Signs and wonders that will bring many to their knees and surrender says the Lord.

There will be a quarantine of those who are out there infecting the masses with dark rhetoric they shall be quarantined and stripped of their voice says the Lord of Hosts this day. However says the Lord there are those who have been faithful, they have been found faithful and I am increasing their voice and influence in this hour in order to reach those under the spells of the enemy and those who have cynical aspirations of leadership that will truly destroy nations if they are allowed to lead. However, I the Lord thy God appoint Kings and Leaders and I say this day the election in the United States shall be even more baffling than the last. There shall be a plot to usurps votes and steal votes, but it will be outed right before the beginning of November and the perpetrators prosecuted says the Lord God for their crimes. However says the Lord I am doing a mighty work and there will be events that will lead up to the elections that will even leave the most radical commentators scratching their heads not able to put the pieces together of what is happening because this will be spirit driven, this election and the natural will yield to what I the Lord decree and release on scrolls in the Spirit says the lord. Candidates will out themselves and each other and those whom have dipped into the honeypot of election funds to fund the most lavish and environmentally unfriendly of luxury items shall be exposed and caught RED HANDED says the Lord. I am crushing the fist of socialism and communism in more than one country says the Lord for I the Lord do not seek rule that oppresses but that frees those to glorify and serve their Father in Heaven says the Lord.

NOTE: A tidal wave says the Lord thy God this day you will see a tidal wave Heading up to November, it shall be triggered by a violent shaking Says the Lord thy God this day.

NOTE: Watch the Philippines says the Lord, a major event!!

Phenomenon's will break out across the earth that will be compared to biblical events they will be very similar in nature get ready get ready says the Lord for what pharaoh witnessed at the hand of Almighty God the countries that have hardened their hearts and are serving a false versions of Me will see these biblical phenomenon's break out and it will be historical says the Lord thy God this day.

NOTE: Watch the Panama Canal.

NOTE: Protests breaking out across south America the people are desperate says the Lord and I the Lord will answer their cries says the Lord.

NOTE: Hearing mail fraud watch says the Lord.

NOTE: Oil will be discovered in an area thought to have none!! A RICH reserve a WEALTH says the Lord for the earth has resources that have been hidden for such a time as this and I the

216

Lord thy God am causing a shaking and the earth to give them up says the Lord this day.

NOTE: The earth shall leak oil in areas an anointing of the ground says the Lord for the earth cries out and I the Lord am answering that cry says the Lord God Jehovah.

NOTE: A massive mudslide and a giant hole opening up in the earth will be part of the phenomenon that occurs this year as the shaking, shifting, and releasing across the earth takes place says the Lord this day.

NOTE: I am overturning verdicts says the Lord and I am setting captives free says the Lord thy God this day.

Hollywood will be embroiled up to their necks in a massive abuse scandal where celebrities were involved, the minutes and notes of secret meetings that have taken place amongst Hollywood's elite will expose how they are, the tactics they are using in the spirit, with sound, with costume with

undertones in movies to indoctrinate and infect similar to mind control, it shall be exposed the documents leaked by a few I have convicted says the Lord to release them. Hollywood will not quickly dig out of this one says the Lord God this day. However, there are those who will be freed through this and testify to their many levels of indoctrination and the fracturing of souls a huge scandal says the Lord however it is time for this to be exposed.

Pray for the life of Jennifer Lopez's daughter for she has indoctrinated her in on a grand stage and the child is the enemies for the taking as tribute says the Lord thy God pray for her life to be spared and her soul to be saved for a grave event has been planned and it will shatter Jennifer Lopez's world and her god will be the very one who has done it and she will have a choice for I set this day before them life and death and blessing and cursing, choose life that you and your seed may live says the Lord of Hosts this day.

Humble yourselves before me in this hour and listen for I am giving instruction says the Lord. You have walked forth from the fire unharmed says the Lord thy God this day the enemy could not sift you says the Lord and those who submit and surrender in humility and obedience I the lord am set to give unto them a double portion of wisdom and might for this hour for the Lords people will speak out in this hour and baffle the scholars, baffle the experts because I the Lord do not conform to such I do not bow to any man or institution and My fire will come forth from My chosen My faithful in this hour like never before it will be hot it will be convicting and My power will come forth that the people of the earth will feel they will feel the intensity and fire and ROAR of My power for I the Lord thy God shall Rule Over All Rebellion this year and will subdue it and impale that spirit that it shall not freely roam to execute the orders it has been given for the HEAT will be in the words of My anointed and this salt the salt and fire shall be penetrating and purging in this hour and the Holy Fire and the deep seasoning of the Words My anointed My children speak forth will purge and expose for I the Lord God am adding salt and fire to force a purge in this hour of those who have been spewing sulfur who have been speaking for serpents and for those who Want to assassinate the plans in the lives of My children, that assassinating spirit shall be turned on its own says the Lord thy God this day watch and see!!! There will be major key strategic Victories this year that shall pave the way for My power to break loose and break forth and Spring up in the Spring, accelerated growth shall be the portion of My faithful ones and there shall be signs and wonders that cannot be covered up for in this hour there shall be a push back and as pharaoh's army was pushed back By my fire and then swallowed by the sea there shall be a push back and there are those who will be swallowed up for their rebellion. Praise Me My Children, Seek me, Put on your whole Armor and decree and speak in faith and TRULY BELIEVE release the power in unison and watch it multiply and take down strongholds and underground dwellings and the earth will begin to truly now see the power in prayer and the power in Serving a Mighty God. What a Mighty God you serve My Children! Remember that and speak it forth in Faith and watch the Mighty Now in this Hour Manifest.

God bless you in the name of Yeshua My precious Children!! In Jesus name.

Visit Amandagrace4him.blogspot.com for full transcripts authentic and timely prophetic word.

https://www.youtube.com/watch?v=VYRGePNX1DE

The Birth of the Millennial Reign of Christ on Earth
Melissa Redpill the World

What we are all experiencing worldwide is not just another political event. As QAnon post 2937 says (available at https://qanon.pub/).

"This is not simply another four-year election. This is a crossroads in the history of our civilization that will determine whether or not we, the people, reclaim control over our government. -POTUS" He's not just talking about the U.S. Government, or any single nation's government. He means Reclaim Control Over the Governing of the World from the worldwide criminal mafia.

This will transform the world for 1,000 years! Literally.

Where do I get that?

From the Bible is all. This is the Great Awakening.

We are fighting the New World Order Beast in this epic Battle of Armageddon.

Good versus Evil.

We are embarking on 1,000 years of peace and health and wealth for all of humanity!

The Bible calls this the Millennial Kingdom of Christ as in-
"His Kingdom come, His will be done on earth as it is in Heaven."
The Kingdom of Christ is when:

• Christ assumes His authority as King on earth,

• Christ with His Army remove those who have usurped His throne,

• The "Good Guys" finally rule the earth with Him, straightening out this whole mess the Deep State criminals have made!

No matter what the enemy tries, there's nothing he can do to stop this! As Q said from the beginning,

Big. Bigger! BIGGEST!!!

This truly is the BIGGEST!

That sounds Impossible! Outrageous! Too good to be true!

But the Bible is chock-full of this promise.

Sadly most 'Bible scholars" don't recognize it yet. Just like so-called "scholars" have missed what the LORD was doing from time immemorial! Just like we have been under mass deception by "experts" for years! You are welcome to simply believe what religious pundits, and political pundits, and media pundits, and every other pundit says, OR You are invited to join the white hats in the fight to take back our world, and have your eyes opened to what the LORD has promised over and over in His Word, and how He is fulfilling those promises in our Day! (see FreedomForce.LIVE)

How do I know this is true? You mean, beside the Trump presidency overturning the entire world's corrupt systems?

Because the LORD gave us a sign in the heavens.

You've probably heard of it.

It's called the Sign of the Son of Man. Its very specific details are described in Revelation 12:1-2.

What a wonder!

Is there a woman? Check. (Virgo in Biblical Astronomy represents God's people/the Bride of Christ.)

222

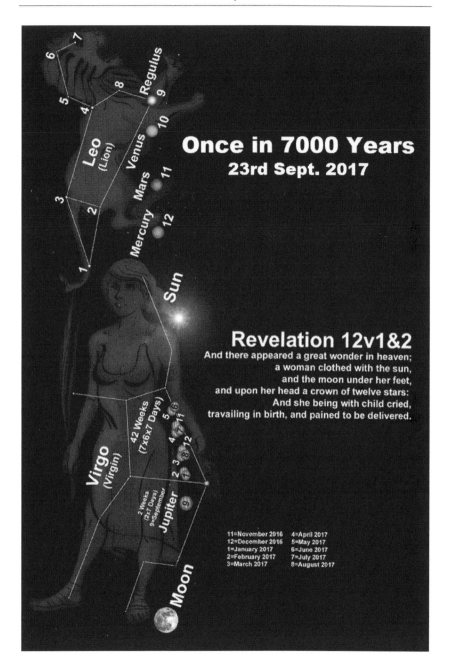

Is she clothed with the sun? Check.

Is the moon under her feet? Check.

Are there twelve stars on her head? Check. Check. Check.

(There are always the nine stars of Leo "crowning" Virgo's head, but in this wonder, three "wandering" stars come into perfect alignment to create Nefertiti's crown.)

What is so wonderful about this wonder is that not only does it match Revelation 12:1-2 to the letter, which has never happened before, but something else amazing happens.

Did you notice that a star enters her "womb?" That's Jupiter. Jupiter's Biblical Astronomy name is Melchizedek - the "priest who lives forever." And did you notice what Jupiter does? It does a loop of clockwork precision inside Virgo's "womb."

I can personally attest to this happening. As I watched the motion of Jupiter inside Virgo night after night, I wondered and prayed what could this mean? I now know the answer.

This is the Birth of the Millennial Reign of Christ on Earth.

No doubt about it.

Right after this sign, which is actually a four-phase sign that completes on December 21st, 2020, the entire world began to wake up. Right after this sign on September 23, 2017, Q began posting in October 2017. And the world will never be the same again!And are you ready for the cherry on top?

Guess what day Jupiter entered Virgo to begin this amazing four-phase earth-shattering wonder.

The day Donald J. Trump was elected as President of the United States of America.

Welcome to the Millennial Reign of Christ on Earth.

https://www.youtube.com/channel/
UC1Zyam1xYQSUxh8gUDek2Vg

Restoration of the Miraculous

BethAnon

We have been raised in a world that abhors the miraculous and loves deception for its own sake. To distract human beings from the obvious glory of God and creation that abounds with every breath. We have been taught to scoff at apparitions of the Mother Mary or of Jesus Christ himself. Miraculous healings are happening all the time and yet just like the apparitions, we don't hear about them on the fake news because they never wanted us to find God, to have an intimate personal relationship with God, and to know Him as our best friend and most intimate companion.

That time is over as we drain the swamp and enter a period of acceptance, realization, repentance, contrition, knowledge of the self, authentic change, amendment, humility, humbleness, and service to humanity through understanding of God within ourselves and our brothers and sisters all over the world. As we come out from the evil influences of the Luciferian agenda and their massive programming of godlessness, we see with new eyes the beauty of other human beings and the animals and all of creation itself and make a decision to live this precious life in consciousness with a heart pierced with love and a conscience that precedes all our actions. Instant karma becomes a blessing instead of a curse when we live consciously. At some point I may attempt a book describing a compilation of the miraculous which is only a shadow of the miracles taking place before our eyes every second of every day. Miraculous thinking is a new way to look at life and is the exact opposite of what has been foisted on us in the world for centuries. Of course, devotion and oneness with our Creator has always been happening and I will enjoy bringing together some of these beacons of light here in the future.

Let's face it. We only have had the luxury of being lost to be found. The great deceiver could only do so much to muddy the waters of consciousness. Now that evil is behind us, we can choose clarity every time. One by one, drop by drop, breath by breath, consciousness rises, our experience of life gets better and better. Proof is in the moment we are living in, within us.

We never needed corroboration from the 'world'. What we are looking for is inside of us...always has been.....always will be. Now is the time to take advantage of our opportunity to embrace this life with every breath. By standing up in our authentic divinity and being fully human ourselves we allow others to join the party. Love wisdom compassion and kindness are contagious. Once we realize the beauty within ourselves, we are able to see the same beauty in others.

We become what we behold which is why I love to focus on all the wonderous and marvelous things that are happening on this beautiful blue planet earth. We were made to sing the praises. Let's do it! Let's bring the Kingdom of Heaven to earth as we were directed to long ago by Jesus Christ in the Lord's prayer.

How We Realized Trump is Leading Our Earth into the Golden Age

Lindsay and Conner

L indsay and Conner created Nova Gaia, a public platform filled with information to help bring Awareness, Freedom, Truth, and Remembrance of our original blueprints and the profound missions we all came here to fulfill.

"We not here to be politically correct, nor are we here to offend anyone. We are simply stating our truth and perceptions backed by very clear evidence and facts that we have compiled over many years of research before Trump became the President of the United States, as well as what has transpired over the last three years. We fully understand that there have been many people who are not aware of what Trump is actually doing and of the goodness that has been unfolding since 12/21/2012, because the mainstream media has intentionally failed to report it. This article is specifically intended to reach those people. We want to help everyone who reads this to have more awareness, to think for themselves, and to see a broader and higher perspective regardless of what you already "think" you know, we simply have come to the realization that absolutely nothing is as it seems from the world view that we were presented in mainstream education and that we have gotten from the media. It is only up to you to truly find out the truth for yourself. Truth brings awareness, and awareness leads to transformation. How are we going to build a new world based on new values and principles with a solid foundation of pure love, unity, and compassion if we do not first come to the innerstanding of what has been? The path of awareness is what leads us all to truly unifying as one human race."

Lindsay: "The very first thing that came into my awareness that triggered a sort of awakening for me as far as Trump goes, actually came from an astrology article. Some of the best astrologers I have ever come across, Starseed Astrology, put out a prediction of Trump winning the 2016 election, during the primaries, long before he was duly elected as President of the United States. They have since predicted many other things regarding the Trump administration, such as Kavanaugh's confirmation, the Farm Bill, the Rehabilitation of the U.S. Economy, and many more. It is pretty profound to see that the stars truly have aligned to give Trump and the Earth Alliance backing him a successful presidency."

Connor: "This is not to say that Trump has lived as a Saint, and yet, his bravery is profound, and let anyone among us who has never acted unskillfully or unconsciously cast the first judgment. I went back out to Standing Rock on 1/20/2017, which was Trump's inauguration day, because I thought he was bought by big oil. I learned so much from all of the brilliant beings who assembled in the fulfillment of the ancient Hopi Rainbow Prophecy. Despite growing up identifying as a Democrat, thinking they were the good guys, I saw through the divide and conquer red vs blue drama once I started doing my own research in 2012. By the time the 2016 elections unfolded, I was relieved that Hillary was not elected, because I knew the depths of unconsciousness that was embodied by Bill Clinton, who attended the Bilderberg Groups meeting in 1991, the year that my Spirit entered my Earthsuit. I also had seen the corruption of the Clinton Foundation, and the chaos caused by the State Department while under Hillary's control. During the elections, I was sifting through Wikileaks' release of the Podesta emails, containing pedophile code, and was also aware of what an NYPD chief said he saw on Anthony Wiener's laptop, who is a registered sex offender and was the husband of Huma Abedin, Hillary's top aid. I also knew of Seth Rich who, was murdered during the elections, after Wikileaks leaked the DNC and Podesta emails, which the Mainstream Media called a "botched robbery" but what was more likely an assassination as retribution by the Podestas, Clintons, and Deep State for Seth Rich leaking the emails to Wikileaks. Julian Assange has said several times that the DNC emails came from a leak, not a hack, and it has since been proven, that the emails from the DNC data base were downloaded onto a flash drive, not hacked through the internet. Then I saw Deep State operatives within the US intelligence community saying that Trump colluded with Russia to win the presidency, and from the moment I heard it, I felt it was a deception. One recent example is here, and one of these men seems to be on the verge of being indicted, with his emotions running high. Russia collusion and calling Wikileaks a front for Putin were propaganda pieces from the Deep State, fabricated in an attempt to undermine Trump's presidency, and to stir up Cold War animosities, while trying to undermine the record of perfect truth that Julian Assange and his team have co-created."

"Lindsay and I shared these perspectives when we met on April 4th, 2018, and our intuitive sense has been proven correct with the publishing of the Mueller investigation, which found no collusion between the Trump campaign and Russia. Just this one fact, has given many beings who have been on the anti-Trump-train pause. The Steele Dossier was artificially created as an "insurance policy" just incase Trump won and then this fake and deceitful narrative was pushed by unconscious actors within our intelligence communities and media, to pitch the American people against the first President that has not been controlled by the Cabal since Kennedy was assassinated. Despite knowing all of this, at the time, I was unaware of the role that Trump is actually playing. It has taken several more years of research to see it clearly, and what follows in this article is a summary of those discoveries. When a being learns to break through propaganda and mind control (MK Ultra), they often see how unconscious, his- story was; how dark, sadistic, and evil (LIVE spelled backwards) the global elitist, celebrities, "royals" and politicians were. This was all behind the curtains of the conquered and controlled 4th estate. The mainstream media, comprised of just 6 massive conglomerates whose Chairmen, Chairwomen, President or CEO was invited to the annual Bilderberg Group meeting, a highly secretive club, which almost none of the legacy media outlets have reported on ever since its conception in 1954."

"Please pause for a moment and reflect. Have you ever heard of this group before? If not, no worries, the majority of people are just hearing of this now. As of 2011, at the end of the old cycle, it is estimated that only one in 5,000 people knew of the Council on Foreign Relations (CFR), and they actually interact openly with the US government. Even less people knew the true power that these groups have wielded. If you had heard of the Bilderberg Group, or the CFR, could you explain them to someone? Or are you one of the ever growing few who has researched all of this for yourself extensively? If the majority of beings are just becoming aware of these groups now, how is it possible that they were hidden for so long? If you were unaware of this secretive-elitist-club of global-power-brokers, what other vitally important truths and realities have you yet to become aware of or remember?"

To expand your awareness of truth on Our Earth, we offer the following books:

1. *None Dare Call it Conspiracy* by Gary Allen
2. *Our Occulted History* by Jim Mars
3. *The Creature from Jekyll Island* by G. Edward Griffin
4. *The Deep State* by Mike Lofgren
5. *The Federal Reserve Conspiracy* by Antony C. Sutton
6. *The Money Mafia* by Paul T. Hellyer
7. *The Rise of the 4th Reich* by Jim Marrs
8. *The Synchronicity Key* by David Wilcock
9. And last but not least,*The True Story of The Bilderberg Group* by Daniel Estulin

"For many decades, alternative media and many of our planet's best journalists have been writing about and shining a light onto the violent consolidation of resources and power that these groups have participated in for thousands of years, hiding behind a network of investment banks, governments, secret societies, and corporations.

There has been a massive coordinated effort that has led to almost no corporate media articles that cover the reality of these groups. Through operations like Operation Mockingbird, the media along with the personalities within them were bought and paid for since the conception of NBC, ABC, and CBS, and certain truth and topics have been off limits. This manipulation of the press in the US goes back to the Investment House of Morgan, which bought up enough newspapers to influence America to join WW1, because 3/4 of the external funding for the Allies came from the Bank of Morgan, which was using propaganda to protect its investments, while driving up inflation from the newly created Federal Reserve system. When you integrate these facts into your awareness, you begin to open your consciousness to the possibilities and realities of what else has been hidden? The most recently created of these groups that make up what has been called The Three Sisters, was the Trilateral Commission (TC), formed in 1973. One rare exception to the media blackout on these groups can be found in this article from 1977 by the Washington Post (WaPo):"

"Trilateralists are not three-sided people. They are members of a private, though not secret, international organization put together by the wealthy banker, David Rockefeller, to stimulate the establishment dialogue between Western Europe, Japan and the United States...But here is the unsettling thing about the Trilateral Commission. The President-elect is a member. So is Vice- President-elect Walter F. Mondale. So are the new

Secretaries of State, Defense and Treasury, Cyrus R. Vance, Harold Brown and W. Michael Blumenthal. So is Zbigniew Brzezinski, Carter's national security adviser, who is a former trilateral director. Also a bunch of others who will make foreign policy for American in the next four years."

"After this article was published, the NWO/Cabal gave Catherine Graham membership in the TC to go along with her memberships in both the Bilderberg Group and CFR, after which, WAPO did not run another exposé on the TC until 1992, when this article was published, but the article is written in a more mocking tone, whereas the 1977 article was more about speaking truth to corruption, hierarchy, and power, or perhaps it was just a clever way for Catherine Graham to ensure her membership in the newest Globalist group. Through media control, these organizations have cloaked themselves behind the red and blue divide and conquer programming, and the existence of the Bilderberg Group as a shadowy club of global power brokers was denied all the way up until 2006, when the group formally acknowledged it's existence with the creation of the site "The Friend's of the Bilderberg's", which is now simply BilderbergMeetings.org"

"Below is a list of prominent figures who have attended Bilderberg meetings, many of them in Violation of the Logan Act: David Rockefeller, Zbigniew Brzezinski, Henry Kissinger, Bill Clinton, Tony Blair, David Cameron, Bill

Gates, Prince Charles, Gerald Ford, Jeff Bezos, Margaret Thatcher, Condoleezza Rice, Eric Schmidt, John Edwards, Prince Philip, Colin Powell, Timothy Geithner, Rick Perry, Laurence Summers, John Carey, Queen Beatrix of the Netherlands, George P Schultz, Peter Sutherland, Angela Merkel, Robert Zoellick, and many other beings who have been princes and queens, from "royal" bloodlines, prominent politicians, chairmen and women of the largest transnational corporations, directors of intelligence agencies, presidents of central banks, and influential intellectuals from the halls of poison ivy, along with many directors of the most well funded tax-exempt think tanks.

When a being looks closely enough, at the true power hierarchy that has been on our Earth, seeing through the divide and conquer political puppet show we learned in school, to the true power structure that ran our planet, The Powers That Were, we

233

then realize there has been a darker shadow within humanity than what Trump has embodied."

"In contrast to the convicted serial pedophile, satanic ritualistic abuser of children, Jimmy Saville, who owned charities that ran children's hospitals, and was Knighted by the Queen of England in 1990, Trump's alleged "gropings" are placed in perspective, not to say that he has not felt the karmic repercussions from anytime in the past, he acted out of alignment with his highest expression of Self. As we all have at some point in this life, or in past incarnations of this Earth timeline, all happening in the eternal NOW. When you learn of the real life Hollywood horror movie 9th Circle, Masonic, and Order of the Eastern Star black magic rituals, you realize that Trump knew some of these people personally, but did not participate in the black magic or pedophilia. From Aug Tellez who has been cleared to bring forth information regarding the Secret Space Program, Solar Warden, Corruption, & The Unveiling, "Current President Donald J. Trump was present as well. It's funny, because saying his name gives me a few flash backs of the events and there is some hope there for me. He was not involved in the pedophilia, the crime-rings, the sacrifice, the torture. He was either protected by a higher-race of beings, a purer human civilization, or they were simply not torturing him so to produce the idea that he was protected. However, he did not torture myself or anyone else and was not involved in the depravity, he "said no to evil", however, presidents are not permitted to make decisions without the support of the people. They cannot say, "well, I want change, so here it is". The people are the true guides and as long as people listen to liars and fools they will not have any of their power."

"To our knowledge, there is no eyewitness or survivor testimony online of Trump engaging in MK ultra, Monarch, or Satanic ritual abuse. This stands in stark contrast to the Bush and Clinton old world actors, which both have had many accounts in books and in video testimony from beings who have been ritualistically raped and abused by these crumbling dynasties, surviving the trauma, and then risking their lives to share their first hand experiences.

Once we realize how dark our Earth drama has been, we can see how far we have already risen."

"From this cosmic and also liberating perspective, we see the transition more clearly, the evolutionary revolutions that are accelerating with each new plasma blast of higher coherence cosmic rays, that the old world Pharmakos hierarchy tried to convince us caused cancer, with transnational corporations that created paid programming, to tell us to put on sunscreens that have revealed themselves to be carcinogenic. From a more wholesome and higher dimensional perspective (which is available to all of us) we realize that Trump was not a part of the human trafficking, child slave rape trade, and perverted religious ritualistic abuse, nor was he helping to create the privately owned central bank fraud, global financial deception and debt slavery systems, in an attempt to create the New World Order and enslave all of humanity.

Once we learn of this pinnacle of power that is dissolving more each hour, we also learn of the Global Earth Alliance, comprised of beings who are following the call of their heart and spirit to rise up as one humanity and soon we will now all hear it, the call to love one and all. Letting crumble the old world systems, organizations, and hierarchical structures that were created and sustained by the bloodlines who once controlled the capstone of conquest on our planet, through secrecy, violence, blackmail, usury, deception and bribery."

Lindsay: "All of the justice and positive transitions that are currently unfolding at this moment in time are according to a sort of script, or what many call "The Plan", which originated decades ago, during the Korean War, when the US military and intelligence community learned that the UN was sharing US strategy with the Koreans. By the time JFK saw the plan, it was already 5 inches thick, and this lead him to take action to dismantle the Nazi infiltrated CIA and expose the secrecy, while acknowledging that he knew of the plot to enslave all men, women and children in our Constitutional Republic. He issued Executive Order 11110, allowing the Treasury to bypass the FED and create over 4 billion dollars without interest. "

"1963 - Kennedy's Green Hilton Agreement with President Sukarno, was signed on November 14th, and was an agreement between the United States and Indonesia, which would have began unlocking the Collateral Accounts, allowing the US Treasury to once again back US currency,with precious metals, thus bypassing the privately owned Federal Reserve System and the interest that US citizens have paid to the FED.

1963 - Kennedy's Assassination, on November 22nd (only 8 days after signing the Green Hilton Agreement) Kennedy was assassinated, and an abundance of evidence points to the CIA/Cabal/Corporatocracy, who were protecting their ability to create and control US currency, inflation, and interest rates via the FED. "

"After Kennedy's assassination, more focus was brought to this global movement for liberation of Our Earth from international banking interests, rogue intelligence agencies, and the secret societies that have shaped and controlled global markets for centuries. After decades of quiet planning we are now watching this plan be carried out with precision. Ever since October 28, 2017, millions of people have gradually become aware of this plan as The Great Awakening, through the QAnon movement, which has grown impressively around the world. It has allowed people to do their own research to come up with their own opinions and perspectives about what is really going on, since the mainstream media has refused to report the truth. Once you go down the rabbit hole of research, it is extremely hard to deny the cold hard evidence that the internet provides us with. Not to mention, the thousands of books that are cited as the number codes for every single Q post. It is simply impossible for any of this to actually be a "conspiracy theory" like the media portrays it to be, and if it was, why would they be trying so hard to discredit all of this?

Well, welcome to the Age of Aquarius, where the truth will always prevail."

"On December 21st, 2017, Donald Trump passed an Executive Order that shook the world, despite mainstream media completely ignoring it. It is hands down the most important executive order in the history of the United States.

From Dr. Michael Salla's Exopolitics article: "Something very profound happened in the U.S. on December 21st with the passage of President Donald Trump's "Executive Order Blocking the Property of Persons Involved in Serious Human Rights Abuse or Corruption." The order declared a state of national emergency concerning human rights and corruption, and named specific individuals and organizations that would have their bank accounts and assets frozen regardless of where in the world the abuses had occurred.

While the mainstream media has largely ignored Trump's Executive Order, the alternative media has been paying close attention. Many have noted the Executive Order is far more significant than what it appears to be on the surface. Rather than just freezing the financial resources of foreign citizens linked to the Russian sphere of influence, as it superficially appears to do, it is really targeted at members of the "Deep State" (aka Cabal or Illuminati) that have been involved in human trafficking, pedophilia and systemic corruption all over the planet."

Jim Stone, a freelance writer, writes: "The executive order is presented as a national emergency up front, right in the beginning. At first it reads like he's going after foreigners which are named directly in an annex at the end. That's not what this is. The first part of the order only cements the second part of the order, to prevent American criminals from running away to foreign countries and being supported by foreigners.

To sum this up:

No swamp critter can accept help from another swamp critter in getting away. Child traffickers and other human rights abuses are covered, the stealing of and misuse of government funds is covered, all items are covered for foreigners and U.S. citizens, any foreigners who have assets in the U.S. that have done anything against the U.S. for the purpose of supporting the American swamp will have those assets seized, anyone in violation of anything in this executive order will have their assets seized."

Dr. Salla: "The Executive Order and the language it uses really does mark a momentous event. Quite simply, it marks a transfer of political power from the Deep State to the U.S. military in terms of who is really in control of the U.S Republic.

It's no secret that Donald Trump has surrounded himself with senior military officers who share his desire to "drain the swamp". His Chief of Staff, John Kelly, is a retired four star USMC general; his Secretary of Defense, James Mattis, is also a retired four star

USMC general; his National Security Advisor, James McMaster, is an active duty three star US Army general; his head of the National Security Agency, Mike Rogers, is an active duty four star Navy Admiral; the head of the Secret Service, Randolph Alles is a retired two star Marine General; and the list goes on."

This executive order also explains why, since 2017, an enormous amount of sealed indictments have been racking up in the tens of thousands, where in any normal year the amount of sealed indictments has been between 1,000 - 5,000. There are over a hundred thousand now. All sealed indictments can be looked up on Pacer.gov." "There have also been thousands of resignations of corporate CEOs since this Executive Order was signed, to be specific, as of April 15th, 2019 the number was 7,568 and an updated list of resignations can be found at www.qmap.pub.

One of the main topics the Trump administration has taken action on is human trafficking, also known as modern day slavery, and it is one of the main reasons why there are over 100,000 sealed indictments and counting. The term "draining the swamp" is no longer just a catch phrase when you realize these indictments are specifically targeting every single individual that has been complicit in, or taken part in, any form of human slavery and abuse.

https://www.whitehouse.gov/briefings-statements/president-donald-j-trump-taking-action-end- human-trafficking/

"No one said that uprooting a 6,000 year old death cult would be easy.

This executive order, and all of the accountability that has happened since, shows us that the end of the old cabal powers has already happened, and the 3D Earth quarantine matrix is dissolving more every single day as high vibrational photonic light from the Great Central Sun infuses Gaia and all of humanity with pure Divine Source energy. Ever since the end of the Mayan Calendar on 12/21/2012, a 26,000 year cycle officially ended, marking the completion of the dark age and the beginning of a brand new 7th dimensional Golden Age on Gaia where evil physically can no longer exist."

"Not only has this time on the planet been prophesied by many indigenous tribes and prophets, but the current astral alignments and aspects happening in our galaxy are telling us that we as a species are currently ascending to much higher frequencies and dimensions along with the earth as the veils between worlds dissolve. Gaia's electromagnetic frequency is also known as the Schumann Resonance, her normal base frequency is 7.83 hertz, it now gets up to 70 hertz on a consistent basis as the sun continues to send solar flares and massive waves of Christened Crystalline Consciousness energy to the earth. We are ascending and there is nothing that can stop it. It is why you are here right now, it is why everything is changing so rapidly and drastically, and it is why a 6,000 year old paradigm is crumbling and a new earth, Nova Gaia, is emerging before our very eyes."

"The reformation of the IMF and World Bank is now in process: https://home.treasury.gov/news/press- releases/sm649

This is now being made possible by the BRICS Alliance, which is a key creator of GESARA, and has emerged as an alternative global lender with the opportunity to truly uplift and benefit all nations of Earth, in contrast to the Bretton Woods Banks, which intentionally put developing nations into perpetual debt so that the global financial order, along with the corporations that they have controlled, could set up military bases in that nation and take their resources for a fraction of the price. John Perkins was trained by the NSA to be an Economic Hitman, and he details the corruption of the World Bank and IMF in his book 'The

New Confessions of an Economic Hitman'. The IMF's structural adjusting was often referred to as austerity, or as Draconian, which likely has its roots in the energy of conquest that has been embodied by many Draco reptilians.

As of March 29, 2019, the gold standard is slowly but surely becoming a reality, https://www.stalkerzone.org/basel-3-a-revolution-that-once-again-no-one-noticed/ with announcements from key Nations such as China and Zimbabwe becoming more audible."

Connor: "Also on March 29, 2019, Brexit was legally completed, and this ended the City of London's underground control over the global financial system, which the families who controlled the privately owned BANK OF ENGLAND, VATICAN BANK, FEDERAL RESERVE, EUROPEAN CENTRAL BANK, INTERNATIONAL MONETARY FUND, WORLD BANK, BANK OF INTERNATIONAL SETTLEMENTS, CHASE MANHATTAN (Morgan, Warburg & Rockefeller), BANK OF AMERICA (Rothschild), CITI BANK (Rothschild), GOLDMAN SACHS (Mercy House), etc. had cultivated for over a century. The bloodlines behind these institutions have been acting out the programs of global domination and colonization for over 6,000 years since Babylon, the etymology of which is "Gates of Gods". With love and compassion in our hearts, we look from the knowing of oneness and equality through the Archontic Artificial Intelligence programs into the spirits and hearts of the Annunaki "Royal" Bloodlines (Vampires of myth), Set (Ancient Egypt), Satanic (Masonic), The Draco Reptilians (Demons), and the Sirian Wolfen beings (Werewolves).

Many of these beings did their best to suppress our multi-dimensional consciousness within our Earth-suits so that they could deceptively rule over us as our creators, when in reality these beings had nothing to do with the creation of our spirit, they simply found a way to suppress our true capacity, in Earth-suits programmed in forgetfulness and sensory perception limitations. We have only seen 1% of the electro-magnetic spectrum, imagine the gifts and abilities awaiting to be activated in the 97% of our DNA that the western Pharmakos medical empire labeled as "junk DNA". The capstone of the Annunaki has been referred to as Anu, who was the false, patriarchal God in the bible and in all hierarchal, dividing, and fear based world religions. Through in vitro fertilization, the Annunaki and their cohorts inserted their "royal" genetics into the human template to create two sub-species within the human template that have competed to most skillfully suppress Gaia's ascension, and our multi-dimensional human spirit, within the programmed limitations of our earth-suits. In this war on consciousness, many have lived in the experience of the reptilian brain program of survival of the fittest, also expressing in its more subtle form as student master relationships, to create the controlling power pyramid."

"Humanity has reclaimed Our Sovereign Wholeness and Infinite Abundance, from what was an artificial Babylonian debt slave matrix, that brutally leveraged the 3 arms of fiat money, fractional reserve banking, and privately owned central bank fraud in its attempt to consolidate all of the wealth and human labor power of the planet, so that the Annunaki "royals" could return to Earth and insert themselves as the rulers of humanity and Our Earth without resistance. We are now standing in the power of love, cultivating patience, compassion, empathy and wisdom as we evolve toward, and honor, the golden rules of "do no harm and do unto others as you would have them do unto you."

"This transition is part of an ongoing process, as humanity and Our Earth ascend to a higher dimension and density upon this beautiful blue, green and rainbow being. It is vitally important to innerstand these exponential positive transitions, and to add our collective energy, words, actions, and faith to our co-created Love Revolution in every moment that we ripple into eternity. For a timeline of events that have unfolded since the 12/21/2012 Precession of the Equinox date transpired, visit our information hub, specifically the "Our Evolution" section of www. OurglassEarth.com

"Dark to Light, in forgiveness lies the end of the wheel of karma. Empathy is a key to our divinity, and compassion brings inner peace even when standing in the turmoil of our collective shadow, which is being exposed to higher coherence and higher dimensional light with every passing moment, day, week, month, year, forever now in eternity, I Am, We Are.

When we see the truth through the propaganda, we all have a front row seat to the greatest story ever told on Our Planet.

The truth is stranger than fiction, the more you know. With Divine Love and Service.

Lindsay and Connor
Nova Gaia
www.novagaia.love

Remarks to the 73rd Session of the United Nations General Assembly

President Trump

September, 2018
United Nations Headquarters New York, NY

"**M**adam President, Mr. Secretary-General, world leaders, ambassadors, and distinguished delegates: One year ago, I stood before you for the first time in this grand hall. I addressed the threats facing our world, and I presented a vision to achieve a brighter future for all of humanity." Today, I stand before the United Nations General Assembly to share the extraordinary progress we've made.

In less than two years, my administration has accomplished more than almost any administration in the history of our country.

America's — so true. (Laughter.) Didn't expect that reaction, but that's okay. (Laughter and applause.)

America's economy is booming like never before. Since my election, we've added $10 trillion in wealth. The stock market is at an all-time high in history, and jobless claims are at a 50-year low.

African American, Hispanic American, and Asian American unemployment have all achieved their lowest levels ever recorded. We've added more than 4 million new jobs, including half a million manufacturing jobs.

We have passed the biggest tax cuts and reforms in American history. We've started the construction of a major border wall, and we have greatly strengthened border security.

We have secured record funding for our military — $700 billion this year, and $716 billion next year. Our military will soon be more powerful than it has ever been before.

In other words, the United States is stronger, safer, and a richer country than it was when I assumed office less than two years ago.

We are standing up for America and for the American people. And we are also standing up for the world.

This is great news for our citizens and for peace-loving people everywhere. We believe that when nations respect the rights of their neighbors, and defend the interests of their people, they can better work together to secure the blessings of safety, prosperity, and peace.

Each of us here today is the emissary of a distinct culture, a rich history, and a people bound together by ties of memory, tradition, and the values that make our homelands like nowhere else on Earth.

That is why America will always choose independence and cooperation over global governance, control, and domination.

I honor the right of every nation in this room to pursue its own customs, beliefs, and traditions. The United States will not tell you how to live or work or worship.

We only ask that you honor our sovereignty in return.

From Warsaw to Brussels, to Tokyo to Singapore, it has been my highest honor to represent the United States abroad. I have forged close relationships and friendships and strong partnerships with the leaders of many nations in this room, and our approach has already yielded incredible change.

With support from many countries here today, we have engaged with North Korea to replace the specter of conflict with a bold and new push for peace.

In June, I traveled to Singapore to meet face to face with North Korea's leader, Chairman Kim Jong Un.

We had highly productive conversations and meetings, and we agreed that it was in both countries' interest to pursue the denuclearization of the Korean Peninsula. Since that meeting, we have already seen a number of encouraging measures that few could have imagined only a short time ago.

The missiles and rockets are no longer flying in every direction. Nuclear testing has stopped. Some military facilities are already being dismantled. Our hostages have been released. And as promised, the remains of our fallen heroes are being returned home to lay at rest in American soil.

I would like to thank Chairman Kim for his courage and for the steps he has taken, though much work remains to be done. The sanctions will stay in place until denuclearization occurs.

I also want to thank the many member states who helped us reach this moment — a moment that is actually far greater than people would understand; far greater — but for also their support and the critical support that we will all need going forward.

A special thanks to President Moon of South Korea, Prime Minister Abe of Japan, and President Xi of China.

In the Middle East, our new approach is also yielding great strides and very historic change.

Following my trip to Saudi Arabia last year, the Gulf countries opened a new center to target terrorist financing. They are enforcing new sanctions, working with us to identify and track terrorist networks, and taking more responsibility for fighting terrorism and extremism in their own region.

The UAE, Saudi Arabia, and Qatar have pledged billions of dollars to aid the people of Syria and Yemen. And they are pursuing multiple avenues to ending Yemen's horrible, horrific civil war.

Ultimately, it is up to the nations of the region to decide what kind of future they want for themselves and their children.

For that reason, the United States is working with the Gulf Cooperation Council, Jordan, and Egypt to establish a regional strategic alliance so that Middle Eastern nations can advance prosperity, stability, and security across their home region.

Thanks to the United States military and our partnership with many of your nations, I am pleased to report that the bloodthirsty killers known as ISIS have been driven out from the territory they once held in Iraq and Syria. We will continue to work with friends and allies to deny radical Islamic terrorists any funding, territory or support, or any means of infiltrating our borders.

The ongoing tragedy in Syria is heartbreaking. Our shared goals must be the de-escalation of military conflict, along with a political solution that honors the will of the Syrian people. In this vein, we urge the United Nations-led peace process be reinvigorated. But, rest assured, the United States will respond if chemical weapons are deployed by the Assad regime.

I commend the people of Jordan and other neighboring countries for hosting refugees from this very brutal civil war.

As we see in Jordan, the most compassionate policy is to place refugees as close to their homes as possible to ease their eventual return to be part of the rebuilding process. This approach also stretches finite resources to help far more people, increasing the impact of every dollar spent.

Every solution to the humanitarian crisis in Syria must also include a strategy to address the brutal regime that has fueled and financed it: the corrupt dictatorship in Iran.

Iran's leaders sow chaos, death, and destruction. They do not respect their neighbors or borders, or the sovereign rights of nations. Instead, Iran's leaders plunder the nation's resources to enrich themselves and to spread mayhem across the Middle East and far beyond.

The Iranian people are rightly outraged that their leaders have embezzled billions of dollars from Iran's treasury, seized valuable portions of the economy, and looted the people's religious endowments, all to line their own pockets and send their proxies to wage war. Not good.

Iran's neighbors have paid a heavy toll for the region's [regime's] agenda of aggression and expansion. That is why so many countries in the Middle East strongly supported my decision to withdraw the United States from the horrible 2015 Iran Nuclear Deal and re-impose nuclear sanctions.

The Iran deal was a windfall for Iran's leaders. In the years since the deal was reached, Iran's military budget grew nearly 40 percent. The dictatorship used the funds to build nuclear-capable missiles, increase internal repression, finance terrorism, and fund havoc and slaughter in Syria and Yemen.

The United States has launched a campaign of economic pressure to deny the regime the funds it needs to advance its bloody agenda. Last month, we began re-imposing hard-hitting nuclear sanctions that had been lifted under the Iran deal. Additional sanctions will resume November 5th, and more will follow. And we're working with countries that import Iranian crude oil to cut their purchases substantially.

We cannot allow the world's leading sponsor of terrorism to possess the planet's most dangerous weapons. We cannot allow a regime that chants "Death to America," and that threatens Israel with annihilation, to possess the means to deliver a nuclear warhead to any city on Earth. Just can't do it.

We ask all nations to isolate Iran's regime as long as its aggression continues. And we ask all nations to support Iran's people as they struggle to reclaim their religious and righteous destiny.

This year, we also took another significant step forward in the Middle East. In recognition of every sovereign state to determine its own capital, I moved the U.S. Embassy in Israel to Jerusalem.

The United States is committed to a future of peace and stability in the region, including peace between the Israelis and the Palestinians. That aim is advanced, not harmed, by acknowledging the obvious facts.

America's policy of principled realism means we will not be held hostage to old dogmas, discredited ideologies, and so-called experts who have been proven wrong over the years, time and time again. This is true not only in matters of peace, but in matters of prosperity.

We believe that trade must be fair and reciprocal. The United States will not be taken advantage of any longer.

For decades, the United States opened its economy — the largest, by far, on Earth — with few conditions. We allowed foreign goods from all over the world to flow freely across our borders.

Yet, other countries did not grant us fair and reciprocal access to their markets in return. Even worse, some countries abused their openness to dump their products, subsidize their goods, target our industries, and manipulate their currencies to gain unfair advantage over our country. As a result, our trade deficit ballooned to nearly $800 billion a year.

For this reason, we are systematically renegotiating broken and bad trade deals.

Last month, we announced a groundbreaking U.S.-Mexico trade agreement. And just yesterday, I stood with President Moon to announce the successful completion of the brand new U.S.-Korea trade deal. And this is just the beginning.

Many nations in this hall will agree that the world trading system is in dire need of change. For example, countries were admitted to the World Trade Organization that violate every single principle on which the organization is based. While the United States and many other nations play by the rules, these countries use government-run industrial planning and state-owned enterprises to rig the system in their favor. They engage in relentless product dumping, forced technology transfer, and the theft of intellectual property.

The United States lost over 3 million manufacturing jobs, nearly a quarter of all steel jobs, and 60,000 factories after China joined the WTO. And we have racked up $13 trillion in trade deficits over the last two decades.

But those days are over. We will no longer tolerate such abuse. We will not allow our workers to be victimized, our companies to be cheated, and our wealth to be plundered and transferred. America will never apologize for protecting its citizens.

The United States has just announced tariffs on another $200 billion in Chinese-made goods for a total, so far, of $250 billion. I have great respect and affection for my friend, President Xi, but I have made clear our trade imbalance is just not acceptable. China's market distortions and the way they deal cannot be tolerated.

As my administration has demonstrated, America will always act in our national interest.

I spoke before this body last year and warned that the U.N. Human Rights Council had become a grave embarrassment to this institution, shielding egregious human rights abusers while bashing America and its many friends.

Our Ambassador to the United Nations, Nikki Haley, laid out a clear agenda for reform, but despite reported and repeated warnings, no action at all was taken.

So the United States took the only responsible course: We withdrew from the Human Rights Council, and we will not return until real reform is enacted.

For similar reasons, the United States will provide no support in recognition to the International Criminal Court. As far as America is concerned, the ICC has no jurisdiction, no legitimacy, and no authority. The ICC claims near-universal jurisdiction over the citizens of every country, violating all principles of justice, fairness, and due process. We will never surrender America's sovereignty to an unelected, unaccountable, global bureaucracy.

America is governed by Americans. We reject the ideology of globalism, and we embrace the doctrine of patriotism.

Around the world, responsible nations must defend against threats to sovereignty not just from global governance, but also from other, new forms of coercion and domination.

In America, we believe strongly in energy security for ourselves and for our allies. We have become the largest energy producer anywhere on the face of the Earth."

The United States stands ready to export our abundant, affordable supply of oil, clean coal, and natural gas.

OPEC and OPEC nations, are, as usual, ripping off the rest of the world, and I don't like it. Nobody should like it. We defend many of these nations for nothing, and then they take advantage of us by giving us high oil prices. Not good.

We want them to stop raising prices, we want them to start lowering prices, and they must contribute substantially to military protection from now on. We are not going to put up with it — these horrible prices — much longer.

Reliance on a single foreign supplier can leave a nation vulnerable to extortion and intimidation. That is why we congratulate European states, such as Poland, for leading the construction of a Baltic pipeline so that nations are not dependent on Russia to meet their energy needs. Germany will become totally dependent on Russian energy if it does not immediately change course.

Here in the Western Hemisphere, we are committed to maintaining our independence from the encroachment of expansionist foreign powers.

It has been the formal policy of our country since President Monroe that we reject the interference of foreign nations in this hemisphere and in our own affairs. The United States has recently strengthened our laws to better screen foreign investments in our country for national security threats, and we welcome cooperation with countries in this region and around the world that wish to do the same. You need to do it for your own protection.

The United States is also working with partners in Latin America to confront threats to sovereignty from uncontrolled migration. Tolerance for human struggling and human smuggling and trafficking is not humane. It's a horrible thing that's going on, at levels that nobody has ever seen before. It's very, very cruel.

Illegal immigration funds criminal networks, ruthless gangs, and the flow of deadly drugs. Illegal immigration exploits vulnerable populations, hurts hardworking citizens, and has produced a vicious cycle of crime, violence, and poverty. Only by upholding national borders, destroying criminal gangs, can we break this cycle and establish a real foundation for prosperity.

We recognize the right of every nation in this room to set its own immigration policy in accordance with its national interests, just as we ask other countries to respect our own right to do the same — which we are doing. That is one reason the United States will not participate in the new Global Compact on Migration. Migration should not be governed by an international body unaccountable to our own citizens.

Ultimately, the only long-term solution to the migration crisis is to help people build more hopeful futures in their home countries. Make their countries great again.

Currently, we are witnessing a human tragedy, as an example, in Venezuela. More than 2 million people have fled the anguish inflicted by the socialist Maduro regime and its Cuban sponsors.

Not long ago, Venezuela was one of the richest countries on Earth. Today, socialism has bankrupted the oil-rich nation and driven its people into abject poverty.

Virtually everywhere socialism or communism has been tried, it has produced suffering, corruption, and decay. Socialism's thirst for power leads to expansion, incursion, and oppression. All nations of the world should resist socialism and the misery that it brings to everyone.

In that spirit, we ask the nations gathered here to join us in calling for the restoration of democracy in Venezuela. Today, we are announcing additional sanctions against the repressive regime, targeting Maduro's inner circle and close advisors.

We are grateful for all the work the United Nations does around the world to help people build better lives for themselves and their families.

The United States is the world's largest giver in the world, by far, of foreign aid. But few give anything to us. That is why we are taking a hard look at U.S. foreign assistance. That will be headed up by Secretary of State Mike Pompeo. We will examine what is working, what is not working, and whether the countries who receive our dollars and our protection also have our interests at heart.

Moving forward, we are only going to give foreign aid to those who respect us and, frankly, are our friends. And we expect other countries to pay their fair share for the cost of their defense.

The United States is committed to making the United Nations more effective and accountable. I have said many times that the United Nations has unlimited potential. As part of our reform effort, I have told our negotiators that the United States will not pay more than 25 percent of the U.N. peacekeeping budget. This will encourage other countries to step up, get involved, and also share in this very large burden.

And we are working to shift more of our funding from assessed contributions to voluntary so that we can target American resources to the programs with the best record of success.

Only when each of us does our part and contributes our share can we realize the U.N.'s highest aspirations. We must pursue peace without fear, hope without despair, and security without apology.

Looking around this hall where so much history has transpired, we think of the many before us who have come here to address the challenges of their nations and of their times. And our thoughts turn to the same question that ran through all their speeches and resolutions, through every word and every hope. It is the question of what kind of world will we leave for our children and what kind of nations they will inherit.

The dreams that fill this hall today are as diverse as the people who have stood at this podium, and as varied as the countries represented right here in this body are. It really is something. It really is great, great history.

There is India, a free society over a billion people, successfully lifting countless millions out of poverty and into the middle class.

There is Saudi Arabia, where King Salman and the Crown Prince are pursuing bold new reforms.

There is Israel, proudly celebrating its 70th anniversary as a thriving democracy in the Holy Land.

In Poland, a great people are standing up for their independence, their security, and their sovereignty.

Many countries are pursuing their own unique visions, building their own hopeful futures, and chasing their own wonderful dreams of destiny, of legacy, and of a home.

The whole world is richer, humanity is better, because of this beautiful constellation of nations, each very special, each very unique, and each shining brightly in its part of the world.

In each one, we see awesome promise of a people bound together by a shared past and working toward a common future.

As for Americans, we know what kind of future we want for ourselves. We know what kind of a nation America must always be.

In America, we believe in the majesty of freedom and the dignity of the individual. We believe in self-government and the rule of law. And we prize the culture that sustains our liberty -- a culture built on strong families, deep faith, and fierce independence. We celebrate our heroes, we treasure our traditions, and above all, we love our country.

Inside everyone in this great chamber today, and everyone listening all around the globe, there is the heart of a patriot that feels the same powerful love for your nation, the same intense loyalty to your homeland.

The passion that burns in the hearts of patriots and the souls of nations has inspired reform and revolution, sacrifice and self-lessness, scientific breakthroughs, and magnificent works of art.

Our task is not to erase it, but to embrace it. To build with it. To draw on its ancient wisdom. And to find within it the will to make our nations greater, our regions safer, and the world better.

To unleash this incredible potential in our people, we must defend the foundations that make it all possible. Sovereign and independent nations are the only vehicle where freedom has ever survived, democracy has ever endured, or peace has ever prospered. And so we must protect our sovereignty and our cherished independence above all.

When we do, we will find new avenues for cooperation unfolding before us. We will find new passion for peacemaking rising within us. We will find new purpose, new resolve, and new spirit flourishing all around us, and making this a more beautiful world in which to live.

So together, let us choose a future of patriotism, prosperity, and pride. Let us choose peace and freedom over domination and defeat. And let us come here to this place to stand for our people and their nations, forever strong, forever sovereign, forever just, and forever thankful for the grace and the goodness and the glory of God.

Thank you. God bless you. And God bless the nations of the world.

Thank you very much. Thank you. (Applause.)

END

What Donald Trump and King David Have in Common

Garrett Ward Sheldon

2019

Around the middle of Barack Obama's second term, I began to hear from several ministers that their congregations (of different denominations) had begun to spontaneously and fervently pray for our country.

These were not the generic "God Bless America" prayers; they were heartfelt anguish over America's drift from God's Truth and way, begging for God's mercy and grace to give us another chance.

Like the old Anglican general confession, they were admissions that "we as sheep, have gone astray" and "Lord have mercy upon us!"

There seemed to be a recognition that our country's inexorable departure from divine standards of morality—fidelity, honesty, decency, responsibility—had now come home to roost in broken marriages, shattered families, damaged parenthood, shady business practices, and political corruption. Moral breakdown, in turn, created much needless suffering: crime, drug addiction, mental illness, and a rising suicide rate, especially among the young. We seemed on the brink of losing everything: social order, the rule of law, freedom of religion, any meaning of happiness. Millions of Christians were crying out to God to save us from this destruction, perversion, depravity, indecency, profanity, hopelessness and pain.

Then Donald Trump was elected president. Some have suggested that he was God's answer to those prayers. Others have regarded that suggestion as blasphemous and dangerous. I find the answer in another traditional prayer in the Anglican Liturgy: that "God will answer our prayers in the time and in the way that is best for us."

Trump may seem an unlikely vessel of God's providence and grace. But it may help to understand how this could be the case by looking at the Biblical character that I think he most resembles: King David of Israel.

David was an unlikely Leader of God's nation, but he was chosen by the Almighty for some very specific reasons: he defended his people's honor and God's ways. His very human moral failings caused him great pain, and although he was able to establish his nation, God did not let him (because of his sins) build the temple.

President Trump once said how much he appreciated the tremendous support of Evangelical Christians, "even though I don't deserve it." Both remind me of God's promise to Abram and his people Israel: "I will bless those who bless you, and curse those who curse you."

David was an unlikely candidate for king of Israel. When the Prophet Samuel came to anoint one of Jesse's sons for the kingship, David wasn't even there—he was out tending his sheep. But David had done something as a shepherd that qualified him to be king. When his flock had been attacked by ferocious animals (lions and bears) he single-handedly and fearlessly defended his sheep. This is the first duty of a ruler: to protect his people. Our American tradition, viewed in light of the social contract theory of John Locke, posits that free individuals form a government explicitly to protect our natural rights to life, liberty, and property.

President Trump's chief concern with protecting America from military threats, from unfair trade practices and from the drugs and crime of illegal immigration all show this essential concern for the government preserving its people.

Despite his courage and devotion to duty, David was still viewed with skepticism. His inexperience disqualified him to rule in the eyes of his father and brothers. When David's resolve was tested by the attack of the monster warrior Goliath, his comrades insisted he put on all the accoutrements of battle: armor, a helmet, a coat of mail and an enormous sword. David found he could not move weighted down by this equipment: he couldn't be himself. One thinks of Trump rejecting all the "requirements" of running for president: lobbyists and consultants, advisors and party connections, interest groups, even daily intelligence briefings. He said, "I cannot be myself in all this garb!"

So, David faced a massive army and giant warrior with his staff, a slingshot, and a few stones. The monster killer Goliath mocked him: "Am I a dog that you come out to meet me with sticks?!" Goliath told David he would kill him, cut him into pieces, and feed him to the birds and the beasts. David proclaimed that he came "in the name of the Lord of hosts, the God of the armies of Israel whom you have defied." He proceeded to kill the enemy with one small stone from his slingshot. The powerful enemy army fled in fear and King David established Jerusalem as the capital of Israel.

President Trump confirmed that by recognizing Jerusalem as the capital of Israel by moving the U.S. embassy there.

King David was not a perfect man and he suffered much for it. His infidelities caused him to lose a son; other family members rebelled against him. He was misunderstood and persecuted. His sins disqualified him from building the temple, leaving that honor to his son Solomon. But like another rescuer of Israel, Esther, he was "for such a time as this."

And so is President Trump

"Man without God" versus "God without Man"
Dr. Dmitry Radyshevsky

D r. Dmitry Radyshevsky is a Harvard educated theologian, political analyst and writer. Author of "Universal Zionism" and "The New Maccabees". Dmitry is the founder of Jerusalem Summit—a think-tank dedicated to uniting the free world around Jerusalem, and a co-founder of Knesset's Christian Allies Caucus.

God's grand design is to bring all His creation to Unity in Him. The road to this Unity is given in His Word: it is a voluntary way of grace and love. This is the JERUSALEM WAY.

The Great Deceiver is the "ape of God": he offers humanity an alternative way to Unity: way of the forced universalization. This is the BABYLON WAY.

In the 20th century we had a clash of two competing projects of Babylon: Nazism and Communism.

Nazism offered a shortcut to global unity via a radical division of mankind into the "right" race and the "wrong" races subject to enslavement or extermination.

Communism was another temptation of a shortcut to Heavens on Earth: via a radical division into the "right" class, or proletariat, and the "wrong" classes subject to destruction or re-education.

The West leaned on its Judeo-Christian values, on faith and sacrifice to defeat Nazism and then Communism.

Yet having won the Cold War, the West immediately gave in to another temptation: another dead-end shortcut to Heavens on Earth—unifying all nations in consumerism, atheism and hedonism.

The radical Left who have hijacked the Western intellectual agenda and proudly call themselves *neo-Marxists* are in fact *neo-pagans* striving for justification and legalisation of any sin or perversion which do not cause immediate physical or financial damage, for the total priority of "individual rights" over common interest—ultimately, to the arch-paradigm *Man without God*.

This post-Christian West removed God from the agenda, but the Islamic East put God back in, as best as he could.

Islam refused to accept this godless version of End of History and pushed for its own path to Heavens on Earth: a radical division of mankind into the "faithful" and the "infidels," who need to be destroyed or forced to worship Allah.

Islam offers the End of History as the global Islamic theocracy, total priority of a religious dogma over individual rights, cult of totalitarian deity with total disregard to human rights and human dignity—in short, *God without Man*.

Islam forces it on the world by waging Jihad—demographic, economic, political, propagandistic and terrorist.

These two demons, two dead-end Babylon ways of imposing unity, Globalism and Islamism, two global projects, leading only to death ad destruction, "Man without God" fighting "God without Man," were fighting each other only until we, believers, Jews and Christians, did not put our acts together and remembered that we are called to offer the only alternative to humanity's salvation: **God Meeting Man**.

We have remembered that the solution is—Man and God walking and working together, in Love and Partnership, keeping faith and Biblical commandments, and respecting human liberty and dignity at the same time.

We have recalled that Judeo-Christian unity and Judeo-Christian revival is the only hope for humanity: the only way to defeat aggressive Post-liberalism and militant Islamism.

We have recalled all that—and elected President Trump, a God-given global leader of our Biblical resistance.

That made the two archenemies of God—the radical Left and Islamists—unite against the Judeo-Christian civilization, against Israel, against President Trump and against the Bible-believing Americans.

Have you ever wondered why the atheistic, hedonistic, sexually perverse radical Left are comrades in arms with the fanatically religious Islamists and the ascetic Chinese Communists? What do they have in common?

Only one thing: hatred towards the God of the Bible.

This *personal* God requires each person to work on his or her personal character: to engage in the personal dialogue with God and to strive towards individual virtues, individual holiness.

This God does not "buy" that all passions and lusts of a man are "holy" even if a man calls them "human rights" and passes laws allowing being proud of these lusts.

This God does not allow the consciousness of a sinful man to absolve his own sin... the man feels this discomfort of the soul and rebels against God. But since he cannot fight an invisible God, he fights His visible and loyal servants: Israel and Bible-believing Christians, and their leader—President Trump.

The same goes for the Islamists and Chinese Communists. The God of the Bible does not consider the blind submission to the 7th century norms of monotheism or to Maoist dogmas, and cruel imposition of these norms on humanity to be a virtue. That's a mechanical, primitive way towards holiness—too simple, too easy, too misguided. Holiness cannot be reached by mechanical performance of rituals, it cannot be imposed by cruelty, it cannot be reached by the blind submission to Allah or to the Communist party. Holiness requires a free dialogue with Creator, it requires submission to the voice of God within us, to our consciousness —not to the external authority, it requires a *hard labour of the soul.* Islamism and Communism conveniently frees a man from this hard labour.

However, God of the Bible does not allow the consciousness of an Islamist or a Communist to busk in the blissful submission to Sharia or Communist Law. God of the Bible disturbs their consciousness—and that provokes their rage.

But again, since Islamists or Communists cannot fight an invisible God, they fight His visible and loyal servants: Israel and Bible-believing Christians, and their leader—President Trump.

This is why President Trump is hated both by the radical Left (including Chinese Communists) and by Islamists.

This is why Israel and Bible-believing Christians are so much hated by the radical Left (including Chinese Communists) and by Islamists. It is not about policy, not about economy, not about racism or immigration. It is about the God of the Bible.

This is why this battle is so vicious, so bitter, so crucial.

This is why we cannot lose this battle and we will *not* lose it.

Because it is not about us. It is about the Source of Life. The Creator.

And He will make sure that His way, the Way of Jerusalem will prevail.

This is why President Trump will prevail.

This is why we vote for Trump.

Archangels & Ascended Masters: A Synthesis of Presidential-Election Prophecies

Christine Preston

C hristine Preston is a messenger who is in daily communication with Archangel Michael and her Ascended Twin Flame Andre, whom she knew as a cousin till he passed away in 1972.

February 18, 2016

Christine: On February 18, 2016 Archangel Gabriel gave me the following message and at that time I didn't have any expectation in regard to the American elections and had little knowledge about them as I live in Britain. This is an extract from that message:

Archangel Gabriel:I have not mentioned a name to reveal who, at the top of the pyramid of great deceit, is going to be stripped of his credibility. I have sent a mental image of who it is to the emissary of this message. This is going to bring great turmoil in the political affairs but will be followed by a great renewal in relation to that mechanism in which those who preside over the people, in a certain nation in particular, are being replaced.

This turn of events will be deserved by those who have betrayed the trust of a Nation that was to be an example of democracy with a Constitution inspired by Saint Germain, and so dear to his heart. The time has arrived when there can no longer be any secret machinations and conspiracies of wars for economic gain and wealth that ends in the pockets of a few. Heaven has decreed 'Enough is enough'. Now is the beginning of that Phase of Enlightenment that starts with a shaking up of the world. I am blowing my trumpet to announce to the world it is time to step upon that Path of the resurrection of civilization.

Mankind must be freed from its misconceptions, its mind set, and place its feet upon the path of enlightenment to recreate a civilization that will be represented in the Galactic Federation of Light. A new Gaia and golden age will then be recreated. We are all working together in unison, in a sacred relationship, to achieve this goal.

February 28, 2016

Christine: Then on February 28 Mother Mary made a revelation concerning the outcome of the presidential elections of 2016, as follows:

Mother Mary: A replacement in governance of that Nation – which was destined to be an example of democracy, and instead has been infiltrated down to its core and leadership by the forces of darkness – is shortly to take place. Of course, if a new President – one who, by the way, needs to be extremely resilient, dynamic and vigorous, to be able to oppose the Establishment – if that one told you that 9/11 was an 'inside job' to create an enemy, create the idea of terrorism, to serve the mechanism of the war industries, the number of doubting Thomas would drop sharply. And I am now revealing that Archangel Gabriel's announcement alluded to this particular topic. We are entering a phase of Disclosure entailing a complete dismantling of the various systems of thought created by the powers of darkness in recent decades. These were also built upon the legacy inherited during thousands of years of slavery under the Anunnaki. I am referring to the system that has kept you in ignorance and darkness.

March 8, 2016

Christine: On March 8, Archangel Michael stated:

Lord Michael: A battle is being waged in the psyche, but before explaining something about this I would like to mention that the forces of darkness, on the astral plane, are still attempting to sabotage the Ascension process and to influence political leaders, the Establishment, the military, and other groups in the financial and business sectors of the big Corporations, to avoid complying with the orders imposed upon them by the Forces of the Light to go ahead with a program of Disclosure concerning the truths that have been suppressed for more than a century. They are trying to avoid it with a number of excuses. They are fearful and reluctant to lose power. Assaults are still taking place upon the light in the lightbearers and there is not one nation without these spiritual beings who are on the path of the Ascension. This is taking place behind the scenes of the political scenarios and you may feel that they make no sense any more. A phase of transition with changes on the political front and financial system will also be initiated, and it will take place because of some events in the USA that will affect the whole world in the sense that as a result the adverse influence from the astral world will be greatly lessened.

March 18, 2016

Christine: Then on March 18, Archangel Michael spoke of something that would happen before it was called the shift to 4th density and explained that some of the events expected in 2012 had not taken place.

Lord Michael: we wanted to convert more souls to a higher frequency of vibration so they could continue to exist on Earth. This is a world in transition and it is being lifted up to a higher dimension in the sense that physicality will still exist but in an exalted way, much like what you think of a Garden of Eden, or Paradise. So on September 28, 2015, something that had been expected to take place in December 2012, finally happened.

March 22, 2016

Christine: Then on March 22, Ashtar Command stated:

Ashtar Command: Dear ones, this is an Alert from Ashtar Command. We are approaching a time of difficulty because of the planetary adjustment that will take place with the process of Disclosure. The Earth has entered a most dense area of the Ring of Light that is called a Photon Belt, and the entire Solar System is being buffeted by electro-magnetic waves.

These waves are instrumental to the Great Awakening as the photonic light and gamma rays of these electro-magnetic surges are stripping the psyche of mankind of negative elements in much the same way as the circles and swords of Blue Flame of Archangel Michael, as well as of the Elohim Hercules and Astrea.

Christine: They said Earth was to play a key role in the manifestation of the Divine Will and we were close to the goal because the planetary body had been swept by a flux of energy that had impacted the Solar System on March 20, 2016, and that on March 22, this stream of light had gone round the world for a second time. They also stated:

Ashtar Command: Those at the top of their pyramid of control have made their move like in a game of chess, to go ahead with a scheme designed long ago. They have tried various tactics to create a global conflict and weaponize space. They did not understand that the process of Ascension is a cosmic one and that it is also affecting the planetary bodies of the Solar System. They discovered that they could not leave Earth, nor run away with their secret technology and spacecraft. They would love to declare ownership of the Solar System. They intended to use their holographic technology to stage an alien invasion such as the one of 'Independence Day' or 'The War of the Worlds.' They are being kept under surveillance of the Galactic Federation of Light and Ashtar Command which would not allow it. We are coming close to a time when some replacement in power, in just a few months from now, will also create a more favorable climate for disclosure. We can see that Victory is very close, and we rejoice. A new perception of Reality of the whole situation upon Earth is being received. Enlightenment is also playing a part in the whole process, and you will be looking forward to the progress of the Third Wave when the energies peak at the end of the year.

March 29, 2016

Christine: On March 29, Archangel Michael declared that Disclosure would take place God's Way and there would not be any delays. He explained again that the forces of darkness have created scenarios to create wars and are still attempting to incite conflicts, but are failing. He also said that the two first Waves of souls functioning in a realm of awakened consciousness were influencing the Media and the political scene.

April 23, 2016

Christine: Then, on April 23, André stated:

André : About the Presidential Elections we are still saying that Donald Trump is going to win them. Of course, it's a very delicate matter to make such a prediction where you stand, but we have seen the certainties in the timelines. There is a situation with who is pulling the strings in the political scenes of the world. With regard to Donald Trump, we see that there is a need for a candidate to possess great strength and stamina in present circumstances, and we see that the next President will have a fight with the Establishment and need to oppose it so that Disclosure can occur. If the dark ones, the Illuminati, or Cabal, attempt to control him by threat, blackmail, or anything of the kind, we will be intervening with Ashtar Command, the air division of the Great White Brotherhood. The Cabal is being given a chance to turn to the Light.

May 27, 2016

Christine: In Time of Transition and Reunion, published on May 27, 2016, my ascended twin flame, André, stated:

André: Back on February 18 and 28, 2016, when Archangel Gabriel and Mother Mary first disclosed that it was Donald Trump who will be elected President, we gave you these prophecies and continued to inform you that he was still on track. He has now won the necessary delegates for this to become a reality and he is receiving a different kind of attention from the media.

The Elections will play an important role in the changes that will not only transfigure the American Continent, but the whole world. The Earth is the planet that was to play a key role in the Ascension to bring physicality to a higher place.

April 29, 2016

Christine: On April 29, Archangel Michael stated:

Lord Michael: The world is emerging into a better reality in which America will become the example the founding Fathers wanted it to be. It was Saint Germain's dream, and he is causing it to unfold at the moment, as the Dark is on the run.

May 5th, 2016

Christine: On May 5th, Mother Mary gave me a message entitled 'Prophecy regarding the Elections'. I had 35 videos published at the time and now the number is 83. So please listen to this one as well as the one entitled 'Renewed Prophecy for the Elections' published by Matt Muckleroy. An important part of the first video is where I have explained:

I would like to inform you that on February 28, 2016 I received a message from Mother Mary saying that Donald Trump will be the elected president. I didn't hesitate to post the message on my Facebook page and to have it published as a video although predictions are a bit tricky because - as they say - prophecies are not set in stone, and that is because they depend on mankind's actions, and there are many timelines. Some new events can change the prophecy. However in this case I was assured that there was a certainty about this.

They looked at the timelines and saw the future. Normally they see the possibilities, or probabilities, as well as what is certain. In this case, my daily contacts [which are constant where my ascended twin flame is concerned] were adamant and kept on saying day-after-day, week-after-week: 'we are still saying that Donald Trump will make it' or something of the kind. They have explained that the forces of the Light are supporting him because of the need to oppose the Establishment. It's not just happened by coincidence, i.e. they are not supporting him because he happens to be aligned with the Divine Will. No, it's like he has incarnated for this mission and there has been manipulations to get to this point. It is in relation to the Ascension and the fact that the Earth and Solar System are in a galactic alignment, and crossing an area in space that is intense in photonic light. This is having an influence upon mankind. It is causing an awakening and a liberation from the forces of darkness that have been controlling mankind. Light transmutes darkness. After my explanations I repeated the statement Mother Mary made on February 28:

February 28, 2016

Mother Mary: A replacement in governance of that Nation —which was destined to be an example of democracy, and instead has been infiltrated down to its core and leadership by the forces of darkness - is shortly to take place. Following this a phase of disclosure will begin with the scandalous matter of betrayal related to 9/11. I am Mother Mary, confirming to Christine that this notion is correct. She takes my dictation and doesn't know what is coming next. But while listening to one of Donald Trump's speeches recently, something he said made her suspect that Archangel Gabriel's last announcement concerning a disclosure may have been related to that subject of 9/11. Some ideas concerning a disclosure on that subject have spread many years ago, but in the mainstream media this is still regarded as a conspiracy theory. However, of course, if a new President - one who, by the way, needs to be extremely resilient, dynamic and vigorous, to be able to oppose the Establishment - if that one told you that 9/11 was an 'inside job' to create an enemy, create the idea of terrorism, to serve the mechanism of the war industries, the number of doubting Thomas would drop sharply. And I am now revealing, as Christine is noting word for word, in this method of dictation, that Archangel Gabriel's announcement alluded to this particular topic. Christine: After Donald Trump was nominated to represent the Republican Party, Nigel Farage was interviewed in the United States. And he has been interviewed again a few days ago after the first Debate had taken place. He also recognised the parallel between what is going on in the United States with that battle for Brexit in Britain, as being to do with an opposition to the Establishment. Archangel Michael made a comment that related to Mark Taylor's Prophecy, given to him in 2011. I learned about it in May and Archangel Michael told me he was the one who revealed it to Mark Taylor, but being Christian, the latter speaks of the Spirit of the Lord. On May 11, Archangel Michael said to me:

Lord Michael: With regards to the video entitled 'Prophecy regarding the Elections,' it has caused some bewilderment. However, some people were already given such a prophecy many years ago. The prophesied election of Donald Trump is in relation to the need to oppose the Establishment and large Corporations. If some people see a division occurring, remember that you are now living in the predicted time of great tribulations called the Apocalypse.

May 27, 2016

Christine: In Time of Transition and Reunion, published on May 27, 2016, my ascended twin flame, André, stated:

André: Back on February 18 and 28, 2016, when Archangel Gabriel and Mother Mary first disclosed to you that it was Donald Trump who will be elected President, we gave you these prophecies and continued to inform you that he was still on track. He has now won the necessary delegates for this to become a reality and he is receiving a different kind of attention from the media. A battle has already been won in regards a certain dissemination of misrepresentation for a political agenda. Once the strings of control are totally severed the Leaders of the Nations will be freed to make changes to spread peace around the world. It will be freed from that captivity under the forces of darkness that sought to precipitate more and more chaos upon the surface of this globe to serve their own agenda. The Elections will play an important role in the changes that will, not only transfigure the American Continent, but the whole world, because it was the nefarious activities of the War Industries that caused the decline along the lines plotted for many decades by the Dark Forces.

June 5, 2016

Christine: In the video published on June 5, I explained that I had received a request from Saint Germain, as follows: I have received symbolic images that carry the meaning that the American Elections and Brexit in Britain are like the top of the iceberg of what is going on, and in one of them this dark force was a Dragon that will be wounded when Britain choses to leave the European Union. It needs to be slain in the sense that we have to overcome it, and perhaps that is what will happen as a great turmoil seems to be created in the process of the American Elections. A great awakening is however resulting from it. A great many people are changing their opinion as so many notions are coming out in the open. Saint Germain conveyed to me the idea that the individuals opposing and fighting the Establishment in the process of the American Elections are taking a hard beating. Certain Ascended Masters are closely connected with this struggle. So Saint Germain has asked me to make calls for those who are fighting a battle for Freedom and to see if a video with some prayers can be produced. He is the Hierarch of this New Age of Aquarius and of Freedom.

June 10, 2016

Christine: In 'Broad Vision', June 10, André, my Ascended Twin flame, a judgment is taking place behind the scene of the Elections and revealed that Donald Trump is a soul extension of the Master Saint Germain:

André: Greetings dear ones. We are still saying, as we have before since February 28, that despite enormous difficulties at the moment, Donald Trump is the candidate who will eventually be elected President of the United States as a result of the present Elections and nominations. There is an enormous 'turn around' of opinions as a result of light being cast upon the abominations and deceptions carried out by the Institutions, and there is increased awareness concerning the activities of the major Corporations which are acting as the hands of this shadow government upon the Astral plane. The Archons ruled in Atlantis and rose to power again in the 1980s. Everything they have done was allowed as their judgment has been, and will be, based upon their deeds. Those who were given a second chance could not have been judged before they had committed their crime. So this is the status. Donald Trump will be President by destiny. He is a soul extension of Saint Germain, who is an expert in creating wealth and has a momentum of Light that permits him to win any battle or confrontation with the Dark ones. Keep in mind that extensions, or incarnations of great beings such as Masters, Archangels and Star seeds, are still veiled and do not possess memory of who they are. I have permission to release this information at this time as we know there is no need to keep this a secret from the Lightworkers any more. Saint Germain is the Hierarch of the Aquarian Age and is involved with the Project of Peace, Prosperity and recreation of civilization, which will propulse mankind, and this planet, in a golden age era. He was the one who shouted 'Sign that document!' when the Founding Fathers hesitated and were about to introduce the Constitution, Bill of Rights, etc. in 1776. He appeared and then disappeared in a room within locked doors and this miracle remained a mystery. The Constitution is not in effect any more. Many perversions have been introduced in politics, and Donald Trump has enough strength and abilities for this battle against the power that are keeping mankind captive. A lot has still to happen between now and November 2016. This broad vision of what has happened up to now will help you to keep faith.

You also have a shift in density to look forward to at the end of this year. We are shortly to enter a Time of Transition. As we have said it before, the time ahead is one of Disclosure and then of Transition, with healing and teachings, as well as contacts and great encounters of the inner and outer types. We will be able to meet when you have reached a higher level than the present one upon which you dwell. Ahead and beyond 2016 is a time of reconstruction, of enlightenment, of teaching, of the creation of new Gaia, a time of Great Disclosure to continue unveiling suppressed truths and discovering a new spiritual Science, a time of using new technologies. It's a time when many will be busy with their sacred labors and a time of great discoveries in preparation for a destiny greater and more wonderful than you can yet imagine. It is one of Reunion of twin flames and of other relationships too, of Peace, and of growth, one of Great encounters and of supernatural experiences as you are all progressing upon the path of Ascension, and are discovering the wonders of your inner Selves. Everyone will be learning and working to prepare the collective and the population for that next quantum leap years later, when the human will have conquered illnesses and death and will be Galactic.

Christine: In the video 'Broadcast Love' of June 15, a message from the Master Jesus, I explained: We are having a revolution in spirit and consciousness. The liberation comes from the 7th Ray of Saint Germain, and the impulse of cosmic energies projected to Earth in this Age of Aquarius, the Hierarch of which is Saint Germain, who has been known for centuries as the Count of Saint Germain and has a reputation as the 'man who never dies'.

The Violet Transmuting Flame also is the energy of forgiveness that erases the records, their causes, cores and memory. Its liberating effects will also cause the restoration of the Rights relating to every human being in this time of Transition to a Quantum Leap to the Fifth Dimension in some years to come, in terms of changes to our physicality. The true Democracy of the founding fathers will be resurrected and America is still promised to function as an example to other nations when corruption is abolished and righteousness is resurrected in the land. Its truth and values have been desecrated because of the infiltration of dark powers in the government to its core, and therefore God has not ruled over men. 'God over men' is what government is supposed to be but has not been for many decades. A revolution is taking place but as people are trying to work out who to follow, who is telling the truth, there is a whirlpool of negative reactions as well as an attempt of control on the part of those forces that fear to lose control. However, you can recognize truth when you hear it, if you already know it because you have magnetized the Light of Christ consciousness. The Master Jesus explained that the group of souls which had not yet been anchored in the 5th dimension, as far as consciousness, perception, attitude, or spirituality, goes, would be fished in the net of the 5th dimension by the waves of the photonic light by the end of the year, and he asked our motto to be 'Broadcast Love'.

July 2, 2016

Christine: In 'From Liberation to New Gaia' of July 2, 2016, my twin flame stated:

André: I will demonstrate to you what is happening. We are on the verge of an enormous amount of changes at a very speedy rate which will result with the promised disclosures, though some have already taken place and caused consternation. We, the Forces of the Light, who are opposing those of Darkness, have just had a great victory, as a majority of people in Britain have seen the Light, come to their senses, and rejected the side of the sinister ones, in the process of exercising their right to vote and of their own freewill, and have said 'No' to the European Union. These people who have voted 'Out' have been able to perceive the truth that the sinister forces have attempted to conceal behind the world dramas they fabricate. The dark forces counted on the peoples' reduced spectrum of consciousness, but they had been awakened in the process of Ascension, and Campaigners had outlined the reasons and advantages to reject the European Union, especially as its leadership has never been elected. So a majority of people in Britain have taken their stand against an anti-democratic organization that is linked to the Obama administration as well as the neo—con policy makers governed by the Elite, the Cabal and its servants, the Bankers, who own 95% of the wealth of the world and yet obtained to be bailed out with the peoples' tax monies some years ago. So you get the picture. It is scandalous. The present situation of the Solar System is that it is relentlessly moving within the Stargate towards its final destination, the Constellation of Sirius. It will take its place, as recently stated by Lord Sanat Kumara, as the 8th system that will orbit Sirius A. In the United States of America the battle that represents the other side of the same coin, so to speak, with the presidential Elections, also is one against the same Establishment that has one foot over the new continent and the other over Europe.

July 21, 2016

Christine: In 'Renewed Prophecy and Hope', published on July 21, André stated:

André: I would like to pass on a message of hope with regard to the Elections in America. The vote has been cast and Donald Trump has been elected as a nominee for the Republican Party, and what will follow from this is a nasty battle of wits and words coming from the opposition. As we have said it before, in prophetical messages that have been published in February and then May this year, it will be Donald Trump who will be elected President of the United States of America, and he was the only one who had enough strength for the coming confrontation that will bring deliverance as well as to oppose the Establishment. His appointment is part of a divine Plan to restore order upon earth and release mankind from its captivity to the dark forces.

July 30, 2016

Christine: On July 30, the World Mother declared 'I come with the Ruby Ray' stating: World Mother: I come to intervene in the affairs of the world. I am coming to precipitate certain events in the arena of the world and its political scenes. The American people are about to overcome a great negative power that has held them in great suffering. There are great forces at work which will cause them to awaken to a new perception of Reality through the deliberations taking place for the Presidential Elections.

August 1, 2016

Christine: Then on August 1, Saint Germain confirmed that the World Mother is present to dissolve the core of darkness on the physical plane of the planet that originated from the Draco Constellation, and that contributed to the fall of the planet that existed between Mars and Jupiter that was destroyed and that was called Maldek. He revealed the fact he has more than one incarnation at the moment, and that one of these extensions of himself is indeed Donald Trump whose work it is to oppose the Establishment and lead Earth in to an era of transition and golden age, or the New Age of Aquarius of which he is the Hierarch.

Saint Germain has a deep connection with mankind and his plan including the release of prosperity funds will play a key role in the Age of Transition that will apparently start in a few months.

He was with us as a Leader in the land of Egypt but at the time of a decline from the Golden Age of Lemuria. He said that Hillary Clinton is in the leading position of that conspiracy to cause a downfall of civilization.

May you all be kept safe and secure in the Ascended Masters' Light, Christine

"Prophecies are not set in stone because they rely on man's actions." Christine Preston

"Trump has incarnated for this purpose." Christine

Article below is so full of good inspiring information

Mother Mary, Announcing Acceleration, Christmas Celebrations

December 8, 2016

Christine: Hi Lightworkers, this morning I have received the following telepathic message from Mother Mary. It is as follows:

Mother Mary: Know that you are loved, dear ones. You are doing well. I have been associated with the concept of the Immaculate Conception because I came to Earth with a pure heart to be the Mother of Jesus, Yeshuah, in that moment of time more than 2000 years ago, which it has become traditional to commemorate on December 25, in the Christian tradition, and even in those nations that are not, as this celebration has been amalgamated with the ancient Roman festival of Saturnalia as well as other feasts of Eastern Nordic legends. By that I mean that wonderful story of Father Christmas, or Santa Claus, who is portrayed as coming down chimneys. It's a wonderful idea and you may not know this, but the idea originated from the fact that in the country of origin of this legend the entrance to the peoples' homes was by the roof. We in the heavenly regions, the higher dimensions, are looking forward to the Christmas Season as we can use it to sweep more souls into the Great Fisherman's Net, that cosmic Web of

Ascension into the 5th dimension in consciousness. One of the results of this awakening was the recent shift into 4th density in your physicality, the lower body of your multi-dimensional system of operation, so to speak, and eventually your Reality, as you are creating the 5th kingdom and the process of recreating Gaia has started. There is much to say about what is taking place right now. Progress is being made in the general process of Ascension, as well as the shifting of the physical atoms of planet Earth into 4th density, bringing many changes that are still to be manifested as time goes on after the New Year. At the same time you are being elevated upon the ladder of the dimensions in consciousness. Your attention has been drawn to the fact that there is shortly to be a stepping up of energies once again. The American lands have been the stage of a battle in the psyche, a great Armageddon in which you have seen different views and narratives emerging in your media, reflecting the level at which souls dwell in consciousness. The Presidential elections have been the catalyst for that Harvest of souls in the end time, bringing a victory to the forces of the Light over those of darkness that had for their agenda to keep mankind in captivity with their various systems of control and psychotronic warfare, for their program and manipulations of supremacy and of conquest, even of the whole solar system. But this is over now, or practically so. Dear ones you have entered a new Day, a period of Transition which will bring to you disclosure with enlightenment, as well as the manifestation of Saint Germain's Plan for the Earth. And I have come to this messenger today to announce to you that you will shortly be picking up the pace upon the Path of Ascension and of the Golden Age. You will indeed be on a fast track and experiencing an acceleration now, a quickening, and further awakening as a result of the descent of the Lightbody or Christ consciousness, as well as all of the prodigious contacts you will be experiencing in the years to come. I would also like to inform you that your Galactic family are watching your progress and providing you with assistance in all the ways they can. The acceleration that you are about to experience is the result of the recent progressive shift to 4th density and of the victory of the Light in the matter of the opposition to the darkness of the Establishment, for behind the scenes of what you see with your physical eyes, a conflict with the overlords who held the strings has been taking place. It's happening in other nations too and is a revolution in consciousness demanding Freedom. The door is now opening to the Peace of my son, the Ascended Jesus Christ, as well as Archangel Michael's, and it is descending upon Earth from the higher octaves. Infinite blessings and wishes are coming your way, dear ones. Healing, changes in your DNA, will eventually restore you to full consciousness and a condition in physicality that is not affected by illnesses, changes, and death. That recovery is on the timetables after you have renewed contact with your celestial, ascended, or Galactic, may I say 'so heavenly' family. It has been a difficult year. We looked forward to that confrontation and now, we can celebrate, especially as the Christmas festivities are approaching. We are very joyful and want to let you know that you are very tired because you have lived through years of stress, on adrenaline, as the dark lords have created atrocious conditions, particularly during this last decade. But let's turn to the future now and let's enjoy together the wonders, fairy tales and magic of the Christian tradition of Christmas, as well as its good tidings. The New Year will bring a most wonderful set of events as this is just the beginning of our reunion. You are being caught up in more waves of Ascension, and we are pushing on with an activation, or acceleration, that will eventually manifest a new golden age, and the fulfilment of prophecies. I Am Mother Mary and I am keeping you safe and consecrated in the love of my Immaculate heart. As always, I am interceding for you and mankind, and I am eternally devoted to my tasks upon the Emerald Ray, as a mother and friend. Merry Christmas and Happy New Year, dear ones, Namaste, Mother Mary!

+++

One of the most important lines in President Trump's Rushmore Speech—

"Our children are taught in school to hate their own country and to believe that the men and women who built it were not heroes but were villains. The radical view of American history is a web of lies."

God's Anointed Leader Isn't Always What We Expect

Michelle Fitzpatrick Thomas

January 28, 2020

M ichelle Fitzpatrick Thomas is a Christ follower, wife to Trevor Thomas, and homeschooling mom of four. Her books include *Lord, I Need You*, *Through Deep Waters*, and *Debt-Free Living in a Debt-Filled World*.

Much has been spoken and written lately regarding the evangelical community's feelings toward President Trump, especially since the Christianity Today editorialcalling for his removal from office was published last month. Many evangelicals continue to support him wholeheartedly because he has proven repeatedly that he can be trusted to keep his campaign promises and to govern faithfully and conservatively. Others vow never to support him because they feel that he "embodies the anti-Christian ethic."

President Trump certainly has a "colorful" past, and that is the key reason why I did not support him in the Republican presidential primary of 2016. I just couldn't imagine a man of his moral failings representing this nation and becoming the leader of the free world. However, when it ultimately came down to a choice between Donald Trump and Hillary Clinton on November 8, it was a no-brainer. I would have crawled on my hands and knees to the polls, if necessary, to vote against her. That's exactly what my vote was at that time — a vote against Hillary Clinton.

It turns out, however, that millions of us who held our noses and voted for Trump have been quite pleasantly surprised by his ardent support of the values and policies that we hold dear. He has been the most pro-life president in the history of our nation, and he was the first president ever to attend the annual March for Life on Capitol Hill. He has been a true friend to small business-owners; he has appointed hundreds of wonderful federal judges; he is defending religious liberty; he is improving our international trade relationships; and among many other accomplishments, he is making our military stronger and our nation safer. Despite all of these successes, many persist in demanding the removal of President Trump because they dislike how he conducts himself.

For many evangelicals, the decision to vote for and to continue to support Donald Trump essentially boils down to this: he operates from the Republican Party platform, which represents life; liberty; and conservative, Judeo-Christian values. Whoever his Democrat opponent turns out to be in November, that person will stand on the Democrat Party platform, which is immoral, anti-Christian, anti-God, anti-life, and anti-freedom. Seems pretty clear and simple.

My church went through a study in 2019 called OT19, in which we read much of the Old Testament together. The very same week that the Christianity Today editorial calling for Trump's removal was published, our assigned reading included Isaiah, chapters 44 and 45. In these chapters, the Israelites were captives in Babylon, and God used a non-Israelite, a Persian king named Cyrus, to free His people from captivity and rebuild the temple in Jerusalem.

Speaking to Cyrus, God said (emphasis mine): For the sake of Jacob my servant, of Israel my chosen, I summon you by name and bestow on you a title of honor, though you do not acknowledge me. I am the Lord, and there is no other; apart from me there is no God. I will strengthen you, though you have not acknowledged me, so that from the rising of the sun to the place of its setting men may know that there is none besides me. (Isaiah 45:4-5)

I see some parallels between God's anointing of the Persian King Cyrus and the election of President Donald Trump. Cyrus clearly was not a follower of God, but God anointed him and gave him a "title of honor." Donald Trump has not historically been a follower of God, either, yet God has also bestowed on him a title of honor and given him the role of shepherding the most influential and powerful nation in the history of the world.

There has been much debate about whether President Trump is truly a Christian and whether he is "morally fit" to lead our nation. He certainly has moral shortcomings, as we all have. It is true that only God can judge the hearts of men, but hundreds of trusted evangelical leaders all over the nation, who have spent time with President Trump and advised him and prayed over him, continue to defend and support him. Regardless of Trump's true spiritual condition, which none of us can know with certainty, God has shown clearly in His Word that He can and will use both people who honor and serve Him and people who do not in order to accomplish His purposes on this Earth. When God anointed the foreign, heathen Persian King Cyrus, He said about him, "He is my shepherd and will accomplish all that I please" (Isaiah 44:28).

Cyrus was the tool that God used to bring deliverance and restoration to the Jews thousands of years ago. God has continued to use all sorts of flawed and morally deficient people — Moses,

Samson, Rahab, and Paul are just a few examples — down through the centuries, because He is God and He knows best.

God doesn't need our permission or approval to put His choice of shepherd over us to accomplish His purposes. His ways are higher than our ways, and we can't always understand with our finite minds what He is doing in this world. However, we can see when good and moral fruit is coming from the White House, as it certainly seems to be now. I, for one, am abundantly thankful for the shepherd who has been anointed to watch over our nation. Our responsibility is to continue to pray for our president to make wise decisions. He has the weight of the world on his shoulders, and we, like Aaron and Hur, should help to hold up his hands when he grows weary (Exodus 17:10-13).

Michelle Fitzpatrick Thomas' website is KingdomCrossing.com, and her email is michelle@kingdomcrossing.com.

Proclamation on National Day of Prayer

Donald J. Trump

May 6, 2020

On this National Day of Prayer, Americans reaffirm that prayer guides and strengthens our Nation, and we express, with humility and gratitude, our "firm reliance on the protection of divine Providence." As one Nation under God, we share a legacy of faith that sustains and inspires us and a heritage of religious liberty. Today, we join together and lift up our hearts, remembering the words of 1 John 5:14 that tell us when "we ask anything according to His will, He hears us."

From our earliest days, our dependence upon God has brought us to seek His divine counsel and unfailing wisdom. Our leaders have often encouraged their fellow citizens to seek wisdom from God and have recognized God's power to lead our Nation ahead to brighter days. When the prospects for our independence seemed bleak, General George Washington proclaimed a national day of "fasting, humiliation and prayer, humbly to supplicate the mercy of Almighty God." Following the devastating destruction of the Civil War, President Lincoln delivered his second inaugural address and invoked the power of prayer to "bind up the nation's wounds." And more than 100 years later, President Reagan noted our long reliance on prayer throughout our history, writing that "through the storms of revolution, Civil War, and the great world wars as well as during times of disillusionment and disarray, the Nation has turned to God in prayer for deliverance."

Today, as much as ever, our prayerful tradition continues as our Nation combats the coronavirus. During the past weeks and months, our heads have bowed at places outside of our typical houses of worship, whispering in silent solitude for God to renew our spirit and carry us through unforeseen and seemingly unbearable hardships. Even though we have been unable to gather together in fellowship with our church families, we are still connected through prayer and the calming reassurance that God will lead us through life's many valleys. In the midst of these trying and unprecedented times, we are reminded that just as those before us turned to God in their darkest hours, so must we seek His wisdom, strength, and healing hand. We pray that He comforts those who have lost loved ones, heals those who are sick, strengthens those on the front lines, and reassures all Americans that through trust in Him, we can overcome all obstacles.

May we never forget that prayer guides and empowers our Nation and that all things are possible with God. In times of prosperity, strife, peace, and war, Americans lean on His infinite love, grace, and understanding. Today, on this National Day of Prayer, let us come together and pray to the Almighty that through overcoming this coronavirus pandemic, we develop even greater faith in His divine providence.

In 1988, the Congress, by Public Law 100-307, as amended, called on the President to issue each year a proclamation designating the first Thursday in May as a National Day of Prayer, "on which the people of the United States may turn to God in prayer and meditation at churches, in groups, and as individuals."

NOW, THEREFORE, I, DONALD J. TRUMP, President of the United States of America, do hereby proclaim May 7, 2020, as a National Day of Prayer. I encourage all Americans to observe this day, reflecting on the blessings our Nation has received and the importance of prayer, with appropriate programs, ceremonies, and activities in their houses of worship, communities, and places of work, schools, and homes consistent with the White House's "Guidelines for Opening up America Again."

IN WITNESS WHEREOF, I have hereunto set my hand this sixth day of May, in the year of our Lord two thousand twenty, and of the Independence of the United States of America the two hundred and forty-fourth.

DONALD J. TRUMP

Remarks by President Trump at the White House National Day of Prayer Service

May 7, 2020, Rose Garden, 4:04 P.M. EDT

THE PRESIDENT: Thank you very much. Please. Thank you. Be seated, please. And, Melania, thank you very much, on the second anniversary of the BE BEST Initiative. You've done a fantastic job. And everybody appreciates it. But I want to — (applause) — thank you. And I want to thank you, on behalf of the entire nation, for all that you do for America's children and on fighting the drug addiction problem that we have in this country. It's all over the world. But I want to thank you very much. Great job you do. You work so hard.

On this National Day of Prayer, America is engaged in a fierce battle against a very terrible disease. Throughout our history, in times of challenge, our people have always called upon the gift of faith, the blessing of belief, the power of prayer, and the eternal glory of God.

I ask all Americans to join their voices and their hearts in spiritual union as we ask our Lord in Heaven for strength and solace, for courage and comfort, for hope and healing, for recovery and for renewal.

In recent days and weeks, our country has endured a grave hardship. We pray for every family stricken with grief and devastated with a tragic loss. We pray for the doctors, the nurses, and first responders waging war against the invisible enemy. We pray for the scientists and researchers, who pioneer treatments, that they find therapies and vaccines and that they find them soon. We pray for the frontline workers keeping our nation fed, nourished, and safe and secure. May God watch over them all.

We are honored to have with us today our amazing Vice President, Mike Pence, and his wonderful wife, Karen. Great friends of our nation and great friends of mine and Melania's. And somebody is doing an incredible job, not only as Vice President, but as heading the task force, which has come up with so many solutions and ideas and things that we didn't even think about two months ago.

We're also profoundly grateful to be joined by many faith leaders who are helping to care for our neighbors in their hour of need. Thank you all for providing meals to families, medical supplies to hospitals, and for providing spiritual strength and encouragement to your communities. You're very important people, very respected people, and very much loved people.

In every part of our country, we have seen the Grace of God through the love and devotion of our fellow citizens. As Scripture assures us, "The Lord your God is not [in] your midst, a mighty one who will save." And I think it's — I think it's so true. Think of that: "The Lord your God is in your midst, a mighty one who will save."

We have been reminded once again that God has blessed our land with heroes of faith.

Here with us is Brittany Akinsola from Charlotte, North Carolina. Brittany is a nurse, a pastor, a wife, a mother. When she saw the dire situation in New York City, she volunteered to work at the Samaritan's Purse field hospital in Central Park. There, she worked 13-hour shifts in the intensive care unit for weeks, praying for each patient while giving them the very best care. As Brittany said, "We just keep sharing the love of Christ through our gifts of nursing."

Brittany, America is forever indebted to you and the incredible job you're — you have done. And we very much appreciate it, Brittany. Please come up. Please, come up, Brittany, and say a few words. (Applause.) Thank you.

MS. AKINSOLA: Thank you so much, Mr. President. It has been a great honor and privilege to be able to travel around the world with Samaritan's Purse and help people in their time of crisis and need.

And I most recently had the opportunity to go to New York City, as you shared. And I will tell you that, just to be able to combine both my skills of nursing and the gifting of pastoring at such a time as this in our nation and to serve the people of New York City was truly one of the greatest honors of my life.

And I know that I am one of many frontline workers that are serving our country right now. And so to all of my colleagues at

Samaritan's Purse, and to everyone that is doing such an incredible job sharing their gifts to help those in need, I just want to say thank you so much. Thank you for being just a light of hope in a time that is such a hopeless time for so many people.

I would love to just leave you with a Scripture that has helped me so much through this time. And it's Galatians 6:9, and what it says is, "Let us not become weary of doing good, for at the proper time we will reap a harvest if we do not give up." And the harvest that I'm believing for our country is one of restoration and hope. I am believing for healing in the name of Jesus,

and I am believing that unity — that unity would thrive during this time. So thank you so much, and God bless you all.

THE PRESIDENT: Wow, Brittany. That's great. Wow. Thank you very much. (Applause.) Brittany — no notes, no nothing. You know your stuff, don't you? Huh? Thank you very much. Fantastic person.

Also with us is Mario Salerno, a landlord auto-shop owner in Brooklyn. Last month, Mario waived rent for all 200 of his tenants. Oh, I got to see you on television, actually. I said, "What kind of a landlord is that?" (Laughter.) That's a great landlord, right? That's very nice. I got to see that. He wanted to make sure that they could put food on the table, and he wanted to take care of their families even though he's losing a lot of income — which he could always use. We can always use it. Right, Mario? But that was a big thing. Mario says that's irrelevant compared to the value of human life. Fantastic thing, Mario.

He also believes he has two callings in his wonderful world — usually wonderful world; we live in a world that's very complex — to do good to people and to keep his faith. As Mario puts it, "Faith is a lot more powerful than fear." That's true.

Mario, if you would, would you please step up and say a few words? Thank you very much.

MR. SALERNO: Thank you very much, Mr. President. I'm honored. On this special day of prayer, I have nothing written. I just want to thank the good Lord.

Every morning when I wake up, at 3:30 in the morning, get ready, put my feet, I pray and I ask the good Lord, "Please, conquer this vicious virus. He's making us all stumble." And besides me praying to the Good Lord, I pray for our dear President. And I tell God, "Please, give him the strength and the power, because he's not only our leader of the great United States; the whole world is following this gentleman."

And I can't say anything else, but let's please pray for this wonderful man. Faith before fear. And, Mr. President, I'm honored to be here. And I pray for you every day. God bless America and God bless you, Mr. President. Thank you. (Applause.)

THE PRESIDENT: Thank you, Mario. Wow. That's so great. Thank you, Mario. That's really nice. I appreciate it. And, by the way, I love your tie, but I love your words even more. Thank you very much.

In every age and in every generation, the prayers of our people and the faith of our families has willed us on to victory. No obstacle, no enemy, and no danger can overcome the mighty spirit and soul of our nation.

In every battle against poverty, against disease, against tyranny and evil, we have placed our loyalty in each other and our trust in God. And we have prevailed. We will continue to prevail. We will prevail again. We will vanquish the virus. We will defeat the enemy. We will not fail.

So, once more, we call upon our Creator to guide us through these very complex steps, protect our people, rebuild our communities, and restore our beloved nation to even greater heights. We will never forget, however, those that have been lost, those incredible souls, and the families of those souls that are going through so much. We will never forget you. We will be there for you.

May God continue to strengthen our hearts and sustain our souls. May God continue to shed His divine grace upon this land. And may God forever bless the United States of America.

And now I'd like to ask the faith leaders of our country — some of the most important of our faith leaders, people respected by everybody — to say a few words.

Please, Sister Anida Martinez, if you would, perhaps begin. Sister, thank you very much.

SISTER MARTINEZ: Thank you, Mr. President.

In the name of the Father and of the Son and of the Holy Spirit. Amen. Dear Heavenly Father, I ask you to grant us, in this moment, to be in your most holy presence. In the presence of our mother Mary, of Saint Joseph, our protector and guide, of all the angels and of all the saints, I ask you to please grant us the grace to be one in body and in spirit, all of your children of the Earth. Please be with us so that with one voice, with the voice of the Church, we may pray together to our Lord and Savior Jesus Christ.

Jesus, Son of God, you were sent by the Father to bear our weakness. Be with us in this time of crisis. Merciful savior, heal and comfort the sick, so that with health restored, they may give you praise.

Divine physician, accompany our caregivers so that serving You with patience, they may heal wisely. Eternal wisdom, guide our leaders so that seeking remedies, they may follow Your light. Christ, the anointed, protect us in body and spirit so that freed from harm, we may be delivered from all affliction.

Beloved Son of the Father, grant us the grace to grow in love for Him, that we may love the Lord our God with all of our heart, with all of our mind, and with all of our strength. You who live in reign, in the unity of God the Father with the Holy Spirit, one God, forever and ever. Amen.

We thank you, Father, for this moment. We thank you for your love for us. We ask you, in the name of Christ our Lord, to bless us with His most precious blood, to bless our nation, to bless our world. In the name of the Father, and of the Son, and of the Holy Spirit. Amen.

THE PRESIDENT: Thank you, Sister, very much. Thank you. It's beautiful.

Pujari Harish Brahmbhatt.

MR. BRAHMBHATT: Thank you, Mr. President. In these troubled times of COVID-19, social distancing, and the lockdown, it's not unusual for people to feel anxious or not at peace. The Shanti Paath, or the peace prayer, is a prayer that does not seek worldly riches, success, fame, nor is it a prayer for any desire for heaven. It is a beautiful Hindu prayer for peace — Shanti. It's a Vedic prayer derived from the Yajurveda. And the prayer goes:

Om Dyau Shanti Rantariksha Gwam ShantiPrithvi Shanti Rapah Shanti Roshadhayah Shanti Vanas Patayah Shanti Vishwed Devah Shanti Brahma Sarvag Wam Shanti Shanti Reva Shanti Sa Ma Shanti Redhi Om Shanti Shanti Shanti

The prayer translates into:

Onto the heavens, be peace. Onto the sky and Earth, be peace. Peace be onto the water. Onto the herbs and trees, be peace. Onto all the crops, be peace. Onto Brahma and onto all, be peace. And may we realize that peace. Peace. Peace. Peace.

Thank you.

THE PRESIDENT: Thank you very much. Thank you.

Would Bishop Dwight Green please come up?

BISHOP GREEN: Thank you. Good afternoon to the President, Vice President, and all those that are assembled today at the National Day of Prayer.

Let us pray:

To the eternal sovereign God of creation, You have summoned your people, once again, to prayer. And the presiding Bishop of the Church of God in Christ and the membership of our organization around the world has, for the last 12 weeks, been joined together interceding for the deliverance of our nation and our world that God would deliver us from the coronavirus pandemic and all of other debilitating plagues present in our world.

We believe that the suffering and the loss of life, which continues to threaten the socioeconomic and geopolitical balance of our country can be curtailed when the people of God pray.

You said in Psalms 107: "He will send His word to heal and deliver us from destruction."

Our systems are broken, no longer trusted, nor effective, because we have strayed from your commandments. And our people are wounded, ailing, bewildered, frustrated by empty promises.

We need you to transform us to the likeness of your Son, Jesus the Christ. We need your word of healing that will restore confidence in our justice system that will reflect fairness and provide rehabilitation for redeemable offenders. We need your word to heal that promise quality early childhood education and equitable distribution of opportunities for wealth-building for blacks, browns, and disadvantaged whites.

We need your word of healing that will speak to the physical, emotional, and spiritual deficiencies of our nation; your word that will cause us to recognize we are all God's children and He has called us to love and good works.

You declared a house divided against itself will self-destruct. So, Father, have mercy on us as we repent today for our miscarriage of justice. I repent of all offenses and disobedience of our nation to your commandments, and humbly seek your forgiveness and pray for mercy that you will deliver us from this evil affliction of the coronavirus.

And grant to our President, Mr. Trump, the Vice President, Congress, and the religious leaders of our nation your divine insight to navigate this pandemic, in the name of Jesus Christ the Savior.

And we pray divine comfort for the grieving families of those that have been lost and those that are yet struggling with the affliction inflicted by this virus. We pray your comfort, your deliverance, and your peace.

In Jesus's name, thank God. Amen.

THE PRESIDENT: Thank you, Bishop, very much. Thank you.

Pastor Paula White, please come up. Thank you, Paula.

PASTOR WHITE: What an honor to be here with you, President and First Lady, Vice President, Second Lady. It's a beautiful day to lift up our Lord and Savior. He is a certain God in uncertain times. And the Bible says, if two or three of us agree as touching anything, it will be done.

Job 22, verse 28 says: If you decree a thing and declare a thing, it will be established. So, God, we come in agreement with your word and with your name — the name of Jesus.

Psalm 40, verse 17 says: You are my help and my deliver. Do not delay, Oh God. I declare no more delays to the deliverance of COVID-19. No more delays to healing and a vaccination. No more delays to restoration of this great nation, the United States of America.

For Psalm 71:2 says: In your righteousness, deliver us and rescue us, incline your ear and save us.

Psalm 107 says: You deliver us out of the stress and out of destruction.

Your word will not return void, according to Isaiah chapter 55, verse 11. So I declare your word. I declare divine intervention and supernatural turnaround. You will restore this land.

According to Psalm 118:25: Save our nation, oh Lord, and send prosperity now.

For Deuteronomy 28:8 says: Command your blessing upon this land. You said in Deuteronomy 8:9 to bring us into good land without any lack.

For your word declares in Psalm 33:2: Blessed is the nation whose God is Lord.

So I declare you right now to be Lord over this nation, over the United States of America, and we receive your blessing over any plague, over any economic distress.

You will stay the hand of the enemy, according to Second Samuel chapter 21, verse 16: When 70,000 men died by a plague, David cried out as he covered himself in prayer. And the Lord answered and said, "It is enough."

Stay now thine hand. Lord, let that be the cry today, and let that be your answer. Lord, enough coronavirus, enough to death, enough to fear, enough to poverty. Stay thine your hand.

We pray over President Trump and First Lady, Vice President and Second Lady, and this administration. I declare Psalm 89, verse 21: Let your hand establish President Trump, and let your arm strengthen him. I declare Psalm 98:1 that your right hand and your holy arm will give Him victory. We declare victory in the name of Jesus.

Isaiah 58:11 says: Guide him continually. And you said in Psalm 78:72 that you would guide him by the skillfulness of your hand.

You declared in Psalm 43 that send out your light and truth and let him lead his household, his administration, in the name of Jesus.

Now, Lord, we pray for your mercies, for they are new every single day. And every morning, your mercies are new. Your steadfast love never ceases. I declare new mercies for hospital workers, new mercies for doctors and nurses, moms and dads, pastors and clergies, CEOs and employers, for the President and Vice President.

God, your love is steadfast and it endures forever. So right now, wrap your arms of love around every person who is hurting, every person who is confused, scared, tired, weary sick, lonely. Let them know your love. Let them know that you will never leave them and you will never forsake them.

And in conclusion, I declare Isaiah chapter 43, verse 19: I ask the Lord to do a new thing in our nation by giving waters in the wilderness and streams in the desert.

Malachi 4:2 says: Jesus, arise over the nation with healing in your wings.

President, one last word: Like David, who had had victory, after victory, after victory, after victory, would face his biggest battle — it was called Ziklag. And they would take his wives and his children, and the city would be burned down. And he cried and he wept, and he began to pray out to God. And God gave him a word.

And through fasting and praying, I believe this is the word for you and for this nation: The Lord spoke to him and said: Pursue and go after them, and you shall, without fail, recover all.

Sir, the word of the Lord, I believe, for this nation and for this administration is: You will recover all.

THE PRESIDENT: Well, thank you very much, Paula. Incredible, Paula. Thank you.

Next is Chaplain Ibraheem Raheem. Thank you, Chaplain.

CHAPLAIN RAHEEM: Thank you, Mr. President.

Let us pray:

Gracious and merciful Lord, I pray for our nation. I bring the needs of our citizens before you and ask that you be with all of us through the challenges we endure from COVID-19.

I pray for the victims and families of victims that have lost their lives, as well as those that are fighting for their lives today.

I pray for the many without jobs, food, and shelter. I ask that you would give all of our nation's leaders the wisdom and courage to lead us through this pandemic.

I pray for our President, Vice President, First Lady, and Second Lady. I ask that you help us to work together as a nation. I ask that you bless our Congress and all of those in leadership positions to restore our nation back to full operation. I pray for your protection to cover all of our valiant healthcare workers, our courageous first responders, law enforcement community, and brave men and women of our military. I pray for all essential workers. I pray for the soundness of mind for our governors and judges across the land.

I pray for every faith community and their leaders. And I ask your blessings upon those in my community who are observing the collective fast of Ramadan.

I ask these blessings in your gracious and merciful name. Amen.

THE PRESIDENT: Thank you very much. Thank you very much. Sister Debbie Harrison. Sister Harrison, thank you very much.

SISTER HARRISON: Thank you, Mr. President.

Our Dear Heavenly Father, we are grateful, this day, to be gathered together with representatives from many faiths, united in prayer to appeal to thee thy mercy and grace, and helping us and our nation.

We are grateful to be in a country where we have the right to exercise our religious beliefs. And we pray and cherish that those freedoms that we have will be protected and not be diminished.

We are united in prayer today to ask a special blessing of deliverance—deliverance from this pandemic that has covered the

Earth in a devastating sickness. We ask that our doctors, nurses, and caregivers can be blessed with special protection in recognition of their sacrifices and hard work.

Please bless our scientists and doctors to develop effective treatments for those who are sick and who may become sick. We pray that a safe and effective vaccine can be developed quickly to protect us, so that life can return to normal.

Bless the leaders of this great nation to be inspired by thee, to have wisdom and judgment to make good decisions and to get the economy running again. Amplify their talents.

Bless our leaders to work together in harmony and unity to do what is best for the citizens of this nation.

We pray for those that mourn for lost loved ones and ask that you send thy Holy Spirit to comfort them and give them assurance that they can be reunited again through the power of our savior Jesus Christ's resurrection.

We know that without thy strengthening help, we will fail. But with thy help and tender mercies, we can do all things and we will not fail.

We pray we can look to thee in every thought, doubt not, and fear not.

We love thee, Heavenly Father, and we call down the powers of Heaven to help us, unite us, and deliver us from these troubled times.

I say these things in deep gratitude for all of our blessings in the sacred name of Jesus Christ, our healer and redeemer.

Amen.

THE PRESIDENT: Thank you very much, Sister. Thank you. Rabbi Ariel Sadwin. Thank you, Rabbi.

RABBI SADWIN: Thank you, Mr. President.

King Solomon, in his great wisdom, writes in the second chapter of Song of Songs, "There he stands behind our wall, gazing through the windows, peering through the lattice." The Midrash commentary explains this to be referring to Almighty God at a time when his presence is not visible, nor is it readily apparent. "But fear not," says King Solomon, "he is right there in the background, watching you through the window, and the lattice. (Speaks Hebrew.) Oh, our merciful Father."

This idea is so apparent and reminiscent to this most challenging time during which we find ourselves. Our relationship with you seems so different from what it always has been. We have not been in your house, our holy synagogues, in nearly two months. These sacred places where we go to seek you and to derive inspiration three times a day, every day, are empty, dark, and shuttered. Instead, all we have had is the sanctuary of our own homes and the limited allowable interactions.

There is fear, there is sickness, there is death wherever we turn and whenever we listen. But yet, we know you are still there, watching over us as always. (Speaks Hebrew.) Master of the world, you are the Rofei chol basar, the healer of all flesh. We implore you to eradicate this awful plague from your Earth, heal those who suffer, comfort those who mourn, sustain those who have lost livelihood.

Please bless our President, our First Lady, our Vice President, our Second Lady, and the entire administration, as well as the leaders of state and local governments who must make critical decisions each and every day.

Please bless the doctors, nurses, first responders, and all medical personnel who dedicate their lives to save others. Please bless the selfless community and civic leaders who are doing their part to help those in need. And please bless each and every one of your 330 million children who make up the United States of America.

Amen.

THE PRESIDENT: Thank you, Rabbi, very much.

Now I'd like to ask the Spirit of Faith Christian Center Choir to come up and conclude the event by leading us in the singing of "God Bless America."

Thank you.

MR. BOWMAN, JR.: It is my prayer and desire as we join together to sing "God Bless America" that we will all reciprocate and begin to bless God.

("God Bless America" is sung.)

(Applause.)

THE PRESIDENT: Well, thank you very much. That was — that was great. Thank you.

You know, while you're up here — so this is totally unexpected, but you're so good. Do you have one song that you'd like to sing for the group and for the whole world that's watching right now? You have a lot of cameras out there.

Go ahead. We'll put a little pressure on you. You can handle it.

MR. BOWMAN, JR.: Let's do this.

THE PRESIDENT: Go ahead.

("I Lift My Eyes Up" is sung.)

(Applause.)

THE PRESIDENT: That's fantastic. A lot of people were watching. Thank you. Great talent, beautiful.

Thank you all very much. Great day of prayer. Thank you very much,

Quotes
Donald J. Trump

"Trump comes as advertised.......he is who he is." Trump, Trump, Trump...his name is power."

"He has charisma, a self-confidence, a presence he is electric........on fire."
Nicky Haslam, English Interior Designer

DJT Quotes

"I just don't like wasting time on the past.
Other than learning from the past.......the past is over."

"I'm a big believer in natural ability.
I have a very unique ability to handle pressure.
People don't know that about me.
I have very low blood pressure."

"I was very rebellious. I loved to fight."
(Did Fred suspect his lineage? Divine right?)

"They have unsuccessfully tried to take down
the wrong person. That's treason!"
President DJT 2019

DJT on Military School

> "I evolved in the system. I liked discipline....playing the game...winning the game...setting the terms yourself."

Donald became an officer going from a 'wise guy' to graduating at the top of the heap leading the parade down Fifth Avenue.

DJT was determined to show that he could take the family legacy to a higher place.

Fred would spend less money building better houses and then sell them for more. Donald learned a lot from his father.

More DJT Quotes

> "I love to learn from other people's mistakes.
> I've learned so many lessons by watching other people
> make mistakes. I study other people's mistakes."

> "I've always been counter intuitive."

> "No matter what it is....I have a gift to get
> the best locations for our projects."

> "You have to do many different things to be successful.
> A lot of life is relationships. A lot of great things that
> happened to me is because of relationships."

> "I enjoy what I'm doing."

DJT is a man who loves women and has elevated them to many offices and positions of power.

> "Donald Trump is a force to be reckoned with.
> Everything Donald touches turns to gold......
> better than gold. He is a swashbuckler. He takes chances."

"He always has time for family and friends and
when he says something, he does it."

Regan recognized DJT and told Roger Stone that he needs to
run for office.

"I have a great feeling for this country. I love this
country. Our so-called allies are a disaster for this
country. The Country is acting so weak on Iran."

"When I do something I like to win."

"I am so loyal to people that when people are
disloyal to me I look at them in horror."

"I've never had a failure because I've always
turned my failures into successes."

More Quotes on DJT

"He knew he was going to make a come
back when he was down and out."

"He can talk to anyone."

"Our destiny is not written in Washington.
Its written in our hearts." DJT

"I am the least racist person in the world."

DJT "Not only didn't I back down. I backed up!" DJT

"I love America and when you love something you
protect it passionately—fiercely, even." DJT

Quote from end of 4th of July speech 2019

"We must go forward as a nation with the same unity
of purpose. As long as we never stop fighting for
a better future there will be nothing that America
cannot do. We are one people, chasing one dream
and one magnificent destiny. We all share the same
heroes, the same home, the same heart. and we are
all made by the same Almighty God. The Spirit of
Independence will reign for ever and ever and ever."

"Truth Is A Force Of Nature!"

President Trump after Mueller Testimony

We know our POTUS is a high IQ individual as well as being one of the most prolific men in America. God prepared Trump for his entire life to take on this supreme service and we are so grateful for that.

The Art of the Deal

Think Big & Kick Ass

Think Like a Billionaire

Midas Touch: Why Some Entrepreneurs Get Rich-And Why Most Don't

Never Give Up: How I Turned My Biggest Challenges into Success

Crippled America: How to Make America Great Again

Surviving at The Top

The Art of the Comeback Trump 101-

The Way to Success

Think Like a Champion

Commercial Real Estate Investing 101 How to Get Rich

The Best Real Estate Advice I Ever Received

Why We Want You to Be Rich

The America We Deserve

The Way to the Top-

The Best Business Advice I Ever Received

The Best Gold Advice I Ever Received

A Short List of Truthers
BethAnon

A partial list of wonderful truthers on YouTube and other social media platforms who have inspired me in this Great Awakening in addition to the ones previously mentioned in this book. Truthers are subject to frequent censorship, so you may need to search for them on YouTube, BitChute, Parler, Twitter, or other social media platforms. Like the Bible says in Proverbs 25:2 "It is the glory of God to conceal a thing: but the honor of kings is to search a matter out."

Amanda Grace	Tom Fitton, Judicial Watch
Santa Surfing	Project Veritas
Freedom Force Battalion	SGT Report
In Pursuit of Truth (IPOT)	X22 Report
Jordan Sather	Freya Ferdinand
JoeM	Tiffany Fitzhenry
Lori Colley	Liz Crokin
Linda Paris	Edge of Wonder
Space Shot 76	Operation Freedom
Red Pill 78	Dustin Nemos
Craig Mason	Just Informed Talk
Josh Peck	Greg Hunter

Dave Janda

Corey's Digs

Komorusan Q714

Red Ice TV

Derek Prince

John MacArthur

Blessed to Teach

@Melissa Leggett4

Chris McDonald,

McFiles

Lord's Prophecy

The Sharpening Report

The Bible Project

Amazing Polly

Adrienne Payton-Green

Dinesh D'Souza

Turning Point USA & UK

House of Destiny

Ann Vandersteel

Charles Ward

And We Know

Inthematrixxx

Steve Hilton

Candace Owens

Brandon Straka

Scott Presler

Diamond and Silk

Lara Login

Laura Loomer

Sheila Zelinsky

Anomaly Legendary.vision

EWTN

Steven Crowder

Raymond Arroyo

Sean Hannity

Tucker Carlson

Laura Ingraham

Liz Wheeler OAAN

Kaleigh McEnany

Mark Levi

www.whitehouse.gov

Middle East Peace Plan with Jared Kushner

First Step Prison Plan with Ivanka Trump

www.famm.org

www.#cut50.org

www.qanon.pub

Mark Taylor

Dane Wiggington

www.geoengineeringwatch.org

RelentlesslyCreativeBooks.com

Rockin' the West Coast Prayer Group

'This Video Will Get Donald Trump Elected' on YouTube

Bethanon Reads the Trump Prophecies by Mark Taylor on YouTube

'Nothing to Lose' on Netflix

Evangelist Edir Macedo Mike Adams www.counterthink.com

'Donald Trump and the Art of the Insult' by Joel Gilbert www.strikeforceofprayer.com

So proud of our patriot kindred who compiled the Amazon best-selling book, "QAnon: An Invitation to The Great Awakening" by WWG1WGA. This is a great tool to spread the word.

Kudos to my Sister in Christ, Melissa, at Freedom Force Battalion for her wonderful book, "QAnon and 1000 Years of Peace", also called "QAnon and the Battle of Armageddon, Destroying the New World Order and Taking the Millennial Kingdom by Force." Melissa has a fresh spiritual eye and an abundant overflowing Holy Spirit. Also watch her Mazzaroth-Heavenly Storybook video series! Fantastic Hebrew astrological prophecy in the sky!

'South Dakota' Bruce Issacson's nonpartisan movie on abortion.....worth watching. www.Unplannedfilm.com

"All of creation longs for the revelations of the sons and daughters of God." Romans 8:19

Go forward in God and watch reality and justice unfold as we prepare for a restoration of humanity on this beautiful garden earth.

A Rallying Cry
BethAnon

To all my brothers and sisters being breathed by our Awesome Creator, I beg and implore you to join us in giving all you've got to spreading this message of hope and faith, joy and truth, love and peace to every human soul you come in contact with. This time we are in is an era that our ancestors prayed for; the pivotal moments where we get to stand in our authentic divinity becoming our completely true selves in knowledge wisdom and understanding for the glory of God.

May we get down on both knees and thank the One who breathes us for this magnificent life and for forgiveness for getting caught up in the spell and delusion of the adversary/enemy.

Let us change our ways to be in alignment with the Will of Our Lord as Jesus Christ prayed in His 'Our Father Prayer' so long ago, "Thy Kingdom Come, Thy Will be Done on Earth as it is in Heaven."

We are at a crossroads with every breath, every choice, each action and reaction, and we can respond in positivity only when we are aligned with Divine Providence from the mercy seat within our own hearts. The only place we truly live is here and now, in this present moment.

It's about how deeply we are connected and anchored within the One True God. Our prayers for a heart-drenched mind will help us to be of maximum service to our Almighty Creator and stay in the Full Armor of God to do His Will.

We must take nothing for granted and be willing to give our all for an incredible Victory resulting in Peace on Earth. We always knew that we would get back to the garden, we just didn't know how that would look. In this age of The Great Awakening, when the Kingdom of Heaven is crashing into the World, the light is shining brighter and brighter, bringing revelations and inspiration, all for the benefit of human beings—souls—to know who they really are, to realize their divinity and connection with the One True God.

It is for the Lord of All to reveal Himself to each of us individually, in the center of our being, in the most intimate relationship any of us will ever enjoy. By being awake and in devotion to God, ourselves, we hold the space for others to join the party. Like Q said, "You cannot tell. You must show." When we are in that singularity with our Creator it shows, and love is contagious.

Even in our deepest, darkest hours, we are never abandoned. He keeps us and brings us all home to His Word."

Amen and Amen Selah Alleluia

WWG1WGA

About BethAnon

BethAnon was born on the East Coast, traveled the world, received her college degree in nutrition, worked as editor and co-publisher of the Malibu Chronicle and assisted her soul-mate and twin-flame, British-American husband, Paul, in various endeavors in film and tech businesses. She is the mother of six amazing daughters. They have raised their family, including his son from a previous marriage, in Malibu, California, and continue to reside there today, enjoying the arrival of five grandchildren so far. "I brought Paul back to Malibu in 1983 to make "Heaven at Last" which is a film that was channeled to him, and as I typed it out there were parts of the story that I knew were prophetic."

Here's what Bethanon has to say about her path to assembling the works contained in this book:

"In 1981 God grabbed me by the back of the neck, so to speak, and I knew He was in my heart and I knew that my only prayer was "Thy Will Be Done!" I have led a graced and beautiful life and in 2015 I came across Mark Taylor and his prophecies about Donald Trump. I took them deeper and they resonated in my heart as being authentic. This led to diving into everything 'Trump,' and researching every story for the truth."

"I came across the QAnon and The Great Awakening movement in October 2017 and have enjoyed this wild ride of kindred spirits and have seen people come to God through Q (which is a divine intelligence-group consciousness experience). Now that we, The Remnant, are awake, it's time to use this ammunition we have gathered to wake up our sleeping brothers and sisters around the world as we head for peace on earth after we drain the global swamp. Amen and Amen Selah"

www.heavenatlastmovie.com
bethruffman@gmail.com
www.masterpeacefilms.com

I would like to thank Prem Rawat for the priceless, yet free, beautiful gift of knowledge of the self, that I received from him in 1982. I have been practicing the techniques of knowledge of the self every day since then, which offers me a daily repeatable experience of inner peace and joy with a cup that fills and overflows in my heart center. Over a billion people have heard Prem's message to date via a myriad of media. It is always a breath of fresh air.

www.premrawat.com
www.timelesstoday.com
www.wopg.org (Words of Peace Global)
www.tprf.org. (The Prem Rawat Foundation)

God's Will Be Done

My intention in this compendium was to gather as many authentic prophecies as I could and put them in one place for others perusal. My goal is always to be in alignment with the Will of God. I had a dream once where God was telling me that I was in his 'slipstream'. A slipstream is a region behind a moving object in which a wake of fluid (typically air or water) is moving at velocities comparable to the moving object. Where else would I want to be?

I live a 100% thy Will Be Done life after lots of bumps and bruises from living in my own Self Will. I am so happy to be alive now in these most exciting times. My premise is that 'God's Will be Done on Earth as it is in Heaven.' That is what we pray in the Lord's prayer will manifest in this world. Why not live in heaven on earth now while God made us here alive and trust that our Creator will bring us into His heaven?

If you disagree with what these prophecies say, don't shoot the messenger. I am just a humble servant spreading the Word, who loves Obedience and Clarity because I have learned that God wants the best for us always in all ways. Like Mark Taylor of The Trump Prophecies says, "This is God's Agenda, Heaven's Agenda...not his." It will be done as God wants regardless, because He is our ever-loving Creator. Let's see what unfolds and be shining witnesses of His Glory.

Alleluia Amen Selah To Our Brilliant Contributors

Thank You!
and bless you

This is a big thank you from Monica and me, to all of you who have been so kind and generous in offering to include your work in the group effort of *Love Joy Trump: A Chorus of Prophetic Voices*. Without you this book wouldn't exist, and all of the wonderful messages and vibrations of truth that are going out into the universe, one human being at a time, because of it, would not be possible.

This is the epitome of the genuine affirmation that Teamwork is Divine.

Again, thank you so much for your participation.

I have a feeling that the Lord is smiling on us all.

Onwards and upwards.

Amen Selah

All love,

BethAnon

About Relentlessly Creative Books

If you would like to recieve
notification of upcoming books
by BethAnon or
Relentlessly Creative Books,
please join our email here.
We promise to use the utmost
respect in contacting you.
https://bit.ly/LoveJoyTrump

Relentlessly Creative Books™ offers an exciting new
publishing option for authors. Our "middle-path
publishing" approach includes many of the advantages of
both traditional publishing and self-publishing without the
drawbacks. For more information and a complete online
catalog of our books, please visit us at.
RelentlesslyCreativeBooks.com
books@relentlesslycreative.com

Printed in Great Britain
by Amazon

57984839R00201